ALL ABOUT BIRDS
TEXAS &
OKLAHOMA

PRINCETON

press.princeton.edu

White-breasted Nuthatch ©Evan Lipton/Macaulay Library

ALL ABOUT BIRDS
TEXAS & OKLAHOMA

Published in 2022 by Princeton University Press
41 William Street, Princeton, New Jersey 08540
6 Oxford Street, Woodstock, Oxfordshire OX20 1TR

press.princeton.edu

Requests for permission to reproduce material from this work should be sent to
permissions@press.princeton.edu

Library of Congress Control Number: 2021940662
ISBN: 978-0-691-99006-4
Ebook ISBN: 978-0-691-23012-2

Front cover photo: Golden-fronted Woodpecker ©Daniel M. Grossi/Macaulay Library

Back cover photos (left to right): Blue-gray Gnatcatcher ©Brad Imhoff/Macaulay Library;
Roseate Spoonbill ©Jay McGowan/Macaulay Library; Phainopepla ©Eric Gofreed/Macaulay
Library; Bullock's Oriole ©Matt Davis/Macaulay Library

Cover-flap illustrations: ©2022 Pedro Fernandes except Curve-billed Thrasher, Verdin ©Raisa
Kochmaruk; Cover-flap extracted photos: Black Skimmer, Common Loon, Phainopepla
©Brian L. Sullivan/Macaulay Library; Wood Stork ©David Wilson/Macaulay Library; Anhinga
©Liam Wolff/Macaulay Library; Monk Parrakeet ©Jay McGowan/Macaulay Library; Northern
Shrike ©David Mitchell https://flic.kr/p/9y6tA8

Editor: Jill Leichter

Assistant Editors: Michael L. P. Retter, Caroline Watkins

Photo Editors: Michael L. P. Retter, Jill Leichter

Design concept and layout: Patricia Mitter, Jill Leichter, Diane Tessaglia-Hymes,
Brian L. Sockin, Regina Miles

Printed in Malaysia
10 9 8 7 6 5 4 3 2 1

TABLE OF CONTENTS

WELCOME TO YOUR
ALL ABOUT BIRDS, TEXAS & OKLAHOMA GUIDE

Wherever you live, we hope you'll enjoy the amazing diversity and beauty of the birds around you. Birds stir our imaginations with their songs, dazzling colors, and flight. Whether in the wilderness, on farms, or in the heart of cities, birds open up a door into endless discoveries and fascination with the natural world.

Mallard

So how exactly do you go about identifying an unfamiliar wild bird likely to fly away before you can figure out what it is? This guide will help you with a treasure trove of information, best practices, and advice about bird identification. By starting with the birds in your backyard, neighborhood, and region, you'll get to know more about the diversity, behaviors, and seasonal changes in birds—a foundation for endless explorations.

In these pages, you'll find information about the most common bird species in your region, drawn from the Cornell Lab of Ornithology's comprehensive website, *AllAboutBirds.org*, used by more than 22 million people each year. Each species profile includes a map and four photographs that will help you recognize and appreciate the diversity of birds' plumages within and between species. You will also discover information about the Cornell Lab's vast online resources and learn about the Lab's free **Merlin® Bird ID** app to help you identify the birds around you based on your observations, photographs, and sound recordings.

We've also included a special section about the Cornell Lab's "citizen science" projects—scientific studies driven by contributions from bird watchers just like you—including the Cornell Lab's Project FeederWatch, NestWatch, and Great Backyard Bird Count. Our largest citizen-science initiative, eBird, provides a free portal for you to create and keep your own bird lists while sharing them for use in science, conservation, and outreach. Each year, participants record more than 100 million bird sightings! These projects empower you to participate and contribute to important science, while enjoying the outdoors or the view from your window. So, let's get started and have fun!

Miyoko Chu
Senior Director of Communications
Cornell Lab of Ornithology

Brian Scott Sockin
CEO/Publisher
Cornell Lab Publishing Group

GETTING STARTED

All About Birds is a field guide for new and developing birders, based on *AllAboutBirds.org*, your online guide to birds and birding from the Cornell Lab of Ornithology. The content you will find in this book was curated by some of the world's leading bird experts and is presented in a friendly, easy-to-understand manner, just like the *All About Birds* website.

The first section of this book is presented as **Birding 101**, a primer for beginning and novice birders, but also a refresher for more advanced birders. You will learn how to identify birds with best practices, how to find, watch, and listen to birds, how to choose equipment, and how to take photos of birds (including how to "digiscope" with your smartphone).

The second section, **Attracting Birds to Your Backyard,** shares some of our best advice and tools to help you "birdscape" or create bird-friendly habitat outside your home. We begin with the three essential elements that all birds need to thrive—food, water, and shelter—followed by descriptions of different types of bird feeders and information on bird food options and what to look for when buying or building nest boxes. We also equip you with the things you need to know to attract the birds you want to see at home, and how you can protect and keep them safe while enjoying them.

The third section, **Getting Involved**, shares information about citizen science and how you can participate and contribute to important scientific studies at the Cornell Lab.

The fourth section is the bird field guide, covering 238 species of commonly seen birds in Texas and Oklahoma. Each species page features easy-to-use sections with graphics, cool facts, backyard tips, and more. The diagram on the following page will show you how to navigate the species field guide pages.

SAMPLE PAGE

Common and scientific names

Category for easier searching

MOTTLED DUCK *(Anas fulvigula)* GEESE · DUCKS

ADULT MALE

ADULT

Photos may include immature and adult birds, and breeding and nonbreeding plumages for easier identification year-round.

ADULT FEMALE AND DOWNY YOUNG

ADULT MALE (L) AND ADULT FEMALE (R)

RANGE MAP

Range Map

- Breeding
- Winter
- Year-round
- - - Post-breeding dispersal

SIZE & SHAPE A relatively large duck, similar in size to a Mallard, with a sturdy body, short neck, short tail, and moderately long bill.

Size & Shape

COLOR PATTERN Both sexes are mostly brown and buff, like a female Mallard, but darker and richer in color and with a black patch at the opening of the bill (the gape). The very buffy face and throat lack fine streaking. The back and sides are rich brown streaked with buff. Males have intensely yellow bills; females have greenish yellow to orangish bills, with or without dark markings. White in the tail is an indication that the individual has some Mallard genes; a pure Mottled Duck has a dark tail.

Color Pattern

BEHAVIOR Mottled Ducks are "dabbling ducks" that feed at the surface or tip up to reach submerged vegetation. They rarely dive unless being pursued by a predator.

Behavior

HABITAT Mottled Ducks use shallow freshwater and brackish wetlands, including marshes, ponds, ditches, and flooded agricultural fields for resting, feeding, and nesting.

Habitat

The **Mottled Duck** is reminiscent of a female Mallard or an American Black Duck and is so closely related that hybridization, especially with Mallards, poses a real threat to the Mottled Duck's future. Look for this species in pairs or small flocks, mostly in freshwater marshes near the coast.

All About Birds Texas & Oklahoma **83**

BIRDING 101

FOUR KEYS TO BIRD IDENTIFICATION

To identify an unfamiliar bird, first focus on four keys to identification.

With more than 800 species of birds in the U.S. and Canada, it's easy for a beginning bird watcher to feel overwhelmed by possibilities. Field guides often look crammed with similar birds arranged in seemingly haphazard order. We can help you figure out where to begin.

White-throated Sparrow

First we share where *not* to start. Many ID tips focus on very specific details of plumage called field marks, such as the eyering of a Ruby-crowned Kinglet, or the double breast band of a Killdeer. While these tips are useful, they assume you've already narrowed down your search to just a few similar species. Instead, start by learning how to recognize the group a mystery bird belongs to. You may still need to look at field marks to clinch some IDs. But these four keys—**Size and Shape**, **Color Pattern**, **Behavior**, and **Habitat**—will quickly get you to the right group of species, so you'll know exactly which field marks to look for.

1 SIZE AND SHAPE

Birds are built for what they do. Every part of the bird you're looking at is a clue to what it is.

The combination of size and shape is one of the most powerful tools to identification. Though you may be drawn to watching birds because of their wonderful colors or fascinating behavior, when it comes to making identifications, size and shape are the first pieces of information you should examine. With just a little practice and observation, you'll find that differences in size and shape will jump out at you. The first steps are to learn typical bird silhouettes, find reliable ways to gauge the size of a bird, and notice differences in telltale parts of a bird such as the bill, wings, and tail. Soon, you'll know the difference between Red-winged Blackbirds and European Starlings while they're still in flight, and be able to identify a Red-tailed Hawk or Turkey Vulture without taking your eyes off the road.

Become Familiar with Silhouettes

Often you don't need to see any color at all to know what kind of bird you're looking at.

Silhouettes quickly tell you a bird's size, proportions, and posture, and quickly rule out many groups of birds—even ones of nearly identical overall size.

House Finch

A small-bodied finch with a fairly large beak and somewhat long, flat head. The House Finch has a relatively shallow notch in its tail.

Beginning bird watchers often get sidetracked by a bird's bright colors, only to be frustrated when they search through their field guides. Finches, for example, can be red, yellow, blue, brown, or green, but they're still always shaped like finches. Learn silhouettes, and you'll always be close to an ID.

Judge Size Against Birds You Know Well

Size is trickier to judge than shape.

You never know how far away a bird is or how big that nearby rock or tree limb really is. Throw in fluffed-up or hunkered-down birds and it's easy to get fooled. But with a few tricks, you can still use size as an ID key. Compare your mystery bird to a bird you know well. It helps just to know that your bird is larger or smaller than a sparrow, a robin, a crow, or a goose, and it may help you choose between two similar species, such as Downy and Hairy woodpeckers or Sharp-shinned and Cooper's hawks.

Sometimes you need two reference birds for comparison. A crow is bigger than a robin but smaller than a goose.

Judge Against Birds in the Same Field of View

Your estimate of size gets much more accurate if you can compare one bird directly against another.

When you find groups of different species, you can use the ones you recognize to sort out the ones you don't.

Use size and shape to find the full range of species hiding in a large flock. Amid these Caspian Terns are some smaller Common Terns. You'll also notice a Ring-billed Gull in the front on the left and a larger Herring Gull near the center.

For instance, if you're looking at a gull you don't recognize, you can start by noticing that it's larger than a more familiar bird, such as a Ring-billed Gull, that's standing right next to it. For some groups of birds, including shorebirds, seabirds, and waterfowl, using a known bird as a ruler is a crucial identification technique.

Apply Your Size and Shape Skills to the Parts of a Bird

After you've taken note of a bird's overall size and shape, there's still plenty of room to hone your identification.

Turn your attention to the size and shape of individual body parts. Here you'll find clues to how the bird lives its life: what it eats, how it flies, and where it lives.

Start with the bill—that all-purpose tool that functions as a bird's hands, pliers, knitting needles, knife-and-fork, and bullhorn. A flycatcher's broad, flat, bug-snatching bill looks very different from the thick, conical nut-smasher of a finch. Notice the slightly downcurved bills of the Northern Flickers in your backyard. That's an unusual shape for a woodpecker's bill, but perfect for a bird that digs into the ground after ants, as flickers often do.

Bills are an invaluable clue to identification, but tail shape and wing shape are important, too. Even subtle differences in head shape, neck length, and body shape can all yield useful insights if you study them carefully.

Noticing details like these can help you avoid classic identification mistakes. For example, the Ovenbird is a common eastern warbler that has tricked many a bird watcher into thinking it's a thrush. The field marks are certainly thrushlike—warm brown above, strongly streaked below, even a crisp white eyering. But look at overall shape and size rather than field marks, and you'll see the body plan of a warbler—plump, compact body, short tail and wings, thin, pointed, insect-grabbing bill.

Measure the Bird Against Itself

This is the most powerful way to use a bird's size for identification.

It's hard to judge a lone bird's size, and an unusual posture can make shape hard to interpret. But you can always measure key body parts (e.g., wings, bill, tail, legs) against the bird itself.

Look for details such as how long the bird's bill is relative to the head. That's a great way to tell apart Downy and Hairy woodpeckers as well as Greater and Lesser yellowlegs, but it's useful with other confusing species, too. Judging how big the head is compared to the rest of the body helps separate Cooper's Hawks from Sharp-shinned Hawks in flight. Get in the habit of using the bird itself as a ruler, and you'll be amazed at how much information you can glean from each view. Good places to start include noting how long the legs are; how long the neck is; how far the tail extends past the body; and how far the primary feathers of the wing end compared to the tail.

Hairy vs. Downy Woodpeckers

The Hairy Woodpecker (L) is quite a bit larger than the Downy Woodpecker (R), but this is not obvious unless they are side by side. Looking at relative bill size is a way to distinguish between the two when they are not together. The Downy Woodpecker's bill is proportionally smaller than the Hairy Woodpecker's when compared to head size.

2 COLOR PATTERN

When identifying a bird, focus on patterns instead of trying to match every feather.

A picture, even a fleeting glimpse, can be worth a thousand words. As soon as you spot a bird, your eyes take in the overall pattern of light and dark. And if the light allows, you'll probably glimpse the main colors as well. This is all you need to start your identification.

Use these quick glimpses to build a hunch about what your mystery bird is, even if you just saw it flash across a path and vanish into the underbrush. Then, if the bird is kind enough to hop back into view, you'll know what else to look for to settle the identification.

Imagine that you're on vacation in Yosemite National Park. You see a small, bright-yellow bird flitting into the understory. Yellow immediately suggests a warbler (or the larger Western Tanager). Did you pick up a hint of grayness to the head? Or perhaps some glossy black? Just noticing that much can put you on track to identifying either a MacGillivray's Warbler or a Wilson's Warbler.

Wilson's Warbler

Some birds have very fine differences that take practice even to see at all. But don't start looking for those details until you've used overall patterns to let the bird remind you what it is. Read on for a few tips about noticing patches of light and dark, and the boldness or faintness of a bird's markings.

Light and Dark

When you're trying to make an ID, keep in mind that details can change, but overall patterns stay the same.

Remember that birds molt and their feathers wear. Their appearance can vary if the bird is old or young, or by how well it had been eating last time it molted. And of course, the light the bird is sitting in can have a huge effect on the colors you see.

At a distance and in very quick sightings, colors fade and all that's left are light and dark. It helps to familiarize yourself with common patterns. For example, American White Pelicans are large white birds with black trailing edges to their wings. Snow Geese are similarly shaped and colored, but the black in their wings is confined to the wingtips.

Lesser Scaup

Greater and Lesser scaups are dark ducks with a pale patch on the side; Northern Shovelers are the opposite: light-bodied ducks with a dark patch on the side.

Many birds are dark above and pale below—a widespread pattern in the animal world that helps avoid notice by predators. By reversing this pattern, male Bobolinks, with their dark underparts and light backs, look conspicuous even from all the way across a field.

Other birds seem to be trying to call attention to themselves by wearing bright patches of color in prominent places. Male Red-winged Blackbirds use their vivid shoulder patches to intimidate their rivals (notice how they cover up the patches when sneaking around off their territory). American Redstarts flick bright orange patches in their wings and tail, perhaps to scare insects out of their hiding places.

Red-winged Blackbird

Many birds, including Dark-eyed Juncos, Spotted and Eastern towhees, American Robins, and several hummingbirds, flash white in the tail when they fly, possibly as a way of confusing predators. White flashes in the wings are common, too: look for them in Northern Mockingbirds; Acorn, Golden-fronted, and Red-bellied woodpeckers; Common and Lesser nighthawks; and Phainopeplas.

Bold and Faint

Notice strong and fine patterns.

There are some confusing bird species that sit side by side in your field guide, wearing what seems like the exact same markings and defying you to identify them. Experienced birders can find clues to these tricky identifications by noticing how boldly or finely patterned their bird is. These differences can take a trained eye to detect, but the good news is that there's a great trial case right outside at your backyard feeder.

Male Purple Finch   *Male House Finch*

House Finches are common across most of temperate North America. Much of the continent also gets visits from the very similar Purple Finch. Males of the two species are red on the head and chest and brown and streaky elsewhere. The females are both brown and streaky. So how do you tell them apart? Look at how strongly they're marked.

Male House Finches tend to be boldly streaked down the flanks, whereas male Purple Finches are much paler and more diffusely streaked. Even the red is more distinct, and more confined to the head and breast, in a male House Finch. Male Purple Finches look washed all over, even on the back, in a paler raspberry red.

The all-brown females of these two species are an even better way to build your skills. The streaks on female House Finches are indistinct, brown on brown, with little actual white showing through. If a female Purple Finch lands next to it, she'll stand out with crisply defined brown streaks against a white background, particularly on the head.

Once you've had some practice, these small differences can be very useful. Similar degrees in marking can be seen between the coarsely marked Song Sparrow and finely painted Lincoln's Sparrow, and between immature Sharp-shinned and Cooper's hawks.

BEHAVIOR

3

There's what birds wear, and then there's how they wear it. A bird's attitude goes a long way in identification.

Bird species don't just look unique, they have unique ways of acting, moving, sitting, and flying. When you learn these habits, you can recognize many birds the same way you notice a friend walking through a crowd of strangers.

Chances are you'll never see a Cedar Waxwing poking through the underbrush for seeds, or a Wood Thrush zigzagging over a summer pond catching insects. But similar-sized birds such as towhees and swallows do this all the time. Behavior is one key way these birds differ.

Because so much of a bird's identity is evident in how it acts, behavior can lead you to an ID in the blink of an eye, in bad light, or from a quarter-mile away. Before you even pick up your binoculars, notice how your bird is sitting, how it's feeding or moving, whether it's in a flock, and if it has any nervous habits such as flicking its wings or bobbing its tail.

And remember that to get good at recognizing birds by their behavior, you must spend time watching them. It's tempting to grab your field guide as soon as you see a field mark. Or, after identifying a common bird, you might feel rushed to move on and find something more unusual. Resist these urges. Relax and watch the bird for as long as it will let you. This is how you learn the way a bird acts, how you discover something new...and let's face it, it's probably why you went out bird watching in the first place.

Posture

The most basic aspect of behavior is posture, or how a bird presents itself.

You can learn to distinguish many similarly proportioned birds just from the poses they assume. It's a skill that includes recognizing a bird's size and shape, and adds in the impression of the bird's habits and attitude.

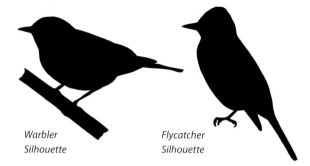

Warblers and flycatchers can be distinguished by posture.

Warbler Silhouette

Flycatcher Silhouette

For example, in the fall season, the small, drab-green Pine Warbler looks similar to the Acadian Flycatcher, right down to the two wingbars and the straight bill. But you're unlikely to confuse the two because their postures are so different. Pine Warblers hold their bodies horizontally and often seem to crouch. Flycatchers sit straight up and down, staying on alert for passing insects.

Horizontal versus vertical posture is the first step. Next, get an impression of the how the bird carries itself. Does it seem inquisitive like a chickadee or placid like a thrush? Does it lean forward, ready for mischief, like a crow? Or is it assertive and stiff, like a robin? Do the bird's eyes dart around after targets, like a flycatcher, or methodically scan the foliage like a vireo? Is the bird constantly on alert, like a finch in the open? Nervous and skittish like a kinglet?

Movement

As soon as a sitting bird starts to move, it gives you a new set of clues about what it is.

You'll not only see different parts of the bird and new postures, you'll sense more of the bird's attitude through the rhythm of its movements. There's a huge difference between the bold way a robin bounces up to a perch, a mockingbird's showy, fluttering arrival, and the meekness of a towhee skulking around.

On the water, some ducks, such as Mallard and Northern Pintail, tip up (or "dabble") to reach submerged vegetation. Others, including scaup and Redhead, disappear from view as they dive for shellfish and other prey. Among the divers, you'll notice that some species, such as eiders, open their wings just before they dive. These ducks flap their wings for propulsion underwater, and they almost always begin a dive this way.

Flight Pattern

Certain birds have flight patterns that give them away.

Almost nothing flaps as slowly as a Great Blue Heron—you can see this from miles away. Learn the long swooping flight of most woodpeckers and you'll be able to pick them out before they've even landed.

Many small birds, particularly finches, have bouncy, roller-coasterlike trajectories caused by fluttering their wings and then actually folding them shut for a split second.

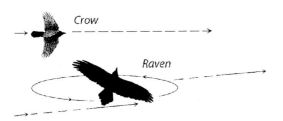

Crows and Ravens

Flight style can be a great way to identify birds at a distance. Although crows and ravens look very similar, they fly quite differently. American Crows flap slowly and methodically, whereas Common Ravens take frequent breaks from flapping to soar or glide.

Birds of prey have their own distinct styles. Red-tailed Hawks and other buteos fly with deep, regular wingbeats or soar in circles on broad wings. Falcons fly with powerful beats of their sharply pointed wings.

Feeding Style

Much of the time that you watch birds on the move, you'll be watching them feed, so it pays to become familiar with foraging styles.

Some are obvious: the patient stalking of a heron; the continual up-and-back sprints of Sanderlings; the plunge of a kingfisher. But you can develop a surprisingly specific impression of almost any bird just from a few seconds of watching it forage.

For example, swallows, flycatchers, vireos, finches, and thrushes are all roughly the same size, but they feed in totally different manners: swallows eat on the wing; flycatchers dart out from perches and quickly return; vireos creep through leaves; finches sit still and crush seeds; and thrushes hop low to the ground eating insects and fruit.

Flocking

A flock of kingfishers? A single starling all on its own? Some species seem to be born loners, and others are never found solo.

Even among flocking birds, there are those content to travel in threes and fours, and others that gather by the dozens and hundreds. A noisy group of yellow birds in a treetop is much more likely to be a flock of American Goldfinches than a group of Yellow Warblers. A visit to northern coasts in winter might net you several thousand Brant, but you'll probably only see Harlequin Ducks by the handful.

You'll often see gulls in flocks on a beach, in a parking lot, or wheeling overhead.

Learning the tendencies of birds to flock and their tolerance for crowding is one more aspect of behavior you can use. Just remember that many species get more sociable as summer draws to a close. After nesting is over and young are feeding themselves, adults can relax and stop defending their territories.

4 HABITAT

A habitat is a bird's home, and many birds are choosy. Narrow down your list by keeping in mind where you are.

Identifying birds quickly and correctly is often about probability. By knowing what's likely to be seen you can get a head start on recognizing the birds you run into. And when you see a bird you weren't expecting, you'll know to take an extra look.

Habitat is both the first and last question to ask yourself when identifying a bird. Ask it first, so you know what you're likely to see, and last as a double-check. You can fine-tune your expectations by taking geographic range and time of year into consideration.

Birding by Probability

We think of habitats as collections of plants—grassland, cypress, pine woods, broadleaf forest. But they're equally collections of birds. By noting the habitat you're in, you can build a hunch about the kinds of birds you're most likely to see.

Of course, if you only let yourself identify birds you expect to see, you'll have a hard time finding unusual birds. The best way to find rarities is to know your common birds first (the ones left over are the rare ones). Birding by probability just helps you sort through them that much more quickly.

Use Range Maps

You don't have to give yourself headaches trying to keep straight every last bird in your field guide. They may all be lined up next to each other on the pages, but that doesn't mean they're all in your backyard or local park.

Make it a habit to check the range maps before you make an identification. For example, you can strike off at least half of the devilishly similar *Empidonax* flycatchers at once, just by taking into account where you are when you see one. Similarly, North America has two kinds of small nuthatches with brown heads, but they don't occur within about 800 miles of each other.

Of course, birds do stray from their home ranges, sometimes fantastically, and that's part of the fun. But remember that you're birding by probability, so first compare your bird against what's likely to be present. If nothing matches, then start taking notes.

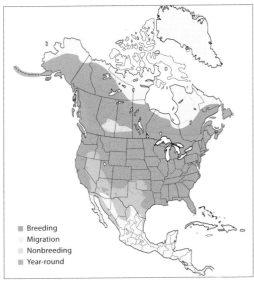

■ Breeding
  Migration
  Nonbreeding
■ Year-round

Range map of the Bald Eagle

Check the Time of Year

Range maps hold another clue to identification—they tell you when a bird is likely to be around.

Many of summer's birds, including most of the warblers, flycatchers, thrushes, hummingbirds, and shorebirds, are gone by late fall. Other birds move in to replace them. This mass exodus and arrival is part of what makes bird watching during migration so exciting.

Use eBird to Help

eBird's online species maps are a great way to explore both range and season. You can zoom in to see bird records from your immediate surroundings, and you can filter the map to show you just sightings from a particular month or season.

Ruby-throated Hummingbird

Another way to focus on the most likely birds near you is to use our free Merlin® Bird ID app for iOS and Android. Merlin takes your location and date, asks you a few simple questions, and gives you a short list of matching possibilities. See page 30 for more on Merlin.

USING FIELD MARKS TO IDENTIFY BIRDS

Once you've looked at Size and Shape, Color Pattern, Behavior, and Habitat to decide what general type of bird you're looking at, you may still have a few similar birds to choose between. To be certain of your identification, you'll need to look at field marks.

Birds display a huge variety of patterns and colors, which they have evolved in part to recognize other members of their own species. Birders use these features (called "field marks") to help distinguish species. Pay particular attention to the field marks of the head and the field marks of the wing.

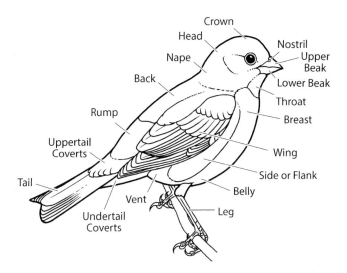

Ornithologists divide a bird's body into topographical regions: beak (or bill), head, back, wings, tail, breast, belly, and legs. To help with identification, many of these regions are divided still further. This diagram shows some of the commonly used descriptive terms.

Field Marks of the Head

When identifying an unknown bird, markings on the head are particularly important, as are beak shape and size. Here are head markings visually displayed to help you along.

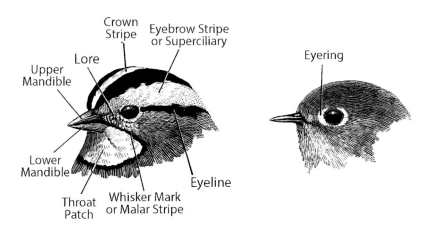

Field Marks of the Wing

A bird's wings are another great place to pick up clues about its identity. In a few groups, notably warblers and vireos, the presence of wingbars and patches of color on the wing can give positive identification even when the bird is in nonbreeding plumage. In other groups, such as flycatchers and sparrows, the absence of wing markings may be important. It also pays to learn the main feather groups, such as primaries, secondaries, tertials, and coverts, and to look for "feather edging"—a different color running along the edges of feathers.

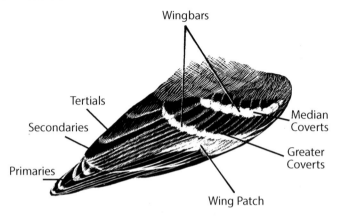

Wingbars

Tertials

Secondaries

Primaries

Median Coverts

Greater Coverts

Wing Patch

USE MERLIN TO SEE THE POSSIBILITIES

Merlin®, an instant bird identification app from the Cornell Lab of Ornithology, can make many identifications simple. It works by narrowing down your choices, prompting you to enter the date, location, and the bird's size, colors, and behavior.

Merlin was designed to be a birding coach for beginning and intermediate bird watchers. Merlin asks you the same questions that an expert birder would ask to help solve a mystery bird sighting. Notice that date and location are Merlin's first and most important questions.

It takes years of experience in the field to know what species are expected at a given location and date. Merlin shares this knowledge with you based on more than one billion sightings submitted to eBird from birders across the world.

Merlin also asks you to describe the color, size, and behavior of the bird you saw. Because no two people describe birds exactly the same way, Merlin presents a shortlist of matching species based on descriptions from Cornell Lab experts as well as thousands of bird enthusiasts who helped "teach" Merlin by participating in online activities.

If you photograph a bird and aren't sure what it is, Merlin can help identify that as well. Using a computer vision system trained on millions of images from the Macaulay Library, the Photo ID tool will help guide you to the right answer.

Much like a modern field-guide app, Merlin also provides world-class photos, ID text, sounds, and range maps. You can browse thousands of stunning images taken by top photographers and listen to a selection of songs and calls for each species. Merlin works all over the world, so no matter where you live or might be traveling, download Merlin for FREE (see page 30 for details).

THE RIGHT STUFF

10 TIPS FOR BEGINNING BIRD WATCHERS

Birding mainly involves patience, careful the wonder and beauty of the natural world overtake you. But having the right equipment can help too:

1 Binoculars

Your enjoyment of birds depends hugely on how great they look through your binoculars, so make sure you're getting a big, bright, crisp picture through yours. In recent years excellent binoculars have become available at surprisingly low prices. So, while binoculars under $100 may seem tempting, it's truly worth it to spend $250 to $300 for vastly superior images as well as lifetime warranties, waterproof housing, and lighter weight. We suggest getting 7-power or 8-power binoculars—they're a nice mix of magnification while still allowing you a wide enough view that your bird won't be constantly hopping out of your image.

2 Field Guides
Field guides like this one focus on the most common species in your area and are meant to be portable. Unlike their digital counterparts, they often earn a special place on windowsills, providing a ready resource at home for hours of study and daydreaming.

3 Bird Feeders
With binoculars for viewing and a guide to help you figure out what's what, the next step is to attract birds to your backyard, where you can get a good look at them. Bird feeders come in all types, but we recommend starting with a black-oil sunflower feeder, adding a suet feeder in winter and a hummingbird feeder in summer (or all year in parts of the continent). From there you can diversify to feeders that house millet, thistle seeds, mealworms, and fruit to attract other types of species. In sections that follow, we describe the main types of bird feeders along with images of what they look like, to help you choose the right feeders for your yard and to attract the birds you want to see.

4 Spotting Scopes
By this point in our list, you've got pretty much all the gear you need to be a birder—that is, until you start looking at those ducks on the far side of the pond, or shorebirds in mudflats, or that Golden Eagle perched on a tree limb a quarter-mile away. Though they're not cheap, spotting scopes are indispensable for seeing details at long range—or simply reveling in intricate plumage details that can be brought to life only with a 20x to 60x zoom. The fact that they are mounted on a stable tripod also helps you see details that can be challenging to appreciate while hand-holding binoculars. And scopes, like binoculars, are coming down in price while going up in quality.

5 Cameras

Affordable modern digital cameras allow even novice photographers to take great photos anywhere, anytime. And even if you don't get a great shot every time, even a blurry photo of a bird can help you or others clinch its ID. Birds are inherently artistic creatures, and more and more amateur photographers are connecting with birds through taking gorgeous pictures. If you don't want to invest in a camera with a big lens or long zoom right away, you can also try digiscoping—fitting your point-and-shoot camera or your smartphone's camera up to a spotting scope or binoculars to get a magnified view.

6 Keeping a List

"Listing" doesn't have to be for hardcore birders only; it's fun to record special moments from your days of birding. Many people save their records online using eBird. A Cornell Lab project, eBird allows you to keep track of every place and day you go bird watching, enter notes, share sightings with friends, and explore the data other eBirders have entered. Learn more about eBird and how to use it for free on pages 59–61.

7 Birding by Ear

Many people love bird sounds—calls, songs, and other avian utterances that fill the air. You can use these sounds as clues to identify species. When you are out in the field, use Merlin® to identify bird song.

8 Visual Bird Identification Skills

Now that we've covered the physical tools that equip you for bird watching, let's loop back to your mental tools. Once you're outside and surrounded by birds, practice the four-step approach to identification that we shared earlier in Birding 101: Size and Shape; Color Pattern; Behavior; and Habitat.

9 Birding Apps and Digital Field Guides

If you have a smartphone, you can carry a bookshelf in your pocket. You've already learned about the free Merlin® Bird ID app, but there are many other resources at your disposal. Download the eBird app to keep track of your bird observations in the field, as well as explore recent sightings and bird lists for nearby hotspots. There are also digital field guides—most of the major printed field guides have an app or eBook version. Some specialized apps cover specific groups of species, such as the Warbler Guide and Raptor ID apps. Others, like LarkWire, focus on helping you learn bird song. Search for them in Apple and Android stores. Our All About Birds species guide (*AllAboutBirds.org*) works on mobile devices, giving you access to free ID information and sound recordings straight from your smartphone's internet browser.

10 Connect with Other Birders

Bird watching can be a relaxing solo pursuit, like a walk in the woods decorated with bird sightings. But birding can also be a social endeavor, and the best way to learn is from other people. A great way to connect with people and birds in your area is to look on **birding.aba.org/**. You'll get emails that will tell you what people have been seeing, announce local bird outings,

and connect you with members of your local birding club. Most regions also have Facebook groups where people share what they've been seeing and welcome newcomers. There's a decent chance that someone's leading a bird walk near you this weekend—and they'd love to have you come along.

LISTENING TO BIRDS

When a bird sings, it's telling you what it is, where it is, and often what is happening.

You can only see straight ahead, but you can hear in all directions at once. Learning bird songs is a great way to identify birds hidden by dense foliage, birds far away, birds at night, and birds that look identical to each other.

And then there's the "dawn chorus," that time as the sun begins to light up the world, when birds join together in a symphony of sound. When you first listen to a dawn chorus in full swing, the sheer onslaught of bird song can be overwhelming. How does anyone begin to pick apart the chirps, whistles, and trills that are echoing out of the woods? The answer, of course, is to concentrate on one bird at a time—and that approach holds true when you're trying to learn individual songs, too. Don't try to memorize each entire song you hear; instead, focus on one quality of the sound at a time. Many birds have a characteristic rhythm, pitch, or tone to their song. Here's how to use them:

Rhythm

Get used to a bird's characteristic tempo as well as the number of distinct sections to its song. Marsh Wrens sing in a hurry, while White-throated Sparrows are much more leisurely.

Repetition

Some birds characteristically repeat syllables or phrases before moving on to a new sound. Northern Mockingbirds do this many times in a row. Though Brown Thrashers sound similar, they typically repeat only twice before changing to a new syllable.

Wood Thrush

Pitch

Most birds sing in a characteristic range, with smaller birds (such as the Cedar Waxwing) typically having higher voices and larger birds (such as the Common Raven) usually having deeper voices. Many bird songs change pitch, so it helps to pay attention to the overall pitch trend in a song. Some birds are distinctive for having steady voices, such as the Chipping Sparrow's trill.

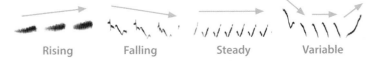

Rising   Falling   Steady   Variable

Tone

The tone of a bird's song is sometimes hard to describe, but it can be very distinctive. As a start, pay attention to whether a bird's voice is a clear whistle, harsh or scratchy, liquid and flutelike, or a clear trill. If you can remember the quality of a bird's voice, it can give you a clue to the bird's identity even if the bird doesn't sing the same notes every time.

- **Buzzy:** Like a bee–a good example would be Townsend's Warbler song.

Buzzy

- **Clear:** Something you could whistle. Northern Cardinals have a clear song, as do Yellow Warblers.

Clear

- **Trilled:** A lot of sounds in a row that are too fast to count (technically, more than 11 sounds per second). Chipping Sparrows and Dark-eyed Juncos sing trills.

Trilled

PHOTOGRAPHING BIRDS

5 BASICS OF GOOD BIRD PHOTOGRAPHY

With the explosion in availability and design of digital cameras, it's now possible for hobbyists to take amazingly good photos. Though your photos may not show up on the cover of *National Geographic*, you can up the "wow" factor by paying attention to a few basics.

Beyond the mechanical aspects of shutter speed, aperture, and ISO (which digital cameras increasingly handle automatically), there is an indefinable something that transforms an image into a work of art. Often thought of as talent, just as often it's the result of hours of practice and attention to detail. Here are five basics of good bird photography to bear in mind:

1 Lighting

The best times to shoot are morning and late afternoon when the light is angled, warmer, and more subdued. It's harder to take a good picture in the middle of a bright, clear day because images end up with too much contrast, where light areas get washed out and shadows turn inky black.

Having the source of light behind and slightly to one side of you creates a more three-dimensional subject. Having your subject backlit rarely works well unless you're deliberately going after a silhouette.

2 Framing

Professionals usually avoid placing any subject in the exact center of a photograph. It tends to be more visually stimulating to see the bird off to one side, facing inward. Our own eyes naturally follow the same trajectory. Luckily, it's easy to crop your image later on to get the framing how you want it, so framing in the field is less important unless you're very close to your subject.

3 Composition

Non-bird elements in your picture can add or detract from a pleasing composition. Branches, shrubbery, rocks, and flowers can be a distraction—or they can be used artfully to frame the bird within the picture. Although you want to avoid having a branch right behind the bird looking like it's growing out of its head, incorporating some part of the bird's habitat often makes a shot better. If the background is too busy, try opening the aperture to blur the background and make your subject stand out.

4 Angle

You can shoot from a position that is higher than your subject, lower, at eye level, or somewhere in between. Each situation can be different—but adjusting your height to shoot the bird at eye level is often a good choice, as it puts the viewer on the same plane as the bird. To get closer to wary birds, you can wear muted clothing, hide behind vegetation, and move slowly and calmly in a zigzag pattern. It is never a good idea to bait a bird or to approach so closely that you flush the bird or alter its behavior.

Sanderling

5 Knowledge of Your Subject

To be the best bird photographer you can be, you really have to know birds. For example, knowing the habitat and behavior of a species allows you to predict where you're likely to find them and anticipate what they might do next. For example, berry bushes attract Cedar Waxwings; herons haunt the edges of marshes and ponds; waterfowl often rest and preen in the same spot every day. Study your subject and you'll know when and where to get the shot.

What Kind of Camera?

We're in a golden age of camera design and there are great options at every level of interest. Serious enthusiasts tend toward DSLR (digital single-lens reflex) or mirrorless cameras with interchangeable lenses, but these can be expensive. At the entry level, so-called "superzoom" cameras can produce surprisingly good results while remaining compact and fairly inexpensive.

DIGISCOPING

Placing the lens of a digital camera to the eyepiece of a spotting scope is called "digiscoping." It's an inexpensive way to take decent pictures without a heavy, expensive telephoto lens.

Both scopes and digital cameras have improved tremendously since the dawn of digiscoping. One of the most significant advances has been the advent of smartphones, which are now arguably the best tool for digiscoping and certainly the most convenient. Scopes, too, have come down in price.

Digiscoped Rose-breasted Grosbeak

There can be different goals in digiscoping. It can be practiced slowly and patiently to capture frame-worthy photos, whether detail-rich or artistically blurred. More often, it's a handy way to capture shots to remind yourself of a special moment or to back up a rare bird report. It's even becoming common for people to record video while digiscoping.

Granted, digiscoping does require a spotting scope, which can cost as much as a camera and telephoto lens—but some birders are happy to put their money toward a scope that can do double duty in both bird watching and photography.

Getting a good image when digiscoping comes down to gathering plenty of light, getting the camera lens the correct distance from the scope's eyepiece, and holding everything steady.

Getting Connected

There are a variety of ways to bring the camera lens and scope eyepiece together. For smartphones, the earliest method involved placing a finger between phone and eyepiece both to steady the lens and keep it at the correct distance. Today you can find phone adapters custom-sized to hold a phone in the proper position—greatly cutting down on fiddling and frustration.

If you don't line up camera and eyepiece perfectly, you may get uneven focus, part of the image cut off, or shadows creeping in as light leaks in between scope and camera lenses. Remember that the many commercial adapters are not universal, so make sure you get what fits your gear.

Standing Steady

The magnification produced by digiscoping is just what you need to pull your subject in close, but it also magnifies small movements from wind or a shaky trigger finger. Keeping extraneous motion to a minimum is of paramount importance. A quality tripod for your scope will provide stable support and prevent your photos from turning into a blurry mess. You'll find that a rock-steady tripod will be well worth it anyway—even in routine bird watching without attaching a camera.

5 TIPS FOR SUCCESSFUL DIGISCOPING

1 Let There Be Light

One cause of blurry photos is low light coming through the scope, which forces a slower shutter speed and increases the effect of motion. Using larger, brighter scopes, such as 85-mm models rather than 65-mm models, results in noticeably better digiscoped photos. If you can change your camera's ISO (a feature

Digiscoped American Goldfinch

becoming more common on smartphones), setting it higher can get you a faster shutter speed.

2 Resist the Zoom

For scopes with a zoom, bear in mind that you quickly lose light as you zoom in. The human eye is good at compensating for this; cameras less so. Take advantage of your camera's many megapixels by shooting at a lower, brighter zoom setting and then cropping later.

3 Capture the Motion

Many cameras and phones have a continuous shooting feature that takes photos one after another. This setting can help you catch birds in just the right pose. As an alternative, consider shooting video of a fast-moving subject—this can be more helpful than still photos when trying to identify a bird later.

4 Try It with Your Binoculars

Sometimes called "digibinning," this advanced technique can sometimes produce decent photos. If you don't already have a spotting scope, it's a less expensive way to get into digiscoping. But be warned: it's hard to hold the binocular-phone combination steady. It's a good idea to start with large, stationary birds such as herons.

5 Practice, Practice, Practice

Fortunately, once you've got the equipment, taking digital photos is virtually free. It may seem impossible at first, but you'll quickly improve as you become comfortable with setting up the scope and handling your camera's controls. Don't be afraid to experiment—you never know what you'll come away with.

ATTRACTING BIRDS TO YOUR YARD

BIRDSCAPING

You can watch birds anywhere.

American Goldfinch

Parks, nature preserves, and wildlife refuges provide some of the most diverse species, but the easiest place to watch birds is your own backyard. Enhancing your yard to attract and support birds is called "birdscaping."

Putting up a feeder is an easy way to attract birds. But if you'd prefer a more natural approach or you want to satisfy more than birds' nutritional needs, consider landscaping your yard—even just a part of it—to be more bird friendly. Even a small yard can provide vital habitat. The core concept is simple—all birds need three basic things from their habitats.

1 Food

Your birds can get food from feeders that you put up. Landscaping your yard to provide the fruit, seeds, beneficial insects, and other small animals that birds feed on adds natural food sources for birds, too.

2 Water

All living things need water to survive. Providing this habitat necessity is one of the quickest ways to attract birds to your property. If there is a water source in your yard, such as a pond, creek, birdbath, or even a puddle, you've probably noticed birds using it. If you don't have a water feature yet, a birdbath is an easy way to provide this habitat need.

3 Shelter

Whether it's protection from the elements, safe places to hide from predators, or secure locations to hide nests, providing shelter is one of the best ways to make your property bird-friendly.

Improve Your Yard

Take a "bird's-eye" look at your backyard. Does it provide those things? If not, there are plants you can grow and many other ways you can enhance your yard to make it safe and inviting for birds. Here are some tips to help you:

1 Evaluate Your Yard
First, take stock of what you already have. Draw a map of your property including buildings, sidewalks, fences, trees, shrubs, feeders, and nest boxes. Note sunny or shady sites, low or wet areas, sandy sites, and plants you want to keep.

2 Start With a Plan
Before you start digging holes and rearranging your yard, develop a planting plan. Draw each new plant onto a piece of tracing paper, then place that over the map of your yard. Once your plants are in, use your map as a reminder about which ones need to be watered and weeded, especially in the first year after planting. Mulch is great for keeping moisture in and weeds out.

3 Think Variety
Try to include variety and year-round value in your planting plan. Look for places to include grasses, legumes, hummingbird flowers, plants that fruit in summer and fall, winter-persistent plants, and conifers for shelter. Plant native species instead of exotics, and look for places to create shelter with a brush pile or standing dead tree.

BIRD FEEDERS

Fifty million people in North America feed birds and it's a great way to attract birds to your backyard. But feeders are not one size fits all—different species are attracted to different designs. Here are the main types of feeders and the types of birds they attract.

Ground

Many species of birds, including sparrows and doves, prefer to feed on large, flat surfaces and may not visit any type of elevated feeder. Song Sparrows and many towhee species, for instance, will rarely land on a feeder, but they will readily eat fallen seed from the ground beneath your feeders. To attract these species,  try spreading seed on the ground or on a large surface such as the top of a picnic table. Ground feeders that sit low to the ground with mesh screens for good drainage can also be used. Make sure that there are no predators around, including outdoor cats.

Large and Small Hopper

A hopper feeder is a platform on which walls and a roof are built, forming a "hopper" that protects seed against the weather. Large hoppers attract most species of feeder birds and will allow larger species, such as doves and grackles, to feed. Small hoppers will attract smaller birds while preventing those larger species from comfortably perching and monopolizing the feeder.

Large and Small Tube

A tube feeder is a hollow cylinder, often made of plastic, with multiple feeding ports and perches. Tube feeders keep seed fairly dry. Feeders with short perches accommodate small birds such as finches but exclude larger birds such as grackles and jays. The size of the feeding ports varies as well, depending on the type of seed to be offered. Note that special smaller feeding ports are required for nyjer (thistle) seed to prevent spillage.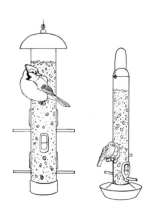

Sugar Water

Sugar-water feeders are specially made to dispense sugar water through small holes. Choose a feeder that is easy to take apart and clean, because the feeder should be washed or run through the dishwasher frequently.

Platform

A platform feeder is any flat, raised surface onto which bird food is spread. The platform should have plenty of drainage holes to prevent water accumulation. A platform with a roof will help keep seeds dry. Trays attract most species of feeder birds. Placed near the ground, they are likely to attract juncos, doves, and sparrows.

Suet Cage

Suet or suet mixes can be placed in a specially made cage, tied to trees, or smeared into knotholes. Cages that are only open at the bottom tend to be starling-resistant but allow woodpeckers, nuthatches, and chickadees to feed by clinging upside down.

Thistle Sock

Thistle "socks" are fine-mesh bags to which birds cling to extract nyjer or thistle seeds. Seed within thistle socks can become quite wet with rain, so only use large ones during periods when you have enough finches to consume the contents in a few days.

Window Feeder

Small plastic feeders affixed to window glass with suction cups, and platform feeders hooked into window frames, attract finches, chickadees, titmice, and some sparrows. They afford wonderful, close-up views of birds, and their placement makes them the safest of all feeder types for preventing window collisions.

FEEDER PLACEMENT & SAFETY

Place feeders in a quiet area where they are easy to see and convenient to refill. Place them close to natural cover, such as trees or shrubs. Evergreens are ideal, as they provide thick foliage that hides birds from predators and buffers winter winds. Be careful not to place feeders too close to trees with strong branches that can provide jump-off points for squirrels and cats. A distance of about 10 feet is a good compromise.

Hummingbird Feeders

Place hummingbird feeders in the shade if possible, as sugar solution spoils quickly in the sun. Don't use honey, artificial sweeteners, or food coloring. If bees or wasps become a problem, try moving the feeder.

Clean and refill hummingbird feeders every few days in a dishwasher or very hot water to prevent dangerous mold. Keep seed and suet feeders clean by washing them periodically in a dishwasher, with soap and very hot water, or with a diluted bleach or vinegar solution.

Window Strikes

Ornithologists estimate that up to *one billion* birds are killed by hitting windows in the United States and Canada each year. Placing feeders close to your windows (ideally closer than three feet) can help reduce this problem. When feeders are close, a bird leaving the feeder cannot gain enough momentum to do harm if it strikes the window.

You can prevent more window strikes by breaking up reflections of trees and open space, which birds perceive as a flight path through your home. Techniques include attaching streamers, suction-cup feeders, or decals to windows, crisscrossing branches within the window frames, or installing awnings or screens. Acopian Bird Savers are closely spaced ropes that hang down over windows. They do the work of tape or decals but are easier to install and can be aesthetically pleasing.

Another method is to attach netting to the outside of the window to buffer the impact. Deer netting (the kind used to keep deer from eating plants in your yard) works well, pulled taut to prevent any entanglements.

To learn more about window crashes, how to prevent them, and more specific solutions to this problem, visit *https://tinyurl.com/preventing-window-crashes*.

BIRD FOOD

Sunflower seeds attract the widest variety of birds and are the mainstay food used in most bird feeders. Other varieties of seed can help attract different types of birds to your feeders and yard and this section highlights many of them. When buying mixtures, note that those that contain red millet, oats, and other fillers are not attractive to most birds and can lead to a lot of waste.

Sunflower Seeds

There are two kinds of sunflower—black oil and striped. The black oil seeds ("oilers") have very thin shells, easy for virtually all seed-eating birds to crack open, and the kernels within have a high fat content, which is extremely valuable for most winter birds. Striped sunflower seeds have a thicker shell, much harder for House Sparrows and blackbirds to crack open. So, if you're inundated with species you'd rather not subsidize at your feeder, before you do anything else, try switching to striped sunflower. Sunflower in the shell can be offered in a wide variety of feeders, including trays, tube feeders, hoppers, and acrylic window feeders. Sunflower hearts and chips shouldn't be offered in tube feeders where moisture can collect. Since squirrels love sunflower seeds, be prepared to take steps to squirrel-proof your feeder if needed.

Safflower

Safflower has a thick shell, hard for some birds to crack open, but is a favorite among cardinals. Some grosbeak chickadees, doves, and native sparrows also eat it. According to some sources, House Sparrows, European Starlings, and squirrels don't like safflower, but in some areas they seem to have developed a taste for it. Cardinals and grosbeaks tend to prefer tray and hopper feeders, which ma these feeders a good choice for offering safflower.

Nyjer or Thistle

Small finches including American Goldfinches, Lesser Goldfinches, Indigo Buntings, Pine Siskins, and Common Redpolls often devour these tiny, black, needlelike seeds. As invasive thistle plants became a

recognized problem in North America, suppliers shifted to a daisylike plant, known as *Guizotia abyssinica*, that produces a similar type of small, oily, rich seed. The plant is now known as niger or nyjer, and is imported from overseas. The seeds are heat-sterilized during importation to limit their chance of spreading invasively, while retaining their food value.

White Proso Millet

White millet is a favorite with ground-feeding birds including quails, native sparrows, doves, towhees, juncos, and cardinals. Unfortunately, it's also a favorite of House Sparrows, which are already subsidized by human activities and supported at unnaturally high population levels by current agricultural practices and habitat changes. When these species are present, you may want to stop offering millet; virtually all the birds that like it are equally attracted to black oil sunflower. Because white millet is so preferred by ground-feeding birds, scatter it on the ground or set low platform feeders with excellent drainage.

Shelled and Cracked Corn

Corn is eaten by grouse, pheasants, turkeys, quail, cardinals, grosbeaks, crows, ravens, jays, doves, ducks, cranes, and other species. Unfortunately, corn has two serious problems. First, it's a favorite of House Sparrows, starlings, geese, bears, raccoons, and deer. Second, corn is the bird food most likely to be contaminated with aflatoxins, which are extremely toxic even at low levels. Never buy corn in plastic bags, never allow it to get wet, never offer it in amounts that can't be consumed in a day during rainy or very humid weather, and be conscientious about raking up old corn. Never offer corn covered in a red dye. Corn should be offered in fairly small amounts at a time on tray feeders. Don't offer it in tube feeders that could harbor moisture.

Peanuts

Peanuts are very popular with jays, crows, chickadees, titmice, woodpeckers, and many other species, but are also favored by squirrels, bears, raccoons, and other animals. Like corn, peanuts have a high likelihood of harboring aflatoxins, so must be kept dry and used up fairly quickly. Peanuts in the shell can be set out on platform feeders or right on a deck railing or windo feeder as a special treat for jays. If peanuts, peanut hearts, or mixtures of peanuts and other seeds are offered in tube feeders, make sure to change the seed frequently, especially during rainy or humid weather, and be sure to completely empty out and clean the tube every time you do so.

Milo or Sorghum

Milo is a favorite with many western ground-feeding birds. On Cornell Lab of Ornithology seed-preference tests, Steller's Jays, Curve-billed Thrashers, and Gambel's Quails preferred milo to sunflower. In another study, House Sparrows did not eat milo. Milo should be scattered on the ground or on low tray feeders.

Golden Millet, Red Millet, Flax, and Others

These seeds are often used as fillers in packaged birdseed mixes, but most birds shun them. Waste seed becomes a breeding ground for bacteria and fungus, contaminating fresh seed more quickly. Make sure to read the ingredients list on birdseed mixtures, avoiding those with these seeds. If a seed mix has a lot of small, re seeds, make sure they're milo or sorghum, not red millet.

Mealworms

Mealworms ae the larvae of the mealworm beetle, *Tenebrio molitor*, and they provide a high-protein treat for many birds. Some people provide live mealworms, while others prefer offering dried larvae. Birds such as chickadees, titmice, wrens, and nuthatches relish this fc and mealworms are one of the few food items that reli attracts bluebirds. Offer mealworms on a flat tray or in a specialized mealworm feeder.

Fruit

Various fruits can prove quite attractive to many species of birds. Oranges cut in half will often attract orioles which will sip the juice and eat the flesh of the orange. Grapes and raisins are a favorite of many fruit-eating birds such as mockingbirds, catbirds, bluebirds, robins, and waxwings. You can also provide a dish of grape jelly for these species, but be sure to avoid jellies containing artificial ingredients like preservatives or sweeteners. Several species are also attracted to the dried seeds of fruits such as pumpkins or apples. Be sure to dispose of any fruit that becomes moldy because some molds create toxins that are harmful to birds.

Sugar Water or Nectar

To make nectar for hummingbirds, add one part table sugar to four parts boiling water and stir. A slightly more diluted mixture can be used for orioles (one part sugar to six parts water). You may want to use regular granulated white sugar rather than raw or cane sugar, which may contain additional ingredients that have unknown effects on hummingbirds. Allow the mixture to cool before filling the feeder. Store extra sugar water in the refrigerator for up to one week (after that it may become moldy, which is dangerous for birds). Adding red food coloring is unnecessary and possibly harmful to birds. Red portals on the feeder, or even a red ribbon tied on top, will attract the birds just as well.

Grit

Birds "chew" their food in the muscular part of their stomac' called the gizzard. To aid in the grinding, birds swallow small, hard materials such as sand, small pebbles, ground eggshells, and ground oyster shells. Grit, therefore, attracts many birds as a food supplement or even by itself. Oyster shells and eggshells have the added benefit of being a good source of calcium, something birds need during egg laying. If you decide to provide eggshells, be sure to sterilize them first. You can boil them for 10 minutes or heat them in an oven (20 minutes at 250°F). Let the eggshells cool, then crush them into pieces about the size of sunflower seeds. Offer the eggshell in a dish or low platform feeder.

WATER SOURCES

Like all animals, birds need water to survive. Though they can extract some moisture from their food, most birds drink water every day. Birds also use water for bathing, to clean their feathers and remove parasites. After splashing around in a bath for a few minutes, a bird usually perches in a sunny spot and fluffs its feathers out to dry. Then it carefully preens each feather, adding a protective coating of oil secreted by a gland at the base of its tail.

Because birds need water for drinking and bathing, they are attracted to water just as they are to feeders. A dependable supply of fresh, clean water is very important. In fact, a birdbath may even bring in birds that don't eat seeds and won't visit your feeders otherwise. Providing water for birds can improve the quality of your backyard bird habitat and should provide you with a fantastic opportunity to observe bird behavior.

Blackburnian Warbler

Birds seem to prefer baths that are at ground level, but raised baths will attract birds as well and may make birds less vulnerable to predators. Change the water daily to keep it fresh and clean. You can also arrange a few branches or stones in the water so that birds can stand on them and drink without getting wet (this is particularly important in winter). Birdbaths should be only an inch or two deep, with a shallow slope.

One of the best ways to make your birdbath more attractive is to provide dripping water. You can buy a dripper or sprayer, or you can recycle an old bucket or plastic container by punching a tiny hole in the bottom, filling it with water, and hanging it above the birdbath so the water drips out. In freezing climates, a birdbath heater will keep ice from freezing. Don't add antifreeze; it is poisonous to all animals, including birds.

To learn more about birdbaths: *https://tinyurl.com/learn-more-birdbaths.*

FEATURES OF A GOOD BIRDHOUSE

IT'S WELL CONSTRUCTED

Untreated Wood – Use untreated, unpainted wood, preferably cedar, pine, cypress, or for larger boxes (owls) non-pressure-treated CDX exterior grade plywood.

Galvanized Screws – Use galvanized screws for the best seal. Nails can loosen over time, allowing rain into the nest box. Screws are also easier to remove for repairs or maintenance. Do not use staples.

IT KEEPS BIRDS DRY

Sloped Roof – A sloped roof that overhangs the front by 2–4″ and the sides by 2″ will help keep out driving rain, while also thwarting predators. Add 1/4″-deep cuts under the roof on all three edges to serve as gutters that channel rain away from the box.

Recessed Floor – A recessed floor keeps the nest from getting wet and helps the box last longer. Recess the floor at least 1/4″ up from the bottom.

Drainage Holes – Add at least four drainage holes (3/8″ to 1/2″ diameter) to the floor to allow any water that enters the box to drain away. Alternatively, you can cut away the corners of the floorboard to create drainage holes.

IT HELPS REGULATE TEMPERATURE

Thick Walls – Walls should be at least 3/4″ thick to insulate the nest properly. (Note that boards sold as 1″ are actually 3/4″ thick.)

Ventilation Holes – For adequate ventilation, there should be two 5/8″-diameter holes on each of the side walls, near the top (four total).

IT KEEPS OUT PREDATORS

No Perches – A perch is unnecessary for the birds and can actually help predators gain access to the box.

Types of Predator Guards – Although predators are a natural part of the environment, birdhouses are typically not as well concealed as natural nests and some predators can make a habit of raiding your boxes. Adding a baffle or guard helps keep nestlings and adults safe from climbing predators. Below are some time-tested options.

←Collar Baffle
A metal collar of about 3 feet in diameter surrounding the pole underneath the nest box.

Stovepipe Baffle→
A more complex pole-mounted baffle. These baffles are generally 8" in diameter and 24"–36" long.

←Hole Guard
A wooden block over the entrance hole that extends the depth of the entrance hole. You can also use an entrance hole guard in combination with a pole-mounted baffle (preferred), or attach it to boxes installed on trees.

Noel Guard→
A wire mesh tube attached to the front of the nest box.

IT HELPS FLEDGLINGS LEAVE THE NEST

Rough Interior Walls – The interior wall below the entrance hole should be rough to help nestlings climb out of the box. For small boxes (wrens and chickadees), plain wood is usually rough enough, but you can roughen smooth boards with coarse sandpaper.

Interior Grooves – A series of shallow horizontal cuts, like a small ladder, works well in medium-sized boxes meant for swallows and bluebirds. Swallows, in particular, need a little help climbing out of boxes.

Duck Boxes – For duck boxes, staple a strip of 1/4"-mesh hardware cloth from floor to hole to help ducklings escape deep boxes..

IT HAS THE RIGHT ENTRANCE SIZE FOR THE RIGHT BIRD

By providing a properly sized entrance hole, you can attract desirable species to your birdhouses while excluding predators and unwanted occupants. Below are the requirements for entrance-hole size for some common species that nest in boxes.

HOLE SIZE	SPECIES
3"	Screech-owls, American Kestrel
2¹/₂"	Northern Flicker
1⁹/₁₆"	Ash-throated Flycatcher, Great Crested Flycatcher, Mountain Bluebird
1¹/₂"	Eastern Bluebird, Western Bluebird, Bewick's Wren, Carolina Wren
1³/₈"	White-breasted Nuthatch, Tree Swallow, Violet-green Swallow
1¼"	Prothonotary Warbler, Red-breasted Nuthatch, Tufted Titmouse
1⅛"	House Wren, chickadees

IT MAKES PLACEMENT AND MAINTENANCE EASY

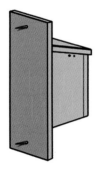

Extended Back

A few extra inches at the top and bottom of your birdhouse can make it easier to mount on a metal pole. Alternatively, you can predrill mounting holes in the back panel before assembly and use a short-handled screwdriver to install the box.

Hinged Door with a Sturdy Closing Mechanism

A hinged side gives you access for cleaning and monitoring your nest box, both of which are important for a successful nesting season. A latch or nail keeps the box securely closed until you are ready to open it.

COMMON NEST BOX PREDATORS

SNAKES – Many snakes are excellent climbers and can easily surmount an unguarded pole. Snakes most likely to climb into birdhouses are generally nonvenomous (such as racers and rat snakes) and helpful at controlling rodents. Avoid installing nest boxes next to brush piles or trees.

RACOOONS – Raccoons are intelligent and can remember nest box locations from year to year. They can be abundant in populated areas. Mount nest boxes on a metal pole equipped with a baffle; avoid mounting them on trees or fence posts.

CHIPMUNKS / MICE – Chipmunks and mice are both nest predators and competitors for nest boxes. To keep chipmunks and mice out, mount boxes away from trees on a metal pole equipped with a baffle.

CATS – Cats are excellent jumpers and can leap to the top of a nest box from a nearby tree or from the ground. Mount your box high enough and far enough from trees so cats cannot spring to the top of the box in a single leap. Keep pet cats indoors for their own safety and that of birds.

INTO DIY?

Visit *nestwatch.org/birdhouses* to get FREE downloadable nest-box plans.

Marbled Godwit ©Luke Seitz/Macaulay Library

GETTING
INVOLVED

CITIZEN SCIENCE

Each month, bird watchers report millions of bird observations to citizen-science projects at the Cornell Lab of Ornithology, contributing to the world's most dynamic and powerful source of information on birds.

The Cornell Lab of Ornithology has been at the forefront of citizen science since 1966. Today, the birding community can use our innovative online tools to tap into millions of records and see how their own sightings fit into the continental picture. Scientists can analyze the same data to reveal striking changes in the movements, distributions, and numbers of birds across time,

and to determine how birds are affected by habitat loss, pollution, and disease.

If you enjoy watching birds, you can help and contribute to science, whether you are a beginner or a seasoned birder. Participating can take as little or as much time as you want—you decide!

There's a Project for Every Bird Watcher
Our fun and meaningful citizen-science projects enable people to watch birds at their favorite locations and share their sightings:

- **eBird** is a powerful tool for keeping track of your sightings and for exploring what others have seen—with global coverage and millions of sightings recorded per month for science and conservation.

- **Great Backyard Bird Count** is possibly the easiest project of all and the best one to start with—a global effort to count birds over one long weekend each February.

- **Project FeederWatch** is a winter project where you count birds at your feeders to help track bird populations and distributions.

- **NestWatch** asks you to report on the nests of birds breeding around you—training and best practices for visiting nests are provided.

- **Celebrate Urban Birds** combines art and science, and encourages participants in urban and rural settings to share their knowledge of local birds and culture.

eBIRD

Since its inception in 2002, eBird has grown into one of the world's largest data sources about living things—thanks to birders contributing a billion or more sightings of birds.

eBird gives birders a convenient, free way to enter, store, and organize their sightings. And it makes those sightings available to others, turning it into a useful resource for studying or finding birds anywhere in the world. Not only that, your sightings power science and conservation, helping scientists identify which species are declining and where best to direct conservation efforts.

Use eBird to start or maintain your birding lists—or use it to find out where and when to go birding. It works all over the world and provides endless ideas about what to do and where to go next. And it's free.

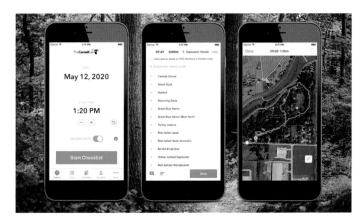

eBird provides easy-to-use online tools for birders and critical data for science. With eBird, you can:

- Record the birds you encounter
- Keep track of birding activity and lists
- Learn where to find birds near you
- Share sightings with other birders
- Contribute to science and conservation

Record and Store Sightings in eBird

eBird allows you to easily record the birds you find. Simply enter when, where, and how you went birding, then fill out a checklist of all the birds you identified with confidence by sight or sound. A free mobile app allows you to create and share checklists faster than ever. Data quality filters check all submissions automatically and local experts review unusual records before they enter the database.

eBird automatically organizes your bird observations into local and national lists, year lists, and more. You can also add photos and sound recordings to your checklists, so you can share your experiences with friends while also powering Merlin Bird ID, an automatic bird identification tool that can help you build skills for better birding. All these features work in any country in the world and are available in many languages.

Explore Data and Learn with eBird

One of eBird's greatest strengths is its ability to show you where and when birds occur, using innovative visualization tools. These free tools are used annually by millions of birders, scientists, and conservationists worldwide. Here are a few:

- **Species Maps:** Choose a species, then explore a map of everywhere it has been reported. Filter the map by date or zoom in to anywhere in the world with pinpoint precision.

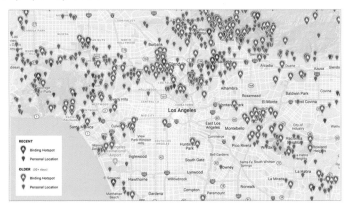

- **Photo and Sound Archive:** Each month, eBirders upload thousands of images and sounds. All of them are searchable in the Macaulay Library archive, so you can explore birds both familiar and new.

- **Explore a Region:** See the full species list, plus recent sightings, photo and audio recordings, best hotspots, and top birders for any county, state, province, or country. The Illustrated Checklist is a living field guide for any region!

• **Seasonal Occurrence Graphs:** Create a customized species list for any region and season. This tool tells you which species to expect when; bars tell you how rare or common each bird is throughout the year.

Seasonal abundance
TheCornellLab Data provided by eBird   Cedar Waxwing (Bombycilla cedrorum) © Brian Sullivan / Macaulay Library

• **Hotspot Explorer:** Use an interactive map to explore popular birding spots anywhere in the world—a great tool for travelers looking for local tips on where to go birding.

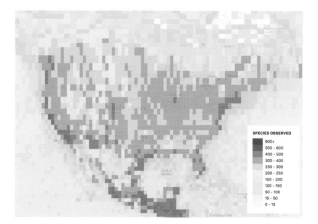

Your Sightings Support Science and Conservation

Every checklist you submit helps scientists better understand when and where birds occur, helping pinpoint where conservation is likely to have the greatest impact on bird populations. Your checklists also help scientists track the health of our bird populations; eBird data helps identify which species may be in trouble and in need of attention. Learn more about eBird and the birds recently seen in your area at *eBird.org*.

GREAT BACKYARD BIRD COUNT

In 1998, the annual four-day Great Backyard Bird Count (GBBC) began in the United States and Canada. It was the first citizen-science program to collect and display bird observation data online on a large scale. Today, the GBBC is one of the most popular annual events among bird watchers and has expanded to include the whole world. More than 200,000 people of all ages and walks of life take part. In 2020, 249,444 counts flooded in, recording a total of 6,942 species of birds—more than half of all bird species in the world!

Why Count Birds?

Scientists and bird enthusiasts can learn a lot by knowing where the birds are. No single scientist or team of scientists could hope to document and understand the complex distribution and movements of so many species in such a short time. Scientists use information from the GBBC, along with observations from other citizen-science projects, to see the big picture about what is happening to bird populations. You can help scientists investigate far-reaching questions, such as these:

- How does weather and climate change influence bird populations?

- Some birds appear in large numbers during some years but not others. Where are these species from year to year, and what can we learn from these patterns?

- How does the timing of bird migrations compare across years?

- What kinds of differences in bird diversity are apparent in cities versus suburban, rural, and natural areas?

Why Is the GBBC in February?

Originally the GBBC was held in the U.S. and Canada each February to create a snapshot of the distribution of birds just before spring migrations ramped up in March. Scientists at the Cornell Lab of Ornithology, National Audubon Society, Birds Canada, and elsewhere can combine this information with data from surveys conducted at different times of the year. In 2013, the count went global, creating snapshots of birds wherever they are in February, regardless of seasons across the hemispheres.

How to Participate

We invite you to participate! Visit *birdcount.org* to find out when the next GBBC is happening (it falls in February during the U.S. Presidents' Day weekend). If you're new to citizen science, you'll need to register for a free online account to enter your checklist counts. If you have already participated in another Cornell Lab citizen-science project, you can use that login information for GBBC.

Once registered, simply tally the numbers and kinds of birds you see for at least 15 minutes on one or more days of the count every February. You can count from any location, anywhere in the world, for as long as you wish. During the count, you can explore what others are seeing in your area or around the world.

To learn more and participate in the Great Backyard Bird Count, visit **birdcount.org**.

The Great Backyard Bird Count is led by the Cornell Lab of Ornithology and National Audubon Society, with Birds Canada and many international partners. The Great Backyard Bird Count is powered by eBird.

BIRD ACADEMY

Whether you're newly curious about the bird songs in your backyard, an avid birder with a life list to tend, or a budding ornithologist, Bird Academy has a course for every bird enthusiast.

Bird Academy courses are entirely online. You can learn at your own pace, return to the material as often as you wish, and there is no deadline to complete them. Take advantage of exclusive learning tools and friendly video tutorials created by our team of expert birders, ornithologists, and educational designers. *The Wonderful World of Owls*, *How to Identify Bird Songs*, *Nature Journaling and Field Sketching*, *Understanding Bird Behavior*, and *Sparrow Identification* are just a few of the courses on offer.

To find out more, visit ***Academy.AllAboutBirds.org.***

Barn Owl

PROJECT FEEDERWATCH

Northern Cardinal

Project FeederWatch is a survey of birds that visit feeders in backyards, nature centers, community areas, and other locales in North America. Each year, tens of thousands of people participate in Project FeederWatch. Annually, FeederWatchers report more than 7 million birds, providing valuable data for monitoring changes in the distribution and abundance of backyard birds. Participants gain from the rewarding experience of learning about birds at their feeders and contributing their own observations to reveal larger patterns in bird populations across the continent.

Why Are FeederWatch Data Important?

With each season, FeederWatch increases in importance as a unique tool to monitor bird species in North America. What sets FeederWatch apart from other monitoring programs is the detailed picture that FeederWatch data provide about weekly changes in bird distribution and abundance. Because participants count and identify all their birds multiple times from the same location, FeederWatch data are extremely powerful for detecting gradual changes in bird populations and ranges through time. FeederWatch data tell us where birds are as well as where they are not, which enables people to piece together accurate population maps. Finally, FeederWatch data provide information on a spatial and temporal scale that could not be collected by any other method than through the efforts of many participants over many years.

How Are FeederWatch Data Used?

The massive amounts of data collected by FeederWatchers across the continent help people understand:

- Long-term trends in bird distribution and abundance
- Invasive species dynamics continent-wide
- Behavioral interactions of birds at feeders
- The timing and extent of winter irruptions of winter finches and other species

- Expansions or contractions in ranges of feeder birds

- How supplementary food and backyard habitat affect birds

- How disease is spread among birds that visit feeders

How to Participate

Anyone interested in birds can participate, including people of all skill levels and backgrounds. FeederWatch is a great project for children, families, individuals, classrooms, retirees, youth groups, nature centers, and bird clubs. You can count birds as often as every week, or as infrequently as you like—the schedule is very flexible. All you need is a bird feeder, birdbath, or plantings that attract birds.

Participants submit their counts using the FeederWatch mobile app or website (*FeederWatch.org*) and have access to a variety of digital resources including detailed counting instructions; information about birds and bird feeding; tools to explore personal and continental data; Winter Bird Highlights, FeederWatch's year-end report; and the digital version of Living Bird, the Cornell Lab's award-winning magazine. There is a small annual participation fee for U.S. residents, and Canadians can join by making a donation of any size to Birds Canada. The participation fee covers staff support, web design, data analysis, and the year-end report. Without the support of our participants, this project wouldn't be possible.

To learn more about Project FeederWatch, visit *FeederWatch.org*.

Project FeederWatch is operated by the Cornell Lab of Ornithology and Birds Canada.

NESTWATCH

NestWatch is a nationwide monitoring program designed to track status and trends in the reproductive biology of birds, including when nesting occurs, how many eggs are laid, how many hatch, and how many young survive. The database is used to study the current condition of breeding bird populations and how they may be changing over time.

Nest of a Song Sparrow.

By finding and monitoring bird nests, NestWatch participants help scientists track the breeding success of birds across North America. Participants witness fascinating behaviors of birds at the nest, and collect information on the location, habitat, species, number of eggs, and number of young. Launched in 2007 with funding from the National Science Foundation, NestWatch has collected more than 400,000 nesting records. Combined with historic data, this information will help scientists address how birds are affected by large-scale changes such as global climate change, urbanization, and land conversion.

How to Participate

Participating in NestWatch is free and just about anyone can do it (children should always be accompanied by an adult when observing bird nests). Simply follow the directions on the website to become a certified NestWatcher, find a bird nest using the helpful tips, visit the nest every 3–4 days to record what you see, and then report this information on the website, or use the mobile app. Your observations will be added to those of thousands of other NestWatchers in a continually growing database used by researchers to understand and study birds. While you contribute extremely valuable information to science, you will also learn firsthand about the breeding behaviors of birds.

To learn more about NestWatch, visit **NestWatch.org**.
Download the mobile app on Google Play or the App Store.

CELEBRATE URBAN BIRDS

Celebrate Urban Birds is a year-round project developed by the Cornell Lab for people in cities, suburbs, and rural areas. It is an easy, fun project for the entire family; no prior knowledge of birds is required, and your data will help scientists understand how birds use green spaces in cities. Since 2007, Celebrate Urban Birds has partnered with 11,000 community organizations and distributed 400,000 educational kits. Educational materials and online trainings are offered in both English and Spanish.

How to Participate

1. Visit *CelebrateUrbanBirds.org* and click "Get Started Now."

2. Learn to identify 16 focal species. You can get additional species lists online at *CelebrateUrbanBirds.org/regional*.

3. Pick a place to watch birds in an area that is 50 feet by 50 feet (the size of half a basketball court).

4. Spend 10 minutes watching birds in the selected area.

5. Repeat observations three times in the same area in one month.

6. Share data online or send to the Cornell Lab by mail.

Every year Celebrate Urban Birds awards dozens of mini-grants to community organizations, including Alzheimer's support groups, youth clubs, oncology centers, businesses, and rehabilitation centers throughout the Americas to lead community activities focused on birds, greening, and the arts. Any community-based organization, especially those led by minoritized communities, are encouraged to apply for a grant. Visit *CelebrateUrbanBirds.org* to order educational materials, apply for a community grant, or find hundreds of fun, creative activities that involve the arts, greening, and birds for people of all ages.

To learn more about CUBs, visit *CelebrateUrbanBirds.org*.

SEVEN SIMPLE ACTIONS TO HELP BIRDS

In 2019, scientists documented North America's staggering loss of nearly three billion breeding birds since 1970. Helping birds can be as simple as making changes to everyday habits.

1 Make Windows Safer, Day and Night

The challenge: Up to one billion birds are estimated to die each year after hitting windows in the United States and Canada.

The cause: By day, birds perceive glass reflections in glass as habitat they can fly into. By night, migratory birds drawn in by city lights are at high risk of colliding with buildings.

These simple steps save birds: On the outside of the window, install screens or break up reflections using film, paint, Acopian BirdSavers or other string spaced no more than two inches high or four inches wide.

2 Keep Cats Indoors

The challenge: Cats are estimated to kill more than 2.6 billion birds annually in the U.S. and Canada. This is the #1 human-caused reason for the loss of birds, aside from habitat loss.

The cause: Cats can make great pets, but more than 110 million feral and pet cats now roam in the United States and Canada. These nonnative predators instinctively hunt and kill birds even when well fed.

A solution that's good for cats and birds: Save birds and keep cats healthy by keeping cats indoors or creating an outdoor "catio." You can also train your cat to walk on a leash.

3 Reduce Lawn, Plant Natives

The challenge: Birds have fewer places to safely rest during migration and to raise their young: More than 10 million acres of land in the United States were converted to developed land from 1982 to 1997.

The cause: Lawns and pavement don't offer enough food or shelter for many birds and other wildlife. With more than 40 million acres of lawn in the U.S. alone, there's huge potential to support wildlife by replacing lawns with native plantings.

Add native plants, watch birds come in: Native plants add interest and beauty to your yard and neighborhood, and provide shelter and nesting areas for birds. The nectar, seeds, berries, and insects will sustain birds and diverse wildlife.

4 Avoid Pesticides

The challenge: More than one billion pounds of pesticides are applied in the United States each year. The continent's most widely used insecticides, called neonicotinoids or "neonics," are lethal to birds and to the insects that birds consume. Common weed killers used around homes, such as 2, 4-D and glyphosate (used in Roundup), can be toxic to wildlife, and glyphosate has been declared a probable human carcinogen.

The cause: Pesticides that are toxic to birds can harm them directly through

contact, or if they eat contaminated seeds or prey. Pesticides can also harm birds indirectly by reducing the number of available insects, which birds need to survive.

A healthy choice for you, your family, and birds: Consider purchasing organic food. Nearly 70% of produce sold in the U.S. contains pesticides. Reduce pesticides around your home and garden.

Orange-crowned Warbler

5 Drink Coffee That's Good for Birds

The challenge: Three-quarters of the world's coffee farms grow their plants in the sun (source), destroying forests that birds and other wildlife need for food and shelter. Sun-grown coffee also often requires using environmentally harmful pesticides and fertilizers. On the other hand, shade-grown coffee preserves a forest canopy that helps migratory birds survive the winter.

The cause: Too few consumers are aware of the problems of sun coffee. Those who are aware may be reluctant to pay more for environmentally sustainable coffee.

Enjoy shade-grown coffee: It's a win-win-win: it's delicious, economically beneficial to coffee farmers, and helps more than 42 species of North American migratory songbirds, including orioles, warblers, and thrushes, that winter in coffee plantations.

6 Protect Our Planet from Plastics

The challenge: It's estimated that 4,900 million metric tons of plastic have accumulated in landfills and in our environment worldwide, polluting our oceans and harming wildlife such as seabirds, whales, and turtles that mistakenly eat plastic, or become entangled in it.

The cause: Plastic takes more than 400 years to degrade, and 91% of plastics created are not recycled. Studies show that at least 80 seabird species ingest plastic, mistaking it for food. Cigarette lighters, toothbrushes, and other trash have been found in the stomachs of dead albatrosses.

Reduce your plastics: Avoid single-use plastics including bags, bottles, wraps, and disposable utensils. It's far better to choose reusable items, but if you do have disposable plastic, be sure to recycle it.

7 Watch Birds, Share What You See

The challenge: The world's most abundant bird, the Passenger Pigeon, went extinct, and people didn't realize how quickly it was vanishing until it was too late. Monitoring birds is essential to help protect them, but tracking the health of the world's 10,000 bird species is an immense challenge.

The cause: To understand how birds are faring, scientists need hundreds of thousands of people to report what they're seeing in backyards, neighborhoods, and wild places around the world. Without this information, scientists will not have enough timely data to show where and when birds are declining around the world.

Enjoy birds while helping science and conservation: Join a project such as eBird, Project FeederWatch, Breeding Bird Survey, or the International Shorebird Survey to record your bird observations. Your contributions will provide valuable information to show where birds are thriving—and where they need our help.

If you don't yet know how to use eBird, we have a free course to help you get the most out of the project and its tools: *https://academy.allaboutbirds.org/product/ebird-essentials/.*

GUIDE TO SPECIES

Vermilion Flycatcher ©Evan Lipton/Macaulay Library

ADULT

ADULT

JUVENILES

ADULT

SIZE & SHAPE The Black-bellied Whistling-Duck is a large, gooselike duck with a long neck, long legs, and short tail. In flight, look for broad wings, a long neck, and a hunched back.

COLOR PATTERN The Black-bellied Whistling-Duck appears dark overall with a chestnut breast and black belly set off by a bright pink bill and legs. It has a grayish face and a broad, white patch in the wings which appears as a stripe down its wing while at rest.

BEHAVIOR Flocks of Black-bellied Whistling-Ducks regularly feed on waste grain in agricultural fields, often at night. Listen for their high-pitched whistles as they travel from feeding fields to roosting sites. They often perch in trees and on logs over water. They nest in cavities and they take readily to nest boxes.

HABITAT Black-bellied Whistling-Ducks roam edges of shallow ponds, golf courses, city parks, and schoolyards. They also frequent agricultural fields, particularly flooded rice fields.

RANGE MAP

■ Breeding
■ Year-round

The **Black-bellied Whistling-Duck** is a boisterous duck with a brilliant pink bill and an unusual, long-legged silhouette. In places like Texas and Louisiana, watch for noisy flocks of these gaudy ducks dropping into fields to forage on seeds or loafing on golf course ponds.

JUVENILE (WHITE MORPH)

ADULTS (WHITE MORPH)

IMMATURE (DARK MORPH)

ADULT (DARK MORPH)

RANGE MAP

- Breeding
- Migration
- Nonbreeding

SIZE & SHAPE The Snow Goose is a medium-sized goose with a hefty bill and long, thick neck. Juveniles are slightly smaller than adults in the fall, and this can be noticeable in flocks during fall and early winter.

COLOR PATTERN The white morph of the Snow Goose is white with black wingtips that are barely visible on the ground but more noticeable in flight. You may also see a dark morph Snow Goose, or "Blue Goose," with a white face, dark brown body, and white under the tail.

BEHAVIOR Snow Geese don't like to travel alone and can form flocks of several hundred thousand. Family groups forage together on wintering grounds, digging up roots and tubers from muddy fields and marshes. In flight, they are steady on the wing with even wingbeats.

HABITAT Snow Geese use agricultural fields, which is one reason their populations are doing so well. During winter and migration, look for them in plowed cornfields, wetlands, lakes, ponds, and marshes where they roost and bathe along shorelines and in open water.

atching huge flocks of **Snow Geese** swirl down from the sky, amid a cacophony of honking, is a little like nding inside a snow globe. These loud, white-and-black geese can cover the ground in a snowy blanket they eat their way across fallow cornfields or wetlands.

ADULT

ADULT

DOWNY YOUNG AND ADULT

ADULTS

SIZE & SHAPE The Canada Goose is a big waterbird with a long neck, large body, large, webbed feet, and a wide, flat bill. Adult Canada Geese can vary widely in size.

COLOR PATTERN Canada Geese have a black head with a white chinstrap, black neck, tan breast, and brown back. At least 11 subspecies of Canada Goose have been recognized. They tend to be smaller as you move northward in summer; plumage is darker as you move westward.

BEHAVIOR Canada Geese feed by dabbling in the water or grazing in fields and large lawns. They are known for their honking call and are often very vocal in flight. They often fly together in pairs or in V formation in flocks, which reduces wind resistance and conserves energy.

HABITAT Canada Geese can be found just about anywhere in the U.S. and Canada, near lakes, rivers, ponds, or other small or large bodies of water, and also in yards, parks, lawns, and farm fields.

RANGE MAP

■ Breeding
Nonbreeding
■ Year-round

The large **Canada Goose**, with its signature white chinstrap, is a familiar and widespread bird of fields and parks. Thousands of "honkers" migrate north and south each year, filling the sky with long V-formations. Every year, more of these grassland-adapted birds are staying put, and some people regard them as pests

ADULT AND DOWNY YOUNG (DOMESTIC TYPE)

ADULT MALE (WILD TYPE)

ADULT (DOMESTIC TYPE)

ADULT (DOMESTIC TYPE)

RANGE MAP

■ Year-round
  Year-round (scarce)

SIZE & SHAPE Muscovy Ducks are large, heavy-bodied ducks with long necks that can make them look like small geese. They have a fairly long bill that slopes smoothly up to the forehead. The tail is fairly long. Males are larger than females; domesticated individuals are often larger than wild.

COLOR PATTERN Wild Muscovy Ducks are mostly black. Adult males have large white patches on the wings; juveniles show much smaller white wing patches. In good light, the black feathers can show a greenish gloss. Domesticated and wild Muscovy Ducks have variable large patches of white to brown feathers, and red facial skin with odd warty growths.

BEHAVIOR Wild Muscovy Ducks are wary birds that feed by dabbling in shallow wetlands. Domesticated ducks can be common at urban parks, mixing with other ducks and taking handouts from park visitors.

HABITAT Wild Muscovy Ducks live in forested wetlands and nest in tree cavities. They forage in shallow wetlands, ponds, and lagoons. Domesticated ducks are common on farms and in parks.

e **Muscovy Duck** causes confusion for bird watchers, as it's distinctive and commonly seen but doesn't pear in some field guides. Wild Muscovy Ducks are forest dwellers that nest in tree cavities and are stricted to south Texas and points south. Domesticated versions occur across much of North America.

BREEDING MALE

BREEDING MALE

DOWNY YOUNG (L) AND ADULT FEMALE (R)

NONBREEDING MALE

SIZE & SHAPE The Wood Duck has a unique shape among ducks—a boxy, crested head; thin neck; and long, broad tail. In flight, they hold their heads up high, sometimes bobbing them.

COLOR PATTERN The male Wood Duck is a gorgeous duck with intricate plumage. In good light, males have a glossy green head with white stripes, a chestnut breast, and buffy sides. The female is gray brown with a white-speckled breast and a white teardrop around the eye.

BEHAVIOR Unlike most waterfowl, Wood Ducks perch and nest in trees and are comfortable flying through woods. Their broad tail and short, broad wings help make them maneuverable. When swimming, the head jerks back and forth much as a walking pigeon's does. You often see Wood Ducks in small groups (fewer than 20), keeping apart from other waterfowl.

HABITAT Look for Wood Ducks in wooded swamps, marshes, streams, beaver ponds, and small lakes. As cavity nesters, Wood Ducks take readily to nest boxes.

RANGE MAP

■ Breeding
■ Nonbreeding
■ Year-round

Wood Ducks are one of the few duck species equipped with strong claws that can grip bark and perch or branches. Soon after hatching, the mother duck leaves the nest and calls to her ducklings to jump down and join her in the water. Ducklings can jump from heights of over 50 feet without injury.

BREEDING MALE

BREEDING MALE

ADULT FEMALE

NONBREEDING MALE

RANGE MAP

■ Breeding
■ Migration
■ Nonbreeding
■ Year-round

SIZE & SHAPE A small dabbling duck, a Blue-winged Teal is dwarfed by a Mallard and only a touch larger than a Green-winged Teal. Its head is rounded, and the bill is on the large side.

COLOR PATTERN Breeding males are brown-bodied with dark speckling on the breast, a slaty-blue head with a white crescent behind the bill, and a small white flank patch in front of their black rear. Females and eclipse males are a patterned brown. In flight, they reveal a bold powder-blue patch on their upperwing coverts.

BEHAVIOR You'll often find Blue-winged Teal with other species of dabbling ducks, where pairs and small groups dabble and up-end to reach submerged vegetation. They are often around the edges of ponds, choosing a concealed spot to forage or rest.

HABITAT Look for Blue-winged Teal on calm bodies of water from marshes to small lakes. The Prairie Pothole Region, full of grassy habitats intermixed with wetlands, is the heart of their breeding range.

irs and small groups of this tiny dabbling duck inhabit shallow ponds and wetlands across much of North nerica. **Blue-winged Teal** are long-distance migrants, with some birds heading all the way to South nerica for the winter, leaving their breeding grounds well before other species in the fall.

NORTHERN SHOVELER *(Spatula clypeata)*

BREEDING MALE

BREEDING MALES

NONBREEDING MALE

ADULT FEMALE

SIZE & SHAPE The aptly named Northern Shoveler has a shovel-shaped bill that quickly sets it apart from other dabbling ducks, even at a considerable distance. It is a medium-sized duck that tends to sit tilted forward in the water, as if its large bill is pulling its front half down.

COLOR PATTERN Breeding male shovelers are bold white, blue, green, and rust, but their most notable feature is their white chest and white lower sides. In flight, males flash blue on the upper wing and green on the secondaries (the speculum). Female and immature shovelers are mottled brown and have powdery blue on the wings (sometimes visible on resting birds), and a very large orange bill. Nonbreeding males sometimes show a white facial crescent near the bill.

BEHAVIOR Northern Shovelers often have their heads down in shallow wetlands, busily sweeping their bills side to side, filtering out aquatic invertebrates and seeds from the water.

HABITAT Northern Shovelers forage in shallow wetlands, coastal marshes, flooded fields, lakes, and sewage lagoons. They nest along the margins of wetlands or in neighboring grassy areas.

RANGE MAP

■ Breeding
  Migration
  Nonbreeding
■ Year-round

Perhaps the most distinctive of the dabbling ducks thanks to its large spoon-shaped bill, the **Northern Shoveler** busily forages, head down, in shallow wetlands. The edges of its uniquely shaped bill have comblike projections, which filter out tiny crustaceans and seeds from the water.

MALE

BREEDING MALE

ADULT FEMALE

ADULT FEMALE

RANGE MAP

- Breeding
- Migration
- Nonbreeding
- Year-round

SIZE & SHAPE Gadwall are about the same size as Mallards, but the bill is noticeably thinner. Gadwall have a fairly large, square head with a steep forehead. In flight, the neck is slightly thinner and the wings slightly more slender than those of a Mallard.

COLOR PATTERN Male Gadwall are gray brown with a black patch at the tail. Females are patterned with brown and buff and have variably orange to black bills. In flight, both sexes have a white wing patch that is sometimes visible while swimming or resting.

BEHAVIOR Gadwall feed with other dabbling ducks, tipping forward to reach submerged vegetation. They sometimes steal food from diving ducks or coots. In winter, you'll often see them in pairs; mates are selected for the breeding season as early as late fall.

HABITAT Gadwall breed mainly in the Great Plains and prairies. On migration and in winter, look for them in reservoirs, ponds, freshwater and saltwater marshes, city parks, or muddy edges of estuaries.

e **Gadwall**'s understated elegance makes this common duck easy to overlook. Males are intricately tterned with gray, brown, and black; females resemble female Mallards, although with a thinner bill and ferent head shape and wing pattern. Gadwall sometimes snatch food from diving ducks and coots.

BREEDING MALE

BREEDING MALE

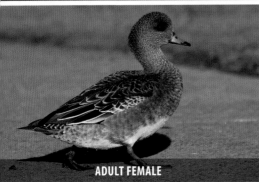

ADULT FEMALE

NONBREEDING MALE

SIZE & SHAPE American Wigeons are medium-sized, compact ducks with a short bill and a round head. They tend to sit on the water with their heads pulled down. They are larger than Green-winged Teal and smaller than Mallards.

COLOR PATTERN Breeding males have a grayish brown head with a white cap and a wide green stripe behind the eye. A pinkish cinnamon body with white patches on the sides of the rump contrasts with black undertail feathers. Females and nonbreeding males are brown with a dark smudge around the eye. Both sexes have a black-tipped gray bill.

BEHAVIOR American Wigeons congregate on lakes and wetlands, nibbling aquatic vegetation on the surface or tipping up for submerged plants. They also waddle through fields, plucking at plants. They are more vocal than many ducks, especially during the nonbreeding season.

HABITAT At all times of year, American Wigeons can be found in freshwater wetlands, lakes, slow-moving rivers, impoundments, flooded fields, estuaries, bays, and marshes.

RANGE MAP

■ Breeding
■ Migration
■ Winter
■ Year-round

Quiet lakes and wetlands come alive with the breezy whistle of the **American Wigeon**, a dabbling duck with pizzazz. Noisy groups congregate during fall and winter, plucking plants with their short gooselike bills from wetlands and fields or nibbling plants from the water's surface.

BREEDING MALE (L) AND ADULT FEMALE (R)

BREEDING MALE

ADULT FEMALE

NONBREEDING MALE

RANGE MAP

- Breeding
- Winter
- Year-round

SIZE & SHAPE Mallards are large ducks with hefty bodies, rounded heads, and wide, flat bills. Like many dabbling ducks, the body is long, and the tail rides high out of the water, giving a blunt shape. In flight, their wings are broad and set back toward the rear.

COLOR PATTERN Male Mallards have a dark, iridescent green head and bright yellow bill. The gray body is sandwiched between a brown breast and black rear. Females and juveniles are mottled brown with orange-and-blackish bills. Both sexes have a white-bordered, blue speculum patch in the wing.

BEHAVIOR Mallards are dabbling ducks and almost never dive. They can be very tame, especially in city ponds, and often group together with other Mallards, other species of dabbling ducks, or even farm ducks.

HABITAT Mallards can live in almost any wetland habitat. Look for them on lakes, ponds, marshes, rivers, and coastal habitats, as well as city and suburban parks and residential backyards.

rhaps the most familiar of all ducks, **Mallards** occur throughout the U.S. and Canada in ponds and parks well as wetlands and estuaries. The male's gleaming green head, gray flanks, and black tail-curl arguably ake it the most easily identified duck. Almost all domestic ducks come from this species.

ADULT MALE

ADULT MALE

ADULT FEMALE

ADULT FEMALE (L) AND ADULT MALE (R)

SIZE & SHAPE The Mexican Duck is similar in size and shape to the Mallard.

COLOR PATTERN Both sexes look similar to a female Mallard, but males are more boldly patterned with dark brown feathers fringed in a paler brown or rufous. The head is a pale brown to brownish gray with a dark eyeline, and the feet are orange. The bill is bold yellow with a black tip. Females are similar but browner, with a variably orange to dull olive bill, with or without black markings.

BEHAVIOR The Mexican Duck is most often seen in pairs or small flocks, often mixed in with Mallards. Like the Mallard, it is a dabbling duck and does not dive. It tips up to feed on plants near the surface of the water.

HABITAT The Mexican Duck favors wetlands, including marshy ponds and rivers. It usually nests on riverbanks but sometimes will choose a nest site far from water.

RANGE MAP

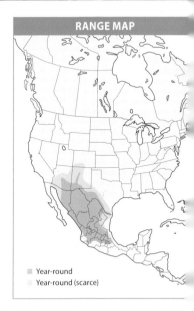

■ Year-round
  Year-round (scarce)

The **Mexican Duck** is closely related to the American Black Duck and the Mottled Duck but is now considered to be a separate species. It is unique in that it is the sole representative of the genus *Anas* to successfully occupy the interior plateau of central and northern Mexico.

ADULT MALE

ADULT

ADULT FEMALE AND DOWNY YOUNG

ADULT MALE (L) AND ADULT FEMALE (R)

RANGE MAP

- Breeding
- Winter
- Year-round
- ••• Post-breeding dispersal

SIZE & SHAPE A relatively large duck, similar in size to a Mallard, with a sturdy body, short neck, short tail, and moderately long bill.

COLOR PATTERN Both sexes are mostly brown and buff, like a female Mallard, but darker and richer in color and with a black patch at the opening of the bill (the gape). The very buffy face and throat lack fine streaking. The back and sides are rich brown streaked with buff. Males have intensely yellow bills; females have greenish yellow to orangish bills, with or without dark markings. White in the tail is an indication that the individual has some Mallard genes; a pure Mottled Duck has a dark tail.

BEHAVIOR Mottled Ducks are "dabbling ducks" that feed at the surface or tip up to reach submerged vegetation. They rarely dive unless being pursued by a predator.

HABITAT Mottled Ducks use shallow freshwater and brackish wetlands, including marshes, ponds, ditches, and flooded agricultural fields for resting, feeding, and nesting.

he **Mottled Duck** is reminiscent of a female Mallard or an American Black Duck and is so closely related at hybridization, especially with Mallards, poses a real threat to the Mottled Duck's future. Look for this ecies in pairs or small flocks, mostly in freshwater marshes near the coast.

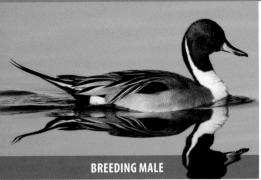

BREEDING MALE

BREEDING MALE

ADULT FEMALE

NONBREEDING MALE

SIZE & SHAPE Northern Pintails are elegant, long-necked ducks with a slender profile. The tail is long and pointed, but it is much longer and more prominent on breeding males than on females and nonbreeding males. In flight, wings are long and narrow.

COLOR PATTERN Breeding males stand out with a white breast and white line down their rich brown head and neck. When molting, both sexes are mottled brown and white with a tan face and a dark bill. In flight, males flash a green speculum and females a bronzy speculum.

BEHAVIOR These dabbling birds use their bills to filter out seeds and insects on the water's surface. They feed on grain and insects in wetlands and agricultural fields. They form groups, often with other ducks, in the nonbreeding season.

HABITAT Northern Pintails nest in wetlands, croplands, grasslands, wet meadows, and shortgrass prairies, and forage in lakes and ponds. When not breeding, look for them in wetlands, ponds, lakes, bays, tidal marshes, and flooded agricultural fields.

RANGE MAP

- Breeding
- Migration
- Nonbreeding
- Year-round

Elegant **Northern Pintails** swim through wetlands and lakes with their long, pointed tails held high. These eager breeders head to the Prairie Pothole Region of the Great Plains, as well as Alaska and other parts of Canada, to nest as soon as the ice breaks up. Though still common, their populations are declining.

BREEDING MALE

BREEDING MALE

ADULT FEMALE

JUVENILE

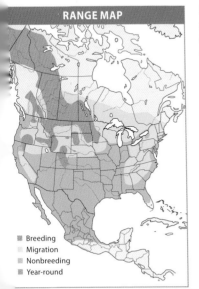
RANGE MAP

■ Breeding
Migration
■ Nonbreeding
■ Year-round

SIZE & SHAPE Canvasbacks are big-headed diving ducks with a gently sloping forehead and a stout neck. The long bill meets a sloping forehead, creating a seamless look. On the water, the Canvasback has an oval body and a short, sloping tail.

COLOR PATTERN Breeding males have a chestnut head and neck set off against a black chest, whitish body, and black rear. Females are pale brown where males are chestnut and black, and have a grayish rather than white body. In late summer and early fall, males have brown heads and necks with a paler body. Males have red eyes, and females have dark eyes.

BEHAVIOR Diving ducks that are gregarious during the nonbreeding season, Canvasbacks form large single-species rafts or mix with Redheads and scaups. They dive underwater to feed on plant tubers, seeds, and clams.

HABITAT Canvasbacks breed in lakes, deep-water marshes, bays, and ponds. In winter, look for them in deep freshwater lakes and coastal waters.

ten called the aristocrat of ducks, the **Canvasback** holds its long sloping forehead high with a distinguished ok. This diving duck eats plant tubers at the bottom of lakes and wetlands. It breeds in lakes and marshes d winters by the thousands on freshwater lakes and coastal waters.

BREEDING MALE

BREEDING MALE

NONBREEDING MALE

ADULT FEMALE

SIZE & SHAPE Redheads are medium-sized diving ducks with a smoothly rounded head and a moderately large bill. They are slightly larger than Ring-necked Ducks, and slightly smaller than Canvasbacks.

COLOR PATTERN Male Redheads are a mixture of cinnamon head, black breast and tail, and gray body. Females and immatures are a plain, mostly uniform brown. Redheads have black-tipped, gray bills, and gray flight feathers.

BEHAVIOR In migration and winter, look for Redheads in large rafts, often with other duck species. They usually dive for their food, although they use shallower water than other diving ducks and may feed by tipping up, like a dabbling duck.

HABITAT Redheads breed mainly in seasonal wetlands such as the Prairie Pothole Region of the Great Plains. In migration and winter, they form large flocks on the Gulf Coast, as well as on lakes, reservoirs, bays, and along the Great Lakes and coastlines across the southern U.S.

RANGE MAP

- ■ Breeding
- ■ Breeding (scarce)
- Migration
- Nonbreeding
- ■ Year-round

With a gleaming cinnamon head setting off a body marked in black and gray, adult male **Redheads** light up the open water of lakes and coastlines. These sociable ducks molt, migrate, and winter in sometimes huge flocks, particularly along the Gulf Coast, where winter numbers can reach the thousands.

BREEDING MALE

BREEDING MALE

IMMATURE MALE

ADULT FEMALE / IMMATURE FEMALE

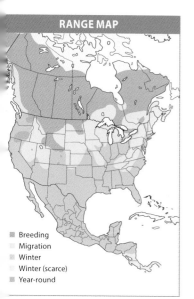

RANGE MAP

- Breeding
- Migration
- Winter
- Winter (scarce)
- Year-round

SIZE & SHAPE The Lesser Scaup is a medium-sized diving duck with a small peak at the back of the head. Behind the small peak, the back of the head is mostly flat, not strongly rounded as it is on Greater Scaup.

COLOR PATTERN Breeding males are black and white with an iridescent purple-to-green head sheen, a barred black-and-white back, a bluish bill, and a yellow eye. Females are delicately patterned brown with a darker brown head and a white patch by the bill.

BEHAVIOR During migration and winter, Lesser Scaup form large flocks on lakes, bays, rivers, and larger wetlands. They tend to form tight groups and mix with other diving ducks such as Canvasbacks and Greater Scaup.

HABITAT During winter, look for Lesser Scaup on inland lakes, reservoirs, coastal bays, and estuaries. During the breeding season, they are more commonly found nesting in marshes of northern North America.

oups of **Lesser Scaup** congregate on bodies of water during migration and winter, sometimes by the ousands. Look for them floating on the surface or diving to eat aquatic invertebrates and plants. Unlike e Greater Scaup's rounded head, the Lesser Scaup's tiny, peaked hat sits near the back of the head.

BREEDING MALE

NONBREEDING MALE

JUVENILE

ADULT FEMALE

SIZE & SHAPE Ruddy Ducks are small and compact with stout, scoop-shaped bills, and long, stiff tails they often hold cocked upward. They have slightly peaked heads and fairly short, thick necks.

COLOR PATTERN Male Ruddy Ducks have blackish caps and white cheeks. In summer, they have chestnut bodies with bright blue bills. In winter, they are dull gray brown with gray bills. Females are brownish with a blurry cheek stripe.

BEHAVIOR Ruddy Ducks dive to feed on aquatic invertebrates, especially midge larvae. They feed most actively at night, so you'll often see them sleeping during the day, head tucked under a wing and tail cocked up.

HABITAT Ruddy Ducks nest in marshes adjacent to lakes and ponds, primarily in the Prairie Potholes Region. In migration, they flock to large rivers, ponds, lakes, and coastal estuaries, frequently mixing with other diving ducks.

RANGE MAP

- Breeding
- Migration
- Nonbreeding
- Year-round

The bright colors and odd behavior of male **Ruddy Ducks** drew attention from early naturalists, though they didn't pull any punches. One 1926 account states, "Its intimate habits, its stupidity, its curious nesting customs and ludicrous courtship performance place it in a niche by itself…"

ADULT MALE

ADULT MALE

ADULT FEMALE

ADULT FEMALE

RANGE MAP

■ Year-round

SIZE & SHAPE Bobwhites are small quail with rounded bodies, small heads, rounded wings, and short tails. The male bobwhite has a small crest that becomes erect when it is alert and its head is raised.

COLOR PATTERN Northern Bobwhites are intricately patterned in brown, rufous, buff, and black. Males have a bold black-and-white striped face with a brown crown and white throat. Females are more speckled with black, brown, and white. They have buffy throats and eyebrows.

BEHAVIOR Northern Bobwhites travel in coveys and run across the ground from the shelter of one shrubby patch to another. When they are flushed, they explode into flight with quick wingbeats and then duck into the nearest cover.

HABITAT Northern Bobwhites live in open pine forests, overgrown fields, shrubby areas, and grasslands. They also like areas managed with prescribed fire, which helps maintain an open, grassy ground layer.

sten for the whistled ringing of the camouflaged **Northern Bobwhite** in the eastern countryside. They ·rage in groups, scurrying between cover or bursting into flight if alarmed. In sharp decline over the last alf-century due to habitat loss and changes in agriculture, bobwhites are a high priority for conservation.

ADULT MALE

ADULT MALE

JUVENILE

ADULT FEMALE

SIZE & SHAPE The Scaled Quail is a compact, chickenlike bird with a small head and distinctive crest. It has a plump body, short tail, and strong legs.

COLOR PATTERN Adult Scaled Quail are pale brownish gray with elegant dark scaling on the neck and breast. The head is plain brown with a pale crest (white in males, buff in females). The back is gray, and the wings are brown and stippled with buff. Juveniles are similar but have a shorter crest, and the upperwing has a more ornate pattern.

BEHAVIOR Scaled Quail forage in small groups (coveys) by walking slowly along the ground, pecking at seeds and insects or nipping vegetation. Males sing from conspicuous perches in spring. Often seen along roadsides in small groups, which usually run away or flush into flight.

HABITAT Look for Scaled Quail in desert grasslands and sparsely vegetated shrublands with plants like yucca, cholla, mesquite, skunkbush sumac, prickly pear, sandsage, pinyon, and juniper.

RANGE MAP

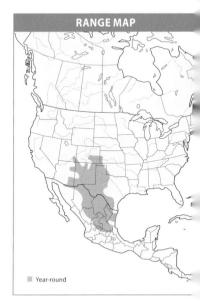

■ Year-round

Groups of **Scaled Quail** scurry through the desert grasslands of the southwestern U.S., calling softly to each other to stay in contact. When encountering people or predators, they dash away or fly a short distance and reassemble. In spring, males perch in the open, singing a short *whock* note.

DISPLAYING ADULT MALE

ADULT MALE

ADULT FEMALE

JUVENILE

RANGE MAP

Year-round

SIZE & SHAPE Wild Turkeys are very large, plump birds with long legs, wide, rounded tails, and small heads on long, slim necks.

COLOR PATTERN Turkeys are dark with a bronze-green iridescence to their plumage. Their wings are barred with white. Their rump and tail feathers are tipped rusty or white. The bare skin of the head and neck varies from red to blue to gray.

BEHAVIOR Turkeys travel in flocks and search the ground for nuts, berries, insects, and snails, using their strong feet to scratch leaf litter out of the way. In early spring, males perform courtship displays in clearings. They puff up their body feathers, flare their tails into a vertical fan, and strut slowly while giving a gobbling call. At night, they roost in trees in groups.

HABITAT Wild Turkeys live in mature forests, particularly those with oak, hickory, or beech trees, interspersed with edges and fields. You may see them along roads and in woodsy backyards.

ok for flocks of **Wild Turkeys** striding around woods and clearings like the miniature dinosaurs they are.
urting males puff themselves up and fill the air with gobbling. The bird's popularity at the Thanksgiving
ole led to a drastic decline in numbers, but they now occur in every U.S. state except Alaska.

BREEDING ADULT

BREEDING ADULT

JUVENILE

NONBREEDING ADULT

SIZE & SHAPE Pied-billed Grebes are small, chunky, swimming birds. They have compact bodies and slender necks, with relatively large, blocky heads and short, thick bills. They have virtually no tail.

COLOR PATTERN These brown birds are darker above and lighter below. In spring and summer, the crown and nape are dark, and the throat is black. While breeding, the bill is whitish with a black band, but yellowish brown the rest of the year. Juveniles have striped faces.

BEHAVIOR Pied-billed Grebes can adjust their buoyancy, using this ability to float with just the upper half of the head above water. They catch small fish and invertebrates by diving or slowly submerging.

HABITAT Look for Pied-billed Grebes on small, quiet ponds and marshes where thick vegetation grows out of the water. In winter, they are found on larger water bodies, occasionally in large groups.

RANGE MAP

- Breeding
- Nonbreeding
- Year-round

Part bird, part submarine, the **Pied-billed Grebe** is common across much of North America. These expert divers inhabit sluggish rivers, freshwater marshes, lakes, and estuaries. Rarely seen in flight and often hidden amid vegetation, Pied-billed Grebes announce their presence with loud, far-reaching calls.

NONBREEDING ADULT

BREEDING ADULTS

NONBREEDING ADULT

NONBREEDING ADULT / IMMATURE

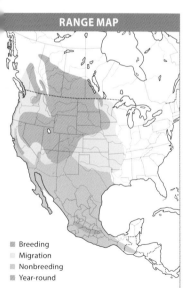

RANGE MAP

- Breeding
- Migration
- Nonbreeding
- Year-round

SIZE & SHAPE The Eared Grebe is a small waterbird with an even smaller head, a thin neck, and a thin bill. It has a sleek back and a tailless, fluffy rear. Breeding birds have a crested or peaked head.

COLOR PATTERN Breeding birds are mostly black with chestnut flanks and golden plumes fanning out from behind the bright red eye. Nonbreeding birds are grayish black overall. The cheeks are smudgy gray and the dark crown extends down past the red eye. A whitish patch on the throat scoops under and up behind the ears.

BEHAVIOR This social bird breeds in colonies and gathers in flocks from the hundreds to the thousands on lakes and ponds during migration and winter. They swim gracefully and jump up slightly before diving underwater for aquatic invertebrates.

HABITAT Eared Grebes breed in shallow lakes and ponds. During migration and in winter, they prefer saltwater habitats and can be found in great numbers in super salty waters with an abundant supply of brine shrimp and flies.

e most abundant grebe in the world, the **Eared Grebe** breeds in colonies in shallow wetlands in western rth America and heads by the thousands to salty inland waters to feast on brine shrimp before heading ther south. In summer, golden wisps fan out from their cheeks. In fall and winter, the wisps are absent.

ADULT

ADULT

ADULT

ADULTS

SIZE & SHAPE Larger and plumper than Mourning Doves, Rock Pigeons are tubby birds with small heads and short legs. Their wings are broad but pointed, and their tails are wide and rounded.

COLOR PATTERN Since pigeons are derived from domestic birds, their plumage is wildly variable. Most birds are a combination of gray, black, white, and/or rusty. Many birds are bluish gray with two black bands on each wing, a black tip to the tail, a white rump, and iridescent neck feathers.

BEHAVIOR Pigeons often gather in flocks, walking or running on the ground and pecking for food. When alarmed, the flock may suddenly fly into the air and circle several times before coming down again.

HABITAT Familiar birds of cities and towns, Rock Pigeons were introduced from Europe in the early 1600s as a food source. They also live on farmlands, and near rocky cliffs. They may gather in large flocks in urban parks where people feed them.

RANGE MAP

■ Year-round
Year-round (scarce)

Common in cities around the world, **Rock Pigeons** were introduced to North America in the early 1600s an now crowd streets and public squares, where they live off discarded food and birdseed. City pigeons nest o buildings and window ledges. In the countryside, they nest on barns, grain towers, natural cliffs, and bridge

RANGE MAP

- Year-round
- Year-round (scarce)

SIZE & SHAPE Eurasian Collared-Doves have plump bodies, small heads, and long tails. The wings are broad and slightly rounded. The broad tail is squared off at the tip, rather than pointed like a Mourning Dove's.

COLOR PATTERN Eurasian Collared-Doves are chalky light brown to gray buff birds with broad white patches in the tail. The collar is a narrow black crescent around the nape of the neck. In flight and when perched, the wingtips are darker than the rest of the wing. Adult and immature birds look alike.

BEHAVIOR These doves perch on telephone poles, wires, and in large trees while giving incessant three-syllable coos. Their flight pattern features bursts of clipped wingbeats and looping glides. When walking, these doves bob their heads and flick their tails.

HABITAT Eurasian Collared-Doves live in urban and suburban areas throughout much of the U.S. except the Northeast. In rural settings, look for them on farms and in livestock yards where grain is available.

d the **Eurasian Collared-Dove** on phone wires and fence posts, giving its rhythmic three-parted coo. s chunky bird gets its name from the black half-collar at the nape of the neck. Introduced to the hamas in the 1970s, they made their way to Florida by the 1980s, then colonized much of North America.

SIZE & SHAPE The Inca Dove is a small and slender dove with a long, square-tipped tail and small head. It has a thin and slightly drooping bill and short legs.

COLOR PATTERN The Inca Dove is the color of desert sands. Its tan feathers are edged in dark brown, creating a scaly pattern over the entire body. Its underparts and face are paler than its back. In flight, the outer wings flash a rich chestnut, and the outer tail feathers flash white. Adult and immature birds look alike.

BEHAVIOR Inca Doves walk quietly on the ground, pushing their heads forward and back as they go. When they take flight, their wings make a dry rattling sound. They are vocal doves, cooing *no-hope* at all hours of the day all year long.

HABITAT Inca Doves frequent areas near people, including cities, towns, parks, and farms. They prefer places with sparse shrub cover and scattered trees, such as palo verde and oak.

RANGE MAP

■ Year-round

The tiny **Inca Dove** blends into its suburban desert habitats until it takes flight, making a rattling whir with its wings. It nods its head with each step and coos a mournful *no-hope* from the trees. After expanding northward in the 20th century, the Inca Dove's range has recently rapidly contracted back to the south.

ADULT MALE

ADULT MALE (L) AND FEMALE (R)

ADULT FEMALE

ADULT MALE

RANGE MAP

Year-round

SIZE & SHAPE Common Ground Doves are tiny doves with short, round wings, short tails, and short, thin bills. They are stocky, with short legs, and they shuffle as they walk.

COLOR PATTERN Common Ground Doves are sandy brown overall, with large, dark spots on the wings. In flight, wings show rich rufous patches. Males have a pinkish wash on the head, neck, and chest, and bluish crowns; females are duller. Both sexes have fine, dark scaling on the neck and chest, and pinkish red bills with a dark tip.

BEHAVIOR These relatively shy birds usually hide in grasslands and small groves of trees. Males sing a series of quiet, moaning coos. They are often seen on the ground at backyard bird feeders eating seeds, grains, and some insects.

HABITAT Common Ground Doves live in open or shrubby areas with tall grasses or groves of trees, including riparian corridors and open savannas. They also live in towns and suburbs, where they frequent yards and hedges.

e sparrow-sized **Common Ground Dove** forages in dusty open areas, feeding beneath grass clumps. Its umage is easy to overlook until the bird takes flight, flashing reddish brown in the wings. These attractive ves are found across the southernmost parts of the U.S., from California to South Carolina.

ADULT

ADULT

JUVENILE

ADULT

SIZE & SHAPE White-winged Doves are plump, medium-sized doves with small heads and short, square-tipped tails. They have relatively long, thin bills.

COLOR PATTERN White-winged Doves are brown with a dark line on the cheek. Each wing has a bold white stripe above, and the tail has white corners. Their faces are marked with a black streak on the cheek, and blue skin around the red eyes.

BEHAVIOR White-winged Doves forage on waste grain and seeds on the ground or take to trees to eat berries. In the Sonoran Desert, they eat saguaro cactus fruits. They often gather in huge flocks for trips between roosting and foraging areas, and during migration. Their long, hooting *whoo-OOO-oo, ooo-oo* calls are an increasingly common sound in the southern U.S.

HABITAT Find these doves in southwestern desert habitat and in cities and suburbs of Texas and the coastal Southeast. They often visit backyards with birdbaths and feeders. Individuals move widely across the continent after the breeding season.

RANGE MAP

■ Breeding
■ Nonbreeding
■ Year-round

Originally a bird of desert thickets, the **White-winged Dove** is now common in cities and towns across the southern U.S. In flight, its subdued wing crescents become flashing white stripes worthy of the bird's common name. Look closely for a remarkably colorful face, with bright red eyes and blue "eye shadow."

ADULT

ADULT MALE

JUVENILE

ADULT

RANGE MAP

- Breeding
- Year-round
- Nonbreeding

SIZE & SHAPE Mourning Doves are plump-bodied and long-tailed, with short legs, a small bill, and a head that looks tiny in comparison to the body. The long, pointed tail is unique among North American doves.

COLOR PATTERN Mourning Doves often match their open-country surroundings in color. They're a delicate brownish gray to buffy tan overall, and a pale peach color below, with pink legs. They have large black spots on their wings and black-bordered white tips to the outer tail feathers.

BEHAVIOR Mourning Doves fly fast on powerful wingbeats, sometimes making sudden ascents, descents, and dodges, their pointed tails stretching behind them.

HABITAT You can see Mourning Doves nearly anywhere except the deep woods. Mourning Doves prefer open fields, areas with scattered trees, and woodland edges, but many roost in woodlots during winter. They feed on the ground in grasslands, agricultural fields, backyards, and roadsides.

he **Mourning Dove's** soft, drawn-out coos sound like laments. Common across much of the continent, his graceful dove perches on telephone wires and forages for seeds on the ground; its flight is fast and traight. When taking off, its wings make a sharp whistling or whinnying sound.

SIZE & SHAPE Greater Roadrunners are large cuckoos with a distinctive shape: long legs, a very long, straight tail, and a long neck. The head has a short crest, and the bill is long, heavy, and slightly downcurved.

COLOR PATTERN They are tan or brown with extensive blackish streaking on the upperparts and chest. The crown is black with small, pale spots, and they have a patch of bare, blue skin behind the eye. The wings are dark with white highlights. Adult and immature birds look similar.

BEHAVIOR Greater Roadrunners spend most of their lives on the ground hunting lizards, small mammals, and birds. They run fast, leaning over parallel to the ground with their tails streaming behind them. They are weak fliers, but may perch above the ground on fence posts and sometimes telephone wires.

HABITAT Greater Roadrunners are characteristic birds of the hot, shrubby expanses of the desert Southwest. They aren't restricted to deserts, though; look for them in open country with patches of shrubs or small trees almost as far east as the Mississippi River. They are also found in towns.

RANGE MAP

■ Year-round

A bird born to run, the **Greater Roadrunner** can outrace a human, kill a rattlesnake, and thrive in the harsh desert of the Southwest. As they run, they hold their lean frames nearly parallel to the ground and rudder with their long tails. They have recently extended their range eastward into Missouri and Louisiana.

ADULT

ADULT

JUVENILE

ADULT

RANGE MAP

■ Breeding
□ Migration

SIZE & SHAPE Yellow-billed Cuckoos are large, long, and slim birds. The bill is almost as long as the head and slightly downcurved. They have a flat head, thin body, and very long tail. Wings appear pointed and swept back in flight.

COLOR PATTERN Yellow-billed Cuckoos are warm brown above and clean whitish below. They have a blackish mask across the face and a yellow eyering. From below, the tail has wide white bands and narrower black ones. The bill is mostly yellow.

BEHAVIOR Yellow-billed Cuckoos forage slowly and methodically in treetops for large, hairy caterpillars—this approach can make them hard to find. However, they are vocal birds, and their slow, rolling, guttural calls are distinctive. They fly in a straight path using sharp wingbeats with a slight pause between them.

HABITAT Look for Yellow-billed Cuckoos among the canopies of broadleaf trees in woodland patches with gaps and clearings. In the West, this species is found only in the cottonwood-dominated forests that line larger rivers running through arid country.

llow-billed Cuckoos are slender, long-tailed birds that stay well hidden in broadleaf woodlands. They ually sit still, hunching their shoulders as they hunt for caterpillars. Fortunately, their drawn-out, knocking ng is very distinctive. They have become rare in the West in the last half-century.

ADULT MALE

ADULT FEMALE

ADULT

ADULT MALE

SIZE & SHAPE Lesser Nighthawks are small nighthawks with rounded wings and a fairly long, notched tail. In flight, they look long and slim, but when perched they look rather full-bodied with a small, flat head. They have a very small, thin bill that is nearly invisible and tiny legs.

COLOR PATTERN Lesser Nighthawks are camouflaged in browns and grays. It is not until they take flight that a distinctive bar across the wingtips is visible. The bar is white on males and cream colored on females. Males and females also have a white stripe across the throat. Males have an additional thin white band across the tail.

BEHAVIOR During the day, Lesser Nighthawks rest, camouflaged on the ground or in a tree or shrub. At dusk and dawn, they fly on buoyant wings, skimming the ground and tops of shrubs and trees to capture flying insects with their mouth agape. Its flight is butterfly-like as it flaps and glides with its wings held in a V.

HABITAT Lesser Nighthawks can be found in deserts, open country, and scrubby areas. They seek out swarming insects, and can be seen feeding in bright lights, such as at sporting events.

RANGE MAP

- Breeding
- Migration
- Nonbreeding
- Year-round

The highly camouflaged **Lesser Nighthawk** sits motionless during the day but takes flight as the desert heat dissipates. It flies like a butterfly on buoyant wings with its mouth wide open, inhaling flying insects. This aerial acrobat nests on the bare desert ground, without putting down even a blade of grass.

ADULT FEMALE

ADULT MALE

ADULT MALE

ADULT MALE

RANGE MAP

- Breeding
- Migration

SIZE & SHAPE Common Nighthawks are medium-sized, slender birds with very long, pointed wings and medium-long tails. Only the small tip of the bill is usually visible, and this combined with the large eye and short neck gives the bird a big-headed look.

COLOR PATTERN Common Nighthawks are camouflaged in gray, white, buff, and black. The long, dark wings have a white blaze about two-thirds of the way out to the tip. In flight, a pale, V-shaped throat patch contrasts with the rest of the plumage.

BEHAVIOR Look for Common Nighthawks flying in the early morning and evening. During the day, they roost motionless on branches, fence posts, or the ground, and can be hard to see. Their buzzy *peent* call is distinctive.

HABITAT Common Nighthawks are most visible when they forage on the wing over cities and open areas near woods or wetlands. They migrate over fields, river valleys, marshes, woodlands, towns, and suburbs.

n warm summer evenings, **Common Nighthawks** roam the skies, giving a sharp, electric *peent* call. These ng-winged birds fly in graceful loops, chasing insects. They are fairly common but declining birds that ke no nest. Their young are highly camouflaged, and even the adults seem to vanish as soon as they land.

SIZE & SHAPE Chimney Swifts are very small birds with slender bodies and very long, narrow, curved wings. They have a round head, short neck, and short, tapered tail that gives them the appearance of a flying cigar. The wide bill is so short that it is hard to see.

COLOR PATTERN Chimney Swifts are dark gray brown all over, slightly paler on the throat. They can appear to be all black from a distance and when backlit against the sky. Adult and immature birds look similar.

BEHAVIOR Chimney Swifts fly rapidly with nearly constant wingbeats, and often twist from side to side and bank erratically. Their wingbeats are stiff, with very little flex at the wrists. They often give a high, chattering call while they fly.

HABITAT Chimney Swifts forage widely, feeding on flying insects. They gather to nest and roost in chimneys and other dim, enclosed areas with a vertical surface on which to cling, like air vents, wells, hollow trees, and caves. They forage over urban and suburban areas, rivers, lakes, forests, and fields.

RANGE MAP

■ Breeding
■ Migration

Best identified by silhouette, the **Chimney Swift** spends almost its entire life airborne. Its tiny body, curvin wings, and stiff, shallow wingbeats give it a flight style as distinctive as its fluid, chattering call. It can't perc clinging instead to vertical walls. This species has sharply declined as chimneys fall into disuse.

ADULT

ADULT

ADULT

ADULT

RANGE MAP

- Breeding
- Nonbreeding
- Year-round

SIZE & SHAPE This is a fairly large swift with a long, slim body and very long, narrow wings that curve like a scimitar. The overall slim outline can make it appear small, especially at a distance.

COLOR PATTERN A blackish brown bird with a white throat and a white stripe down the center of the breast and belly. Upperparts are blackish with white flanks and a white trailing edge to the secondaries (the inner part of the wing). Juvenile coloring is similar to that of an adult but duller.

BEHAVIOR The White-throated Swift catches tiny aerial insects, usually high in the sky. The fast, erratic flight and high-pitched calls are distinctive even when the plumage pattern is hard to see.

HABITAT This swift nests in natural crevices on rocky cliffs or canyon walls, from sea level to high mountain peaks. They forage over virtually any terrestrial habitat that features small aerial insects. They will nest in buildings, bridges, and overpasses, and sometimes in cities.

ook for **White-throated Swifts** on cliffs and canyon walls in western North America. They fly at incredible eeds, pursuing insects. Courting birds dive toward earth, one clinging to the back of the other, separating st above the ground. In cliff crevices, they use saliva to glue their nests to the vertical wall.

ADULT MALE

ADULT MALE

ADULT FEMALE

IMMATURE MALE

SIZE & SHAPE The Ruby-throated Hummingbird is a small hummingbird with a slender, slightly downcurved bill and fairly short wings that don't reach all the way to the tail when the bird is sitting.

COLOR PATTERN Ruby-throated Hummingbirds are bright emerald or golden green on the back and crown, with grayish white underparts. Males have a brilliant iridescent red throat that looks dark when it's not in good light. Immature males have some red feathers on the throat.

BEHAVIOR Ruby-throated Hummingbirds fly straight and fast but can stop instantly, hover, and adjust their position up, down, or backwards with exquisite control. They often visit hummingbird feeders and tube-shaped flowers and defend these food sources against others. You may also see them plucking tiny insects from the air or from spider webs.

HABITAT Ruby-throated Hummingbirds live in open woodlands, forest edges, meadows, and grasslands, and in parks, gardens, and backyards.

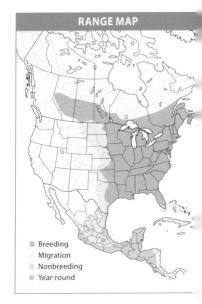

RANGE MAP

- Breeding
- Migration
- Nonbreeding
- Year-round

The **Ruby-throated Hummingbird** is the sole breeding hummingbird in the eastern half of the U.S. and Canada. These precision-flying creatures glitter in the full sun, and are common at feeders and in flower gardens in summer. In early fall, they head south, with many crossing the Gulf of Mexico in a single flight.

ADULT MALE

ADULT MALE

ADULT FEMALE / IMMATURE

IMMATURE MALE

RANGE MAP

- Breeding
- Migration
- Nonbreeding
- Year-round

SIZE & SHAPE The Black-chinned Hummingbird is a small, fairly slender hummingbird with a fairly straight bill.

COLOR PATTERN Males have a velvety black throat which, in perfect light, has an iridescent purple base. Females have a pale throat. In both sexes, the flanks are a dull metallic green, and the bill is black. The female's three outer tail feathers have broad white tips.

BEHAVIOR Black-chinned Hummingbirds hover at flowers and feeders, darting erratically to take tiny swarming insects. They perch atop high snags to survey their territory, watching for competitors to chase off and for flying insects to eat. During courtship and territorial defense, males display by diving 66–100 feet.

HABITAT Look for Black-chinned Hummingbirds at feeders or perched on dead branches in tall trees. They are habitat specialists; found in lowland deserts and mountainous forests, and in natural habitats and very urbanized areas, as long as there are tall trees and flowering shrubs and vines.

ack-chinned Hummingbirds are exceptionally widespread, from deserts to mountain forests, often perching the top of a bare branch. The adult male has no brilliant colors on its throat except a thin strip of iridescent rple bordering the black chin, only visible when light hits it just right. Some winter along the Gulf Coast.

ADULT MALE

ADULT MALE

ADULT FEMALE / IMMATURE

ADULT FEMALE / IMMATURE

SIZE & SHAPE The Calliope Hummingbird is small even for a hummingbird, and its hunched posture makes it look even smaller. It has a short tail and the wings barely extend past the end of the tail. The bill is thin and short for a hummingbird.

COLOR PATTERN The standout feature of a Calliope Hummingbird is the magenta rays on the male's throat. Both sexes are greenish above, but males wear a greenish vest below while females have peachy underparts.

BEHAVIOR These birds take nectar from flowering plants and eat flying insects in midair. They often forage low to the ground. In defense of their breeding territory, they perch on high branches. Displaying males dive in a U-shape.

HABITAT Calliope Hummingbirds breed in mountain meadows, aspen thickets near streams, and open forests that are regenerating from a forest fire or logging. They spend winters in pine-oak forests and scrubby edges in Mexico.

RANGE MAP

- Breeding
- Migration
- Nonbreeding

Magenta rays burst from the throat of the male **Calliope Hummingbird** as it performs U-shaped display dives for females, tail feathers buzzing. This is the smallest bird in the United States, yet it breeds high in the chilly mountains of the Northwest, and travels more than 5,000 miles each year to Mexico and back.

ADULT MALE

ADULT MALE

ADULT FEMALE / IMMATURE MALE

ADULT FEMALE / IMMATURE FEMALE

RANGE MAP

- Breeding
- Migration
- Migration (scarce)
- Nonbreeding
- Nonbreeding (scarce)

SIZE & SHAPE The Rufous Hummingbird is fairly small with a slender, nearly straight bill, a tail that tapers to a point when folded, and fairly short wings that don't reach the end of the tail when the bird is perched.

COLOR PATTERN Male Rufous Hummingbirds are bright rufous on the back and belly, with an iridescent throat that can appear red, orange, gold, or even greenish. Females are green above with rufous-washed flanks, rufous patches in the green tail, and a dark spot on the throat. Adult males have rufous and black tails. Females and immatures also have green and white in the tail.

BEHAVIOR Look for their fast, darting flight and pinpoint maneuverability. They tirelessly chase away other hummingbirds, even in places they're only visiting on migration. Like other hummers, they eat insects as well as nectar.

HABITAT Rufous Hummingbirds breed in open areas, yards, parks, and forests up to treeline. On migration, they pass through mountain meadows as high as 12,600 feet, where nectar-rich, tubular flowers bloom. Their winter habitat in Mexico includes shrubby openings and oak-pine forests at middle to high elevation.

e of the feistiest hummingbirds in North America, the brilliant rufous male and the green-and-rufous ale **Rufous Hummingbird** are relentless attackers at flowers and feeders, going after (if not always eating) even the large hummingbirds of the Southwest, which can be double their weight.

SIZE & SHAPE The Buff-bellied Hummingbird is a medium-sized hummingbird, much larger than a Ruby-throated Hummingbird. Wings are as long as the tail when perched.

COLOR PATTERN Both sexes are metallic bronze green above with a rusty tail and dark wings. They have an iridescent green throat that can appear dark, depending on the light, and a buff belly. The bright red-orange bill is dipped in black. Adult and immature birds look similar.

BEHAVIOR Buff-bellied Hummingbirds defend feeders and flowering trees against other hummingbirds and some insects, such as butterflies and wasps. At feeders in south Texas, they dominate other hummingbirds by chasing them off of feeders and flower sources, probably because they are larger in size. While in pursuit, they give a long call with repeated notes: *see-see-see-see-su-su.*

HABITAT Look for Buff-bellied Hummingbirds in open woodlands, second-growth forests, clearings, scrub, plantations, and gardens. They are often seen at sugar water feeders.

RANGE MAP

■ Nonbreeding
■ Year-round

The **Buff-bellied Hummingbird** regularly disperses to the northeast from its breeding areas in south Texas. This northerly movement is noteworthy among North American hummingbirds. It is probably the least-studied hummingbird that regularly occurs in the United States.

BREEDING ADULT

BREEDING ADULT

JUVENILE

NONBREEDING ADULT

RANGE MAP

- Breeding
- Migration
- Nonbreeding
- Year-round

SIZE & SHAPE Soras are small, chubby, chickenlike rails with long toes. They have stubby bills and frequently hold their tails cocked up.

COLOR PATTERN Soras are mottled gray and brown with white-edged feathers, and a candy-corn-shaped bill. They have a black mask and throat patch, white side lines, and a white patch under the tail. Females are duller than males.

BEHAVIOR Soras walk through shallow wetlands, pushing their head forward with every step while nervously flicking the tail upward. They forage in dense vegetation but may venture into open areas from time to time. Their long toes help them walk on top of floating mats of vegetation.

HABITAT Soras make their homes in shallow freshwater wetlands with dense emergent vegetation. During migration and winter, they also use brackish marshes, flooded fields, and wet pastures.

descending whinny emanates from the depths of cattails and rushes, but the secretive **Sora** rarely ows itself. When it finally appears, the Sora walks slowly through shallow wetlands, a bit like a chicken at has had too much coffee, nervously flicking its tail and exposing the white feathers below.

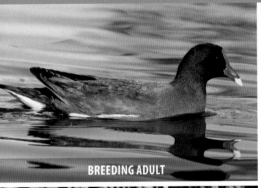

BREEDING ADULT

BREEDING ADULT

JUVENILE

NONBREEDING ADULT

SIZE & SHAPE Common Gallinules are medium-sized marsh birds with long legs and toes. They have a small head, thin neck, and small, thin bill. They frequently hold their wings up, such that the wingtips stick up on the back.

COLOR PATTERN Both sexes are charcoal gray with a white side stripe and white outer tail feathers. Adults have a red shield on their forehead and a red bill tipped in yellow. Juveniles look similar, but lack the red shield and bill.

BEHAVIOR Common Gallinules swim like a duck and walk on top of marsh vegetation. When walking, they tend to crouch and slowly flick their tail up. They often stay close to emergent marsh vegetation but may swim out in the open.

HABITAT Common Gallinules use freshwater and brackish marshes, ponds, and lakes that mix submerged, floating, and emergent aquatic vegetation and are open water all year. They also forage in ditches, canals, and rice fields.

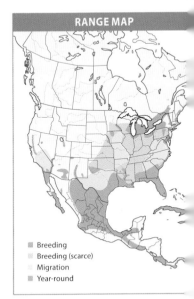

RANGE MAP

- ■ Breeding
- ■ Breeding (scarce)
- ■ Migration
- ■ Year-round

The **Common Gallinule** swims like a duck and walks atop floating vegetation with its long, slender toes. It squawks and whinnies from thick cover in marshes and ponds from Canada to Chile, peeking out of vegetation. Formerly called the Common Moorhen, it is related to coots, rails, and cranes.

ADULT

ADULT

JUVENILE

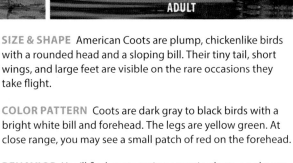

ADULT

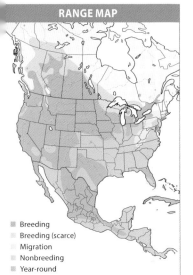

RANGE MAP

- Breeding
- Breeding (scarce)
- Migration
- Nonbreeding
- Year-round

SIZE & SHAPE American Coots are plump, chickenlike birds with a rounded head and a sloping bill. Their tiny tail, short wings, and large feet are visible on the rare occasions they take flight.

COLOR PATTERN Coots are dark gray to black birds with a bright white bill and forehead. The legs are yellow green. At close range, you may see a small patch of red on the forehead.

BEHAVIOR You'll find coots eating aquatic plants on almost any body of water. When swimming, they look like small ducks (and often dive), but on land they look more chickenlike, walking rather than waddling. An awkward and often clumsy flier, the American Coot requires long running takeoffs to get airborne.

HABITAT Look for American Coots at ponds in city parks, in marshes, at reservoirs, along the edges of lakes and in roadside ditches, at sewage treatment ponds, along saltwater inlets, and in saltmarshes.

e waterborne **American Coot** is a reminder that not everything that floats is a duck. A close look at the ot's small head and scrawny legs reveals a very different kind of bird. Common in nearly any open water ross the continent, they're closer relatives of the Sandhill Crane and rails than of Mallards or teal.

ADULT

ADULT

JUVENILE

ADULT

SIZE & SHAPE A chicken-sized rail with a heavy conical bill, short tail (often cocked), a compact body, and very long legs and toes. The Purple Gallinule is slightly smaller than an American Coot and larger than a Sora.

COLOR PATTERN Adults are a medley of purplish head and body, greenish wings and back, a yellow-tipped red bill, baby-blue frontal shield, and bright yellow legs and feet. Juveniles show very little hint of these colors, being mostly brown above, khaki below, with much duller bill and legs. Immatures acquire their colors gradually in their first year.

BEHAVIOR Purple Gallinules forage near the water's edge, walking slowly and investigating vegetation with an outstretched neck or pecking at fruits or tubers. They swim well and sometimes use their long toes to climb bushes and trees.

HABITAT Purple Gallinules are almost always found near fresh water, even during migration. For nesting, they favor freshwater ponds with emergent vegetation, and the species has adapted well to many human-altered environments.

RANGE MAP

■ Breeding
■ Nonbreeding
■ Year-round

Lurking in the marshes of the extreme southeastern U.S. lives the **Purple Gallinule**, one of the most vividly colored birds in all of North America. Watch for these long-legged, long-toed birds stepping gingerly across water lilies and other floating vegetation as they hunt frogs and invertebrates or pick at tubers.

ADULT

ADULT

JUVENILE

ADULT

RANGE MAP

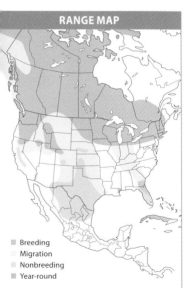

- Breeding
- Migration
- Nonbreeding
- Year-round

SIZE & SHAPE Sandhill Cranes are large, tall birds with a long neck, long legs, and broad wings. The short tail is covered by drooping feathers that form a "bustle." The head is small and the bill is straight and longer than the head. In flight, the straight neck sets cranes apart from herons.

COLOR PATTERN Both sexes are pale gray. Adults have a pale cheek and red skin on the crown. Their legs are black. Juveniles are gray without the pale cheek or red crown. Some birds are stained with rust.

BEHAVIOR Sandhill Cranes forage for grains and invertebrates in prairies, grasslands, and marshes. They do not hunt in open water or hunch their necks the way herons do. Sandhill Cranes form extremely large flocks—into the tens of thousands—on their wintering grounds and during migration. They often migrate very high in the sky.

HABITAT Sandhill Cranes breed and forage in open prairies, grasslands, and wetlands. Outside of the breeding season, they often roost in deeper water of ponds or lakes, where they are safe from predators.

he crimson-capped **Sandhill Crane** has an elegance that draws attention. It breeds in open wetlands, elds, and prairies and forms large groups, filling the air with rolling cries. While populations are generally :rong, some isolated populations in Mississippi and Cuba are endangered.

ADULT MALE

ADULT FEMALE

IMMATURE

JUVENILE

SIZE & SHAPE The Black-necked Stilt is a tall and lanky shorebird with a delicate-looking body. It has very long legs, a long neck, a small head, and a thin, straight bill. It is larger than a Lesser Yellowlegs.

COLOR PATTERN These birds are black above and white below, with white around the eye and rosy pink legs. In females and immatures, the black areas can be brownish.

BEHAVIOR Black-necked Stilts wade into shallow bodies of water in pursuit of tiny aquatic invertebrates. Adults defending nests or chicks fly around and call loudly, sometimes performing a distraction display by feigning injury.

HABITAT Black-necked Stilts are almost always seen near shallow water, including both salt and fresh waters, especially mudflats, salt pans, saltmarshes, and human-modified habitats like sewage ponds, evaporation pools, and flooded fields.

RANGE MAP

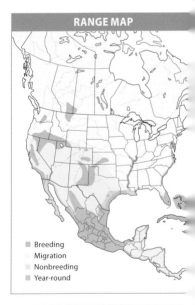

■ Breeding
  Migration
■ Nonbreeding
■ Year-round

Black-necked Stilts are among the most stately of the shorebirds, with long rosy pink legs and elegant plumage. They move deliberately when foraging, walking slowly through wetlands in search of tiny aquatic prey. When disturbed, stilts are vociferous, and their high, yapping calls carry for some distance.

ADULT AND DOWNY YOUNG

ADULT

ADULT

JUVENILE

RANGE MAP

- Breeding
- Nonbreeding
- Year-round
- Year-round (scarce)

SIZE & SHAPE The American Oystercatcher is a large, thickset shorebird with a long, stout bill, a large head, robust neck, and thick legs.

COLOR PATTERN The American Oystercatcher looks black and white from a distance. At closer range, the back and wings are brown, and the head and breast are black contrasting with the white underparts. The bright orange-red bill matches what look like orange eyes, but are actually yellow eyes ringed in red that appear orange from a distance. Juveniles are duller than adults with a dark-tipped bill.

BEHAVIOR American Oystercatchers probe sandy and stony areas for clams, oysters, and other mollusks, which they open by cutting or smashing. Much of their day is spent resting in roosts during high tide. They are vigorous, and very loud, during courtship displays, territorial conflicts, and interactions with intruders.

HABITAT Look for American Oystercatchers in intertidal areas on barrier islands and beaches, saltmarshes, and shellfish reefs.

American Oystercatchers survive almost exclusively on shellfish—clams, oysters, and other saltwater mollusks—and live only in a narrow ecological zone of saltmarshes and barrier beaches. They are sensitive development on the beaches where they nest and are on the Yellow Watch List of Partners in Flight.

BREEDING MALE

NONBREEDING ADULT

JUVENILE

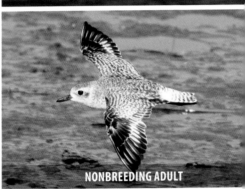

NONBREEDING ADULT

SIZE & SHAPE The Black-bellied Plover is a medium-sized to large shorebird. It has moderately long legs, a short neck and bill, and a large, rounded head.

COLOR PATTERN Breeding males are a dazzling mix of black and white: checkered upperwings, a black face and belly, a white crown, nape, and undertail, and dark legs and bill. Adult females in breeding plumage are similar but with less contrast. Nonbreeding adults are pale gray above and grayish or whitish below. Juveniles are more scaly looking on the back. All plumages show black "armpits" in flight.

BEHAVIOR Black-bellied Plovers move by stop-run-stop, or stop-run-peck, scanning and capturing prey at stops with a single peck or series of pecks. Worms and clams may be shaken vigorously in nearby shallow water to remove mud.

HABITAT Black-bellied Plovers nest in Arctic lowlands on dry tundra. In winter, find them on coastal lagoons and estuaries. Migrants stop along coastlines and in harvested agricultural areas, sod farms, and muddy edges of lakes and rivers.

RANGE MAP

■ Breeding
  Migration
■ Nonbreeding

Black-bellied Plovers are supreme aerialists, and are readily identified at great distance by black axillaries ("armpit" feathers) and their mournful-sounding call. The largest of North America's migratory plovers, it breeds farther north than other species, at the very top of the world, and occurs on six continents.

BREEDING MALE

ADULT (FALL)

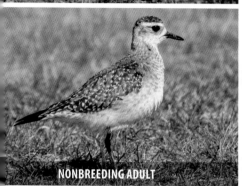

NONBREEDING ADULT

JUVENILE

RANGE MAP

Breeding
Migration
Migration (scarce)

SIZE & SHAPE American Golden-Plovers are stocky, medium-sized shorebirds with moderately long legs, a large, rounded head on a short neck, and a short bill.

COLOR PATTERN In breeding plumage, males have a gold-and-black speckled back offset by black feathers that extend from the face to under the tail. A white crown stripe extends down the side of the neck. Breeding females are paler overall with brown or whitish cheeks. Juveniles are grayish brown overall with a pale eyebrow stripe and a small, almost dovelike head. Adults in nonbreeding plumage are similar to juveniles but less boldly patterned and less golden overall. All plumages have gray underwings without black "wingpits."

BEHAVIOR American Golden-Plovers feed in short vegetation or open areas and move in a stop-run-stop motion, scanning and capturing prey at stops with a single peck or series of pecks.

HABITAT American Golden-Plovers breed on Arctic tundra and winter in grazed grasslands. On migration, they are found on prairie, pastures, golf courses, mudflats, shorelines, and beaches.

A large shorebird of pastures, open ground, and mudflats, the **American Golden-Plover** makes one of the longest migratory journeys of any shorebird. It breeds on the High Arctic tundra of Alaska and Canada and winters in the grasslands of central and southern South America.

ADULT

ADULT

DOWNY YOUNG

ADULT IN PREDATOR DISTRACTION DISPLAY

SIZE & SHAPE Killdeer have the characteristic large, round head, large eye, and short bill of all plovers. They are especially slender and lanky, with a long, pointed tail and long wings.

COLOR PATTERN Both sexes of the Killdeer are brownish tan on top and white below. The white chest is crossed with two black bands, and the brown face is marked with black-and-white patches. The bright orange-buff rump is conspicuous in flight. Downy young have just one black band on the breast.

BEHAVIOR These tawny birds run across the ground in spurts, stopping with a jolt every so often to check their progress, or to see if they've startled up any insect prey. When disturbed, they break into flight and circle overhead, calling repeatedly. Their flight is rapid, with stiff, intermittent wingbeats. To lure predators away from a nest, Killdeer will feign injury with a broken-wing display.

HABITAT Look for Killdeer on open ground with low vegetation (or no vegetation at all), such as lawns, golf courses, driveways, parking lots, and gravel-covered roofs, as well as pastures, fields, sandbars, and mudflats. This species is one of the least water-associated of all shorebirds.

RANGE MAP

■ Breeding
■ Nonbreeding
■ Year-round

The **Killdeer's** broken-wing act leads predators away from a nest, but it doesn't keep cows or horses from stepping on eggs. To guard against large hoofed animals, the Killdeer uses quite a different display: fluffing itself up, displaying its tail over its head, and running at the beast to attempt to make it change its path.

RANGE MAP

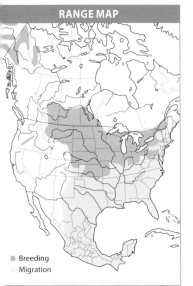

Breeding
Migration

SIZE & SHAPE The Upland Sandpiper is a shorebird with unusual proportions: long legs, a long, thin neck, a small dovelike head, large eyes, and a thin, straight bill. The tail and the wings are long.

COLOR PATTERN Upland Sandpipers are marbled golden brown and blackish above. They are white below, with dark streaks and chevron-shaped markings on the breast and sides. Their throats are white, and they have a white eyering. Adult and immature birds look similar.

BEHAVIOR Upland Sandpipers walk briskly through shortgrass habitats, picking insects and seeds from the ground and vegetation. In breeding season, males perch on fence posts and make circular song flights over the breeding territory, sometimes accompanied by females.

HABITAT Upland Sandpipers nest in grasslands and are most numerous in native prairies in the Great Plains. They also nest in pastures and agricultural fields. During migration and in winter, look for them in shorter vegetation.

small short-billed curlew, the elegant **Upland Sandpiper** paces across grassland habitats throughout the ar. It is considered to be an "indicator species" for the quality of native prairie. Unlike most North merican shorebirds, it avoids wetlands, instead hunting insects with jerky steps and quick jabs at prey.

SIZE & SHAPE The Long-billed Curlew is a large, long-legged shorebird with a very long, thin, curved bill. It has a heavy football-shaped body, a long neck, and a small round head. It is larger than a Whimbrel but smaller than a Cattle Egret.

COLOR PATTERN Long-billed Curlews are speckled and barred in browns above with a pale cinnamon wash throughout and a plain cinnamon belly. The head and neck are pale with faint streaks, and the lower bill is pink at the base. In flight, the wings are mostly cinnamon. Adult and immature birds look similar.

BEHAVIOR The Long-billed Curlew forages for earthworms and other deep-burrowing prey in soft muddy substrates using its long, curved bill. In drier grassland habitats, it pecks at insects. It walks with a strut, pushing its head forward.

HABITAT Long-billed Curlews breed in sparse grasses, including shortgrass and mixed-grass prairies and agricultural fields. In the nonbreeding season, look for them in wetlands, tidal estuaries, mudflats, shallow flooded fields, beaches, and even lawns.

RANGE MAP

- Breeding
- Migration
- Nonbreeding
- Nonbreeding (scarce)

North America's largest shorebird, the **Long-billed Curlew**, is a graceful creature with an almost impossibl long, thin, and curved bill. While the pair works together to incubate the eggs and care for the brood, the female typically leaves 2–3 weeks after the eggs hatch, and her mate is left to care for the young.

BREEDING ADULT

ADULT

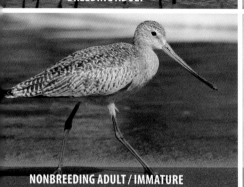

NONBREEDING ADULT / IMMATURE

BREEDING ADULT

RANGE MAP

■ Breeding
□ Migration
■ Nonbreeding

SIZE & SHAPE The Marbled Godwit is a large, long-legged shorebird with an extremely long, slightly upturned bill. A small round head sits atop a thin neck. In flight, its legs stick out beyond the tail.

COLOR PATTERN Marbled Godwits are barred above and below in brown, white, and cinnamon during the breeding season. The bill is black at the tip and orange at the base during the breeding season, and pink during the nonbreeding season, but this distinction can be difficult to see.

BEHAVIOR The Marbled Godwit probes into sand or mud with its long bill for aquatic invertebrates. It sometimes walks while probing or takes a few steps before burying its bill in the mud. It is social outside of the breeding season and forages in groups.

HABITAT Marbled Godwits breed in northern shortgrass prairies near wetlands. During migration and on the wintering grounds, look for them on mudflats, salt ponds, beaches, estuaries, and wetlands.

orebirds have some of the most interesting bill shapes, and the **Marbled Godwit** is no exception with swordlike bill. This well-camouflaged speckled brown bird is especially noticeable on the prairie when it reads its long and pointed wings to take flight.

BREEDING ADULTS

BREEDING ADULT

JUVENILE

NONBREEDING ADULT

SIZE & SHAPE Ruddy Turnstones are short, stocky, oval-shaped shorebirds with stout, slightly upturned bills. They are larger than Spotted Sandpipers but smaller than Willets.

COLOR PATTERN Breeding males have black-and-white markings on the head and throat and a chestnut-and-black pattern on the back. Breeding females are paler. Both have orange legs that are brighter in the breeding season.

BEHAVIOR Ruddy Turnstones flip rocks, pebbles, and seaweed along shorelines in search of food. They rarely wade in waters more than a few inches deep, generally foraging out of the water. On migration and in winter, they gather in groups of 10 to over 1,000.

HABITAT Ruddy Turnstones breed in the tundra of northern North America. On migration and in winter, they use freshwater shorelines, mudflats, rocky shorelines, and sandy beaches further south.

RANGE MAP

■ Breeding
  Migration
■ Nonbreeding

A shorebird that looks a bit like a calico cat, the **Ruddy Turnstone's** orange legs and uniquely patterned black-and-white head and chest make this bird easy to pick out of a crowd. Long-distance migrants that breed in the Arctic tundra, they spend off-seasons on rocky shorelines and sandy beaches on both coasts.

NONBREEDING ADULT

NONBREEDING ADULT

JUVENILE

BREEDING ADULT

RANGE MAP

■ Breeding
Migration
■ Nonbreeding

SIZE & SHAPE Sanderlings are small, plump sandpipers with a stout bill about the same length as the head. Sanderlings are medium-sized members of the genus *Calidris*.

COLOR PATTERN In nonbreeding plumage, they are light gray above and white below, with a blackish shoulder mark. In spring and summer, they are spangled black, white, and rufous on the head, neck, and back. Juveniles have a checkered back and unmarked white underparts. Their legs and bills are black.

BEHAVIOR Sanderlings breed on the High Arctic tundra and migrate south in fall to populate beaches. They gather in loose flocks to probe the sand for marine invertebrates, running back and forth in a perpetual "wave chase."

HABITAT During migration and winter, Sanderlings forage on North American beaches but will also use mudflats in the Midwest. They nest in the High Arctic on gravel patches and low-growing, wet tundra.

e **Sanderling's** black legs blur as it runs back and forth on the beach, picking or probing for tiny prey in e wet sand left by receding waves. Sanderlings are medium-sized sandpipers recognizable by their pale nbreeding plumage, black legs and bill, and obsessive wave-chasing habits.

NONBREEDING ADULT

NONBREEDING ADULT

BREEDING ADULT

JUVENILE

SIZE & SHAPE The Western Sandpiper is a small, portly shorebird with a long, thin bill with a slight droop. It has pointed wings, a short tail, and medium-length legs for its size. Females tend to be larger and have longer bills than males.

COLOR PATTERN Breeding adults have black, brown, rufous, and gold upperparts, with white underparts marked with extensive dark arrow-shaped streaks. They have a rufous crown and ear patch, and dark legs and bill. Nonbreeding adults are pale gray above, whitish below. Juveniles are similar to nonbreeding adults but the upperparts are more vivid in the wings, showing gold and rufous edges to feathers.

BEHAVIOR Western Sandpipers congregate in large flocks on beaches and mudflats. Their toes are adapted for walking and running in short bursts while foraging on beaches. They can often be seen balancing on one leg, or even hopping.

HABITAT Western Sandpipers breed in low coastal tundra with sedges. On migration and in winter, look for them along mudflats, beaches, shores of lakes and ponds, and flooded fields.

RANGE MAP

■ Breeding
  Migration
■ Nonbreeding
  Nonbreeding (scarce)

In migration, the **Western Sandpiper** stages in huge, spectacular flocks, particularly along the Pacific Coast, San Francisco Bay and in the Copper River Delta in Alaska. Estimates suggest that nearly the whole breeding population passes through the Copper River Delta in a few weeks each spring.

NONBREEDING ADULT

BREEDING ADULT

JUVENILE

JUVENILE

RANGE MAP

- Breeding
- Migration
- Nonbreeding
- Year-round

SIZE & SHAPE The Spotted Sandpiper is a medium-sized shorebird with a bill slightly shorter than its head and a body that tapers to a longish tail. They have a rounded breast and usually appear as though they are leaning forward.

COLOR PATTERN In breeding season, Spotted Sandpipers have an orange bill and bold spots on their bright white breast. The back is dark brown. In winter, a Spotted Sandpiper's breast is not spotted; it's plain white, while the back is grayish brown and the bill is pale yellow. In flight, Spotted Sandpipers have a thin white stripe along the wing.

BEHAVIOR Spotted Sandpipers are often solitary and walk with a distinctive teeter, bobbing their tails up and down constantly. When foraging, they walk quickly, crouching low, occasionally darting toward prey, all while bobbing the tail.

HABITAT Find Spotted Sandpipers along streambanks, rivers, ponds, lakes, and beaches. They are one of the most widespread breeding shorebirds in the U.S., commonly seen near fresh water, even in arid or forested regions.

e **Spotted Sandpiper** is the most widespread breeding sandpiper in North America. Female Spotted ndpipers sometimes practice an unusual breeding strategy called polyandry, where a female mates with to four males, each of which then cares for a clutch of eggs.

BREEDING ADULT (EASTERN)

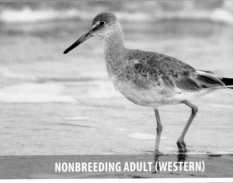
NONBREEDING ADULT (WESTERN)

JUVENILE (EASTERN)

NONBREEDING ADULTS (WESTERN)

SIZE & SHAPE Willets are large, stocky shorebirds with long legs and thick, straight bills considerably longer than the head. Their wings are broader and rounder than those of many shorebirds, and the short tail is squared off at the tip.

COLOR PATTERN Willets are gray or brown birds that, when flying, display a striking white stripe between black patches along each wing. In summer, Willets are mottled gray, brown, and black; in winter they are a plain gray. The legs are bluish gray to olive gray.

BEHAVIOR Willets are often seen alone. They walk deliberately, pausing to probe for prey in sand and mudflats. When startled, they react with a piercing call, often opening their wings and running rather than taking flight.

HABITAT In winter, look for Willets on beaches, rocky coasts, mudflats, and marshes. In breeding season, Western birds nest in grasslands and prairies near fresh water. Eastern birds breed on barrier beaches, islands, and in coastal saltmarshes, and spend the winter in South America.

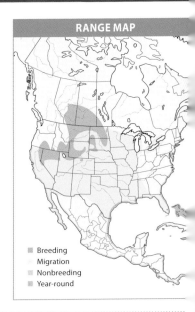

RANGE MAP

■ Breeding
  Migration
■ Nonbreeding
■ Year-round

Like Killdeer, **Willets** will pretend to be disabled by a broken wing in order to draw attention to themselv and lure predators away from their eggs or chicks. Because they find prey using the sensitive tips of their bills, and not just eyesight, Willets can feed both during the day and at night.

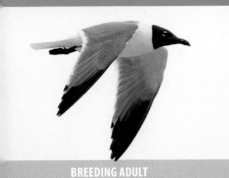

BREEDING ADULT

NONBREEDING ADULT

JUVENILE

IMMATURE (FIRST WINTER)

RANGE MAP

- Breeding
- Year-round
- Summer dispersal

SIZE & SHAPE Laughing Gulls are medium-sized gulls with fairly long wings and long legs that impart a graceful look when they are flying or walking. They have stout, fairly long bills. They are slightly smaller than Ring-billed Gulls.

COLOR PATTERN Adults are dark gray above and white below. Summer adults have a sooty-black hood, white arcs around the eyes, and a reddish bill. In winter, the hood becomes a gray mask on a white head, and the bill becomes black. The legs are reddish black to black.

BEHAVIOR Laughing Gulls eat almost anything, including food they catch or steal, handouts, garbage, and discards from fishing boats. They often congregate in parking lots, sandy beaches, and mud bars.

HABITAT This coastal species is rarely seen far inland. Look for them in plowed fields, garbage dumps, parking lots, and shorelines. They nest, often in large groups, on islands near the shore, away from terrestrial predators.

rling over beaches with strident calls and a distinctive, sooty-black head, **Laughing Gulls** provide sights sounds evocative of summer on the East Coast. You'll run across this handsome gull in large numbers eaches, docks, and parking lots, where it waits for handouts or fills the air with its raucous calls.

BREEDING ADULT

BREEDING ADULT

IMMATURE (FIRST WINTER)

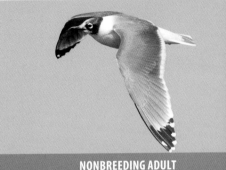

NONBREEDING ADULT

SIZE & SHAPE The Franklin's Gull is a fairly small gull with a short neck and a slim, rather short bill. Like other gulls, the wings are long and the tail is short. It is larger than a Bonaparte's Gull, smaller than a Laughing Gull.

COLOR PATTERN Breeding adult Franklin's Gulls have a black head with white crescents above and below the eye. Upperparts are dark gray; legs and bill are reddish. Nonbreeding adults have a gray half-hood or mask, and bill and legs are dark. In adults, a white crescent separates black wingtips from the gray upperwing.

BEHAVIOR Franklin's Gulls catch insects in the air in flight, or pick prey from the ground as they walk. In the water, they glean prey from the surface while swimming, sometimes swimming in circles to bring prey to the surface.

HABITAT Franklin's Gulls nest in freshwater prairie and open-country marshes with emergent and floating vegetation. They migrate through the continent's center, using agricultural fields, marshes, and reservoirs.

RANGE MAP

■ Breeding
  Migration

A delicate waterbird that nests by the thousands in North American marshes, the **Franklin's Gull** spends winters off the coasts of Chile and Peru. Its buoyant, swift, graceful flight is useful for catching both flying insects and small fish, as well as for making its long migrations.

BREEDING ADULT

NONBREEDING ADULT

IMMATURE (FIRST WINTER)

IMMATURE (SECOND WINTER)

RANGE MAP

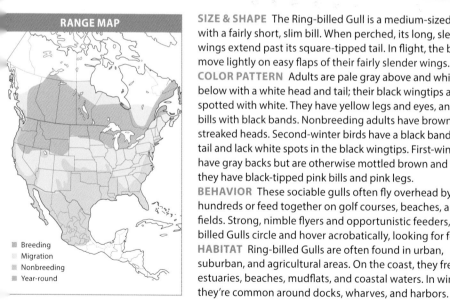

- Breeding
- Migration
- Nonbreeding
- Year-round

SIZE & SHAPE The Ring-billed Gull is a medium-sized gull with a fairly short, slim bill. When perched, its long, slender wings extend past its square-tipped tail. In flight, the birds move lightly on easy flaps of their fairly slender wings.

COLOR PATTERN Adults are pale gray above and white below with a white head and tail; their black wingtips are spotted with white. They have yellow legs and eyes, and yellow bills with black bands. Nonbreeding adults have brown-streaked heads. Second-winter birds have a black band on the tail and lack white spots in the black wingtips. First-winter birds have gray backs but are otherwise mottled brown and white; they have black-tipped pink bills and pink legs.

BEHAVIOR These sociable gulls often fly overhead by the hundreds or feed together on golf courses, beaches, and fields. Strong, nimble flyers and opportunistic feeders, Ring-billed Gulls circle and hover acrobatically, looking for food.

HABITAT Ring-billed Gulls are often found in urban, suburban, and agricultural areas. On the coast, they frequent estuaries, beaches, mudflats, and coastal waters. In winter, they're common around docks, wharves, and harbors.

miliar acrobats of the air and comfortable around humans, **Ring-billed Gulls** frequent parking lots, rbage dumps, beaches, and fields, sometimes by the hundreds. You're most likely to see them far away m coastal areas—in fact, most Ring-billed Gulls nest in the interior of the continent, near fresh water.

BREEDING ADULT

NONBREEDING ADULT

JUVENILE

IMMATURE (SECOND WINTER)

SIZE & SHAPE Herring Gulls are large gulls with hefty bills and robust bodies. In flight, they look barrel-chested and broad-winged compared to smaller gulls.

COLOR PATTERN Breeding adult Herring Gulls are light gray above and white below, with black wingtips, white heads, and pale eyes ringed in red. In winter, dusky brown streaks mark their heads. The legs are dull pink at all ages. Juveniles are tan overall with tan-and-white checkerboarding on their back. Immature plumages are intermediate between juvenile and adult.

BEHAVIOR Herring Gulls patrol shorelines and open ocean, picking scraps off the surface. Rallying around fishing boats or refuse dumps, they are loud scavengers that snatch other birds' meals.

HABITAT Look for Herring Gulls along coasts, and near large lakes and rivers; in summer, look for them as far north as coastal Alaska. They feed in open water, mudflats, plowed fields, and garbage dumps and gather in open space near food.

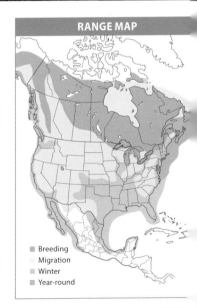

RANGE MAP

- Breeding
- Migration
- Winter
- Year-round

Spiraling above a fishing boat or squabbling at a dock or parking lot, **Herring Gulls** are the quintessential gray-and-white, pink-legged "seagulls." They're the most familiar gulls of the North Atlantic and can be found across much of coastal North America in winter.

BREEDING ADULT

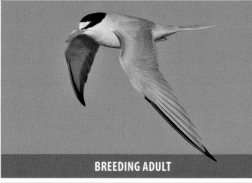

BREEDING ADULT

JUVENILE

IMMATURE (FIRST YEAR)

RANGE MAP

■ Breeding

SIZE & SHAPE The Least Tern, the smallest tern in North America, has narrow pointed wings and a short tail. It is smaller than a Killdeer.

COLOR PATTERN Breeding adult Least Terns have gray backs with white underparts, a black cap, and a white forehead. The yellow bill has a black tip. Nonbreeding adults have a black bill and some gray in the black cap. Immatures have a black leading edge to the wing which appears like a black shoulder when perched.

BEHAVIOR Least Terns feed by plunging into water from flight. They may hover briefly before plunging.

HABITAT Look for Least Terns on coasts, beaches, bays, estuaries, lagoons, lakes, and rivers. They choose to breed on the sandy or gravelly beaches and banks of rivers or lakes, and on rare occasions, on flat rooftops of buildings.

de sandy beaches, lake fronts, and riverbanks are the **Least Tern's** favorite nesting habitats. This small n makes just a scrape in the sand or mud for a nest, which offers little protection from people, velopment, and off-road vehicles. In the past fifty years, their numbers have declined by about 88%.

BREEDING ADULTS

BREEDING ADULT

JUVENILE

NONBREEDING ADULTS

SIZE & SHAPE The Caspian Tern is the largest tern in the world. It has a large bill with a thick base, and a shallow fork in the tail. The large head can look smoothly rounded, squared off, or slightly crested.

COLOR PATTERN Caspian Terns have a black cap, a white body, and a brilliant coral-red bill with a with a dark band near the tip. Nonbreeding adults and immatures have a grayish crown and forehead. Juveniles have black edging to back feathers.

BEHAVIOR Caspian Terns fly over water with the bill pointing down, then plunge into the water to catch fish.

HABITAT Caspian Terns tend to breed in salt marshes and a range of islands, including barrier, dredge-spoil, and freshwater lake and river islands. In migration and winter, they are found along coastlines, large rivers, and lakes. They roost on islands and isolated spits.

RANGE MAP

■ Breeding
  Migration
■ Nonbreeding
■ Year-round

The **Caspian Tern** aggressively defends its breeding colony. It will pursue, attack, and chase predatory birds, and can cause bloody wounds on the heads of people who invade the colony. The entire colony wil take flight, however, when a Bald Eagle flies overhead, exposing the chicks to predation from gulls.

BREEDING ADULT

BREEDING ADULT

NONBREEDING ADULT / JUVENILE

JUVENILE

RANGE MAP

■ Breeding
■ Migration
■ Nonbreeding

SIZE & SHAPE The Black Tern is a small and delicately built waterbird with a thin, pointed bill; long, pointed wings; a shallowly forked tail; and short legs. It is larger than a Least Tern, smaller than a Common Tern.

COLOR PATTERN Adults in breeding plumage are dark gray above with black heads and black underparts. Underwings and undertail coverts are pale. Nonbreeding adults are gray above, whitish below, with a dusky crown, ear patch, and mark at the side of the breast. Juveniles are similar to nonbreeding adults but with a brown scaled pattern to the upperparts.

BEHAVIOR Black Terns forage by flying slowly and either dipping to the water's surface to pick up small fish or insects, or by catching insects on the wing. They breed in colonies in freshwater lakes, making nests on floating vegetation.

HABITAT Black Terns nest in freshwater marshes and bogs and winter in coastal lagoons, marshes, and open ocean waters. Migrants may stop over in almost any type of wetland.

An outlier in a world of white seabirds, breeding **Black Terns** are a handsome mix of charcoal gray and jet black. Their delicate form and neatly pointed wings provide tremendous agility as these birds flutter and swoop to pluck fish from the water's surface or veer to catch flying insects, much as a swallow does.

BREEDING ADULT

BREEDING ADULT

IMMATURE

IMMATURE (FIRST YEAR)

SIZE & SHAPE Common Terns have long, narrow, angular wings and pointed wingtips. Unlike gulls, this tern has a straight, slender bill. The tail is forked, and the legs are short.

COLOR PATTERN Common Terns are pale gray overall with a black cap. Breeding birds have a gray belly and a fully black cap that extends to the back of the neck. They also have a red-orange bill tipped in black and red-orange legs. Nonbreeding birds have a white forehead, a partial black cap, and black legs and bill. Immature birds have a distinctive black bar on the leading edge of the wing.

BEHAVIOR Terns fly gracefully with rowing wingbeats over open waters, diving down to pick fish from or just below the water's surface. They are vocal and gregarious birds that make their presence well known.

HABITAT Common Terns nest on rocky islands, barrier beaches, and saltmarshes and forage over open waters. In the breeding season, they frequent both salt and fresh waters, but in winter, they tend to stick to marine environments.

RANGE MAP

- Breeding
- Migration
- Winter

Common Terns made an unfortunate appearance in women's fashion in the late 19th century. Feathers and sometimes entire terns were mounted on women's hats, resulting in their near extirpation from the Atlantic Coast. The Migratory Bird Treaty Act of 1918 restored their populations by the 1930s.

BREEDING ADULT

BREEDING ADULT

JUVENILE

NONBREEDING ADULT

RANGE MAP

Breeding
Migration
Nonbreeding
Year-round

SIZE & SHAPE The Forster's Tern is a slender, long-tailed, long-winged waterbird with a long, pointed bill and short legs. When perched, the long tail streamers extend past the end of the wings. It is larger than a Black Tern.

COLOR PATTERN Breeding adults are pale gray above and white below, with a black cap, and a black-tipped orange bill. They have silvery gray wingtips and orange legs. Nonbreeding adults have a dark bill, white crown, and blackish eye patch. Juvenile birds are a mottled rusty brown, white, and gray with a black eye patch.

BEHAVIOR Forster's Terns forage by flying slowly over the water to scan for fish, then diving to capture prey. Breeding adults perform spiraling courtship flights and also parade through the colony in tandem with raised bills.

HABITAT Forster's Terns breed in marshes, usually in areas with extensive open water and some floating vegetation. They winter in oceans, bays, and estuaries, close to the coast. Some winter inland near the Gulf of Mexico.

ashing slender, silvery wings and an elegantly forked tail, **Forster's Terns** cruise above the shallow waters of arshes and coastlines. These medium-sized white terns are often confused with the similar Common Tern, ut Forster's Terns have a longer tail and, in nonbreeding plumage, a distinctive black eye patch.

BREEDING ADULT

BREEDING ADULT

NONBREEDING ADULT

JUVENILE

SIZE & SHAPE Royal Terns are large, slender, and long-winged terns. The head is fairly large and often has a ragged crest at the back. Royal Terns have a substantial body, a long, forked tail, and short legs. The bill is long and daggerlike.

COLOR PATTERN Breeding adults are pale gray above and white below, with a black crest and bright orange bill. Nonbreeders have a white forehead with black only at the rear of the crest. The outer primaries of the wing are blackish, and the legs are black. Juveniles are similar but with tan feathers in upperparts, duskier upperwings, and a paler bill.

BEHAVIOR Royal Terns forage by slowly flying above the water's surface, then diving for small fish and crustaceans. They nest in dense colonies on beaches and islands.

HABITAT Look for Royal Terns in the warm, shallow waters of oceans, bays, and rivers, usually close to shore. They nest and roost on barrier beaches, sandy islands, and artificial islands created by dredging. They may be found inland after strong storms.

RANGE MAP

- Breeding
- Migration
- Nonbreeding
- Nonbreeding (scarce)
- Year-round

A sleek seabird of warm saltwater coasts, the **Royal Tern** lives up to its regal name with a tangerine-colore bill and ragged, ink-black crest against crisp white plumage. Royal Terns fly gracefully and slowly along coastlines, diving for small fish, which they capture with a swift strike of their daggerlike bills.

BREEDING ADULT

BREEDING ADULT

JUVENILE

NONBREEDING ADULT

RANGE MAP

Breeding
Nonbreeding
Year-round

SIZE & SHAPE The Black Skimmer is larger than most terns but with similarly elegant, streamlined proportions. It has very long wings and an outsized bill in which the upper half is much shorter than the lower half.

COLOR PATTERN Adults are starkly black above and white below, with a black-and-red bill and orange-red legs. Juveniles are brownish above, with pale-edged wing covert feathers.

BEHAVIOR Skimmers have a distinctive flight style: usually very low to the water with wings held above its body. Long upstrokes and short downstrokes allow the skimmer to stay clear of the water. This creates a characteristic bounding or ranging style to the flight. Juveniles often rest with their body flat on the ground and neck extended.

HABITAT Black Skimmers favor coastal beaches and islands near oceans, including along the Gulf of Mexico, and are occasionally seen inland, especially in sites such as Salton Sea, California, and Palm Beach County, Florida.

e **Black Skimmer** forages in flight, opening its bill and dropping its long lower mandible into the water, imming along until it feels a fish. Then it relaxes the neck, quickly closing its jaws and whipping the fish t of the water. Because these birds feed essentially by touch, they can even forage at night.

BREEDING ADULT

NONBREEDING ADULT

NONBREEDING ADULT / IMMATURE

JUVENILE

SIZE & SHAPE Common Loons are large, diving waterbirds with rounded heads and daggerlike bills. They have long bodies and short tails that are usually not visible. In flight, they stretch out, with a long, flat body and long neck and bill. Their feet stick out beyond the tail (unlike ducks and cormorants), looking like wedges.

COLOR PATTERN In summer, adults have a black head and bill, a black-and-white spotted back, and a white breast. From September to March, adults are plain gray on the back and head with a white throat. The bill also fades to gray. Juveniles look similar, but with more pronounced scalloping on the back.

BEHAVIOR Common Loons are stealthy divers, submerging without a splash to catch fish. Pairs and groups often call to each other at night. In flight, notice their shallow wingbeats and unwavering, straight flight path.

HABITAT Common Loons breed on quiet, remote freshwater lakes of the northern U.S. and Canada, and they are sensitive to human disturbance. In winter and during migration, look for them on lakes, rivers, estuaries, and coastlines.

RANGE MAP

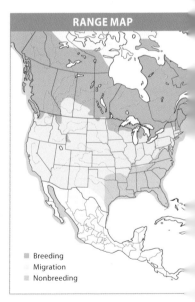

- Breeding
- Migration
- Nonbreeding

The eerie calls of **Common Loons** echo across the clear lakes of the northern wilderness. In winter, look fc them along seashores and on inland reservoirs and lakes. These powerful, agile divers catch small fish in underwater chases. They are less suited to land and typically come ashore only to nest.

ADULT

ADULT

JUVENILE

IMMATURE

RANGE MAP

Migration (scarce)
Breeding
Year-round

SIZE & SHAPE Wood Storks are hefty wading birds with football-shaped bodies perched atop long legs. They have a long neck and a long, thick bill that is curved at the tip. They fly with their neck and legs outstretched but tend to perch with the neck drawn in, giving them a humpbacked appearance.

COLOR PATTERN Wood Storks are entirely white save for their black flight feathers and tail. The head is unfeathered and scaly looking in adults, and variably feathered in immatures.

BEHAVIOR Wood Storks frequently feed in groups with their heads down, feeling for prey in open wetlands. Within the group, they often feed in lines—one after the other. They fly with head and legs outstretched, soaring on thermals like a raptor or vulture.

HABITAT Wood Storks breed in fresh and brackish forested wetlands. They forage in wetlands, swamps, ponds, and marshes, especially those with an open canopy.

Large, white **Wood Storks** wade through southeastern swamps and wetlands and roost and nest in colonies in trees above standing water. Skilled fliers, they soar on thermals with neck and legs outstretched. This bald-headed wading bird stands just over three feet tall, towering above almost all other wetland birds.

BREEDING MALE

BREEDING MALE AND DOWNY YOUNG

ADULT FEMALE / IMMATURE

ADULT FEMALE / IMMATURE

SIZE & SHAPE Anhingas are large and slender waterbirds with long, fanlike tails. They have a long S-shaped neck and a daggerlike bill. They have slim bodies and look rather flattened in flight.

COLOR PATTERN Adult male Anhingas are black with silvery to white streaks on the back and wings. Females and immatures have a pale tan head, neck, and breast. Anhingas' bills are various shades of yellow.

BEHAVIOR Anhingas swim with their bodies partly or mostly submerged and their long, snakelike neck held partially out of the water. After a swim, they perch on branches or logs to dry out, with wings extended. They frequently soar high in the sky.

HABITAT Anhingas inhabit freshwater lakes, ponds, and slow-moving streams with branches near the water for drying themselves. They also use brackish bays and lagoons along the coast, but they avoid extensive open water.

RANGE MAP

■ Breeding
■ Year-round

Look for the snakelike head of the **Anhinga** poking above a lake's surface as it stealthily swims. Underwater it stabs fish with its daggerlike bill. After every dip, it dries itself at the water's edge, silvery wings outstretched and head held high. Once dry, it takes flight, soaring high on thermals, stretched out like a cross.

BREEDING ADULT

BREEDING ADULT

JUVENILES

NONBREEDING ADULT

RANGE MAP

Breeding
Year-round

SIZE & SHAPE A slim waterbird, the Neotropic Cormorant is small for a cormorant, with a long neck, a rather long tail, and a fairly thin, straight bill with a hooked tip. It has broad wings and large webbed feet. It has a proportionately longer tail than the Double-crested Cormorant.

COLOR PATTERN Adults are black with orange skin under the bill; the skin is bordered with a thin white line. In good light, there is a faint olive sheen to the wings. In breeding plumage, adults have a small white tuft of feathers near the ears. Juveniles are similar, but the head, neck, and breast are brownish.

BEHAVIOR Neotropic Cormorants dive from the water's surface, using their feet for propulsion through water. They catch fish underwater, then take prey to the surface and swallow it headfirst. They will also plunge-dive from above the water.

HABITAT Neotropic Cormorants are found in various wetlands, including fresh, brackish, and saltwater habitats. They nest and roost mostly in trees, but also on cliffs and human-made structures.

The **Neotropic Cormorant** looks very similar to the Double-crested Cormorant, and the two species often flock together. Unlike its cousin, the Neotropic Cormorant sometimes plunge-dives for fish from a few feet above the water, but it mostly dives and then darts after fish as it paddles along the water's surface.

NONBREEDING ADULT

BREEDING ADULT

JUVENILES (L) AND NONBREEDING ADULT (R)

JUVENILE

SIZE & SHAPE The Double-crested Cormorant is a large waterbird with a relatively short tail and a small head on a long, kinked neck. The thin, hooked bill is roughly the length of its head. Its heavy body sits low in the water, and it can be mistaken for a loon.

COLOR PATTERN Adults are brownish black with a small patch of yellow-orange skin on the face. Immatures are browner overall, palest on the neck and breast. Breeding adults develop a small double crest of stringy black feathers behind the eyes.

BEHAVIOR Double-crested Cormorants float low in the water and dive to catch small fish. After fishing, they stand on docks, rocks, and tree limbs with wings spread open to dry. In flight, they often travel in V-formation flocks.

HABITAT Double-crested Cormorants are the most widespread cormorants in North America, and they are often seen in fresh water. They breed on coastlines and along large inland lakes. They form colonies of stick nests built high in trees on islands or in patches of flooded timber.

RANGE MAP

■ Breeding
Migration
■ Nonbreeding
■ Year-round

The prehistoric-looking **Double-crested Cormorant** is a common sight around fresh and salt waters across temperate North America—attracting the most attention when standing on docks, rocky islands, and channel markers, wings spread to dry. These solid and heavy-boned birds are experts at diving to catch small fish.

ADULTS / IMMATURES

BREEDING ADULTS

NONBREEDING ADULTS

NONBREEDING ADULT

RANGE MAP

- Breeding
- Migration
- Nonbreeding
- Year-round

SIZE & SHAPE The American White Pelican is a huge waterbird with very broad wings, a long neck, and a massive bill that gives the head a unique, long shape. They have thick bodies, short legs, and short, square tails. A yellow plate forms on the upper bill of breeding adults. The large throat pouch, typical of pelicans, isn't usually obvious.

COLOR PATTERN Adults are white with black feathers visible when the wings are spread. A patch of chest feathers can turn yellow in spring. The bill and legs are yellow orange. Immatures are mostly white, but the head, neck, and back are washed with dusky brown and the bill is dull pink.

BEHAVIOR American White Pelicans feed from the water's surface, dipping their beaks in to catch prey. They often upend but do not plunge-dive. They are among the heaviest flying birds in the world and often travel long distances in large flocks.

HABITAT American White Pelicans typically breed on islands in shallow wetlands in the interior of the continent. They spend winters mainly on coastal waters, bays, and estuaries, or a little distance inland.

One of the largest North American birds, the **American White Pelican** is majestic in the air, soaring with incredible steadiness. On the water, they dip their pouched bills to scoop up fish, or tip-up like dabbling ducks. Sometimes, groups of pelicans work together to herd fish into the shallows for easy feeding.

NONBREEDING ADULT

ADULTS

JUVENILE

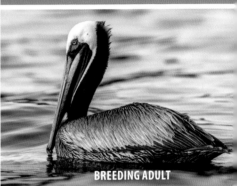

BREEDING ADULT

SIZE & SHAPE Brown Pelicans are huge, stocky seabirds. They have thin necks and very long bills with a stretchy throat pouch used for capturing fish. Their wings are long and broad, often noticeably bowed when the birds are gliding.

COLOR PATTERN Adults are gray brown with pale, yellowish heads and white necks. In breeding plumage, the back and sides of the neck turn a rich, dark reddish brown. Immatures are gray brown above with a pale whitish belly and breast.

BEHAVIOR Brown Pelicans plunge into the water, stunning small fish with the impact of their bodies and scooping them up in their throat pouches. When not feeding, they stand on fishing docks, jetties, and beaches or cruise the shoreline.

HABITAT Brown Pelicans live along seacoasts and are rarely seen inland. An exception is at Salton Sea in California, where they are found in large numbers. They nest in colonies, often on isolated islands free of land predators.

RANGE MAP

- Breeding
- Migration
- Year-round
- - - Year-round (scarce)

Squadrons of **Brown Pelicans** glide above the surf along coasts and feed by plunge-diving from high up, using the force of impact to stun small fish before scooping them up. They are fairly common today—an example of a species' recovery from pesticide pollution that once placed them at the brink of extinction.

ADULT

ADULT

IMMATURE

JUVENILE

RANGE MAP

■ Breeding
■ Nonbreeding
■ Year-round

SIZE & SHAPE This largest of North American herons has long legs, a sinuous neck, and a thick, daggerlike bill. Head, chest, and wing plumes give a shaggy appearance. In flight, the Great Blue Heron curls its neck into a tight S shape; its wings are broad and rounded, and its legs trail well beyond the tail.

COLOR PATTERN Great Blue Herons appear blue gray from a distance, with a wide black stripe over the eye. In flight, the upper side of the wing is two-toned: pale on the forewing and darker on the flight feathers.

BEHAVIOR Hunting Great Blue Herons wade slowly or stand statuelike, stalking prey in shallow water or open fields. Their very slow wingbeats, tucked-in neck, and trailing legs create an unmistakable silhouette in flight.

HABITAT Look for Great Blue Herons in saltwater and freshwater habitats, from seashores, marshes, sloughs, riverbanks, and lakes to backyard goldfish ponds. They also forage in grasslands and agricultural fields.

'hether poised at a river bend or cruising the coastline with slow, deep wingbeats, the **Great Blue Heron** a majestic sight. It will often stand motionless as it scans for prey or wades belly deep with long, deliberate eps. This heron may move slowly, but it can strike like lightning to grab a fish or snap up a gopher.

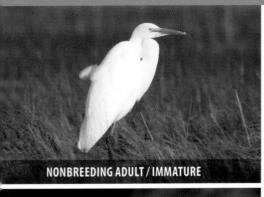

NONBREEDING ADULT / IMMATURE

BREEDING ADULT

NONBREEDING ADULT / IMMATURE

NONBREEDING ADULT / IMMATURE

SIZE & SHAPE Great Egrets are tall, long-legged wading birds with an S-curved neck and a daggerlike bill. In flight, the long neck is tucked in, and the legs extend far beyond the tip of the short tail. During breeding season, long feathery plumes, called aigrettes, grow from its back. They are held up during courtship displays.

COLOR PATTERN Every feather on a Great Egret is white. The bill is solid yellowish orange, and the legs and feet are entirely black. During courtship, the skin patch between the bill and eyes brightens to lime green.

BEHAVIOR You can find Great Egrets wading in shallow water hunting for food. They typically stand still and watch for prey to pass by, and then, with startling speed, strike with a jab of the long neck and bill.

HABITAT Great Egrets live in freshwater, brackish, and marine wetlands. During the breeding season, they are found in nesting colonies on lakes, ponds, marshes, estuaries, impoundments, and islands.

RANGE MAP

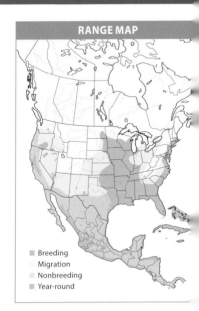

■ Breeding
  Migration
  Nonbreeding
■ Year-round

The pristinely white **Great Egret** gets even more dressed up for the breeding season. A patch of skin on its face turns neon green, and long plumes grow from its back. Called aigrettes, those plumes were the bane of egrets in the late 19th century, when such adornments were prized for ladies' hats.

BREEDING ADULT

NONBREEDING ADULT

IMMATURE

NONBREEDING ADULT

RANGE MAP

- Breeding
- Migration
- Nonbreeding
- Year-round

SIZE & SHAPE Snowy Egrets are medium-sized herons with long, thin legs and long, slender, bills. Their long, thin neck sets the small head well away from the body. It is smaller than a Great Egret and larger than a Cattle Egret.

COLOR PATTERN Adult Snowy Egrets are all white with a black bill, black legs, and rich yellow feet. They have a patch of yellow skin at the base of the bill. Immature Snowy Egrets have greenish yellow running up the backs of the legs.

BEHAVIOR Snowy Egrets wade in shallow water to spear fish and other small aquatic prey. While they use a sit-and-wait technique to capture their food, they may run back and forth through the water with their wings spread, chasing prey.

HABITAT They are most common along the coast but some breed patchily in inland wetlands. Snowy Egrets nest colonially, usually on protected islands, and often with other small herons. They concentrate on mudflats, beaches, and wetlands, but also forage in wet agricultural fields and along the edges of rivers and lakes.

e elegant **Snowy Egret** uses its feet to stir up or herd small aquatic animals as it forages. Breeding Snowy rets grow plumes that once fetched astronomical prices, endangering the species. Through conservation orts in the early 20th century, this species is again common in coastal wetlands.

LITTLE BLUE HERON *(Egretta caerulea)*

ADULT

ADULT

IMMATURE (FIRST SPRING)

JUVENILE

SIZE & SHAPE The Little Blue Heron is fairly small, with a slight body, slender neck, and fairly long legs. It has rounded wings, and a long, straight, spearlike bill that is thick at the base.

COLOR PATTERN Adult Little Blue Herons are very dark all over, with a rich purple-maroon head and neck, and a dark slaty-blue body. They have yellow eyes, greenish legs, and a bill that is pale blue at the base and black at the tip. Immature birds that are molting into adult plumage are a patchwork of white and blue. Juvenile birds are mostly white, except for dusky tips to the outer primaries. Legs are pale green.

BEHAVIOR This bird is a stand-and-wait predator. They watch the water for prey, changing locations by walking slowly or by flying to a completely different site. They nest in trees, usually among other nesting herons and wading birds.

HABITAT Look for Little Blue Herons on quiet waters ranging from tidal flats and estuaries to streams, swamps, and flooded fields. They are usually found in only small numbers at any one water body, often tucked into hidden corners.

RANGE MAP

■ Breeding
■ Breeding (scarce)
■ Migration
■ Nonbreeding
■ Year-round

A small heron arrayed in moody blues and purples, the **Little Blue Heron** is a common but inconspicuou. resident of marshes and estuaries in the Southeast. They stalk shallow waters for small fish and amphibiar with a quiet, methodical approach that can make them surprisingly easy to overlook at first glance.

BREEDING ADULT

BREEDING ADULT

JUVENILE

NONBREEDING ADULT

RANGE MAP

- Breeding
- Nonbreeding
- Year-round
- Year-round (scarce)

SIZE & SHAPE The Tricolored Heron is a medium-sized, delicate, and slim heron with a long, daggerlike bill. Its long, thin neck curves up to its small head. It is larger than a Snowy Egret and smaller than a Great Blue Heron.

COLOR PATTERN Adults are a mix of blue-gray, lavender, and white. Breeding birds have small white plumes at the back of the head, a blue patch around the bill, and pink legs. Nonbreeding birds have yellowish legs and fewer flourishes. Juveniles have a reddish neck.

BEHAVIOR Tricolored Herons gracefully walk through wetlands, but they also run after fish with sharp turns and stops, balancing with their wings. They tend to forage alone or at the edge of flocks of wading birds.

HABITAT Tricolored Herons use coastal estuaries, saltmarshes, mangroves, and lagoons during the breeding season. In the nonbreeding season, they use coastal areas, freshwater marshes, lake edges, canals, and ditches.

...ce known as the Louisiana Heron, the **Tricolored Heron** is a fairly small heron that wades through ...astal waters in search of small fish, often running and stopping with balletic turns and starts. It builds ...ck nests in trees and shrubs, often in colonies with other wading birds.

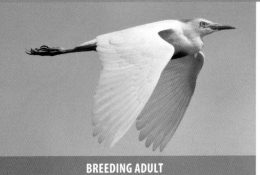
BREEDING ADULT

BREEDING ADULT

NONBREEDING ADULT

JUVENILE

SIZE & SHAPE Compared with other herons, Cattle Egrets are noticeably small and compact. They have relatively short legs and a short thick neck. The straight, daggerlike bill is shorter and thicker than other herons. They have medium-length, broad, rounded wings.

COLOR PATTERN Adult Cattle Egrets are white with a yellow bill and legs. In breeding plumage, they have golden plumes on their head, chest, and back. Juveniles have dark legs and bill.

BEHAVIOR Cattle Egrets stalk insects and other small animals on the ground in grassy fields. They are less often seen in water than other herons. They nest in dense colonies of stick nests in trees or emergent wetlands, often mixed with other species of herons.

HABITAT Cattle Egrets forage in flocks in upland areas such as pastures and fields, generally focusing on drier habitats than other species of white herons.

RANGE MAP

■ Breeding
  Breeding (scarce)
•••• Post-breeding dispersal
  Migration
■ Year-round
  Year-round (scarce)

The short, thick-necked **Cattle Egret** spends most of its time in fields rather than streams, foraging at the fe of cattle, head bobbing with each step, or riding on their backs to pick at ticks. Originally from Africa, it four its way to North America in 1941 and quickly spread across the continent.

ADULT

ADULT

JUVENILE

ADULT

RANGE MAP

■ Breeding
■ Migration
■ Nonbreeding
■ Year-round

SIZE & SHAPE Compared with most herons, Green Herons are short and stocky, with relatively short legs and thick necks that are often drawn up against their bodies. They have broad, rounded wings and a long, daggerlike bill. They sometimes raise their crown feathers into a short crest. They are crow-sized—small for a heron.

COLOR PATTERN From a distance, Green Herons look all dark. Up close, they are deep green on the back with a rich chestnut breast and neck. The wings are dark gray. Juveniles are browner, with pale streaking on the neck and wing spots.

BEHAVIOR Green Herons stand very still at the water's edge as they hunt for food, typically on solid ground or vegetation, seldom wading. In flight, they can look ungainly, often partially uncrooking their necks.

HABITAT Green Herons live near wooded ponds, marshes, rivers, reservoirs, and estuaries. They may nest in dry woods and orchards as long as there is water nearby for foraging.

he dark, stocky **Green Heron** often hides behind leaves at the water's edge, patiently crouching on slender ellow legs to surprise fish with a snatch of their daggerlike bill. They sometimes lure in fish using small ems such as twigs or insects as bait.

BLACK-CROWNED NIGHT-HERON *(Nycticorax nycticorax)*

ADULT

ADULT

IMMATURE (FIRST SUMMER)

JUVENILE

SIZE & SHAPE Black-crowned Night-Herons are medium-sized herons with rather squat, thick proportions. They have thick necks, large, flat heads, and heavy, pointed bills. The legs are short, and the wings are broad and rounded.

COLOR PATTERN Adults are light-gray birds with a neatly defined black back and black crown. Immatures are brown with white spots on the wings and blurry streaks on the underparts. Adults have black bills; immatures have yellow-and-black bills. Juveniles are brown and streaky overall.

BEHAVIOR These herons often spend their days perched on tree limbs or concealed among foliage. They forage in the evening and at night, in water, on mudflats, and on land. In flight, they fold their head back against their shoulders.

HABITAT These social birds tend to roost and nest in groups, although they typically forage on their own. Look for them in most wetland habitats across North America, including estuaries, marshes, streams, lakes, and reservoirs.

RANGE MAP

■ Breeding
  Migration
■ Nonbreeding
■ Year-round

Black-crowned Night-Herons are most active at night or at dusk. Look for their ghostly forms flapping ou from daytime roosts to forage in wetlands. These social birds breed in colonies of stick nests usually built over water. The most widespread heron in the world, it lives in fresh, salt, and brackish wetlands.

ADULT

ADULT

JUVENILE

IMMATURE (FIRST SUMMER)

RANGE MAP

■ Breeding
■ Nonbreeding
■ Year-round

SIZE & SHAPE Yellow-crowned Night-Herons are medium-sized herons with stocky bodies, short, thick necks, and short legs. They have large, blocky heads with thick, relatively short bills. In flight, the wings are broad and rounded.

COLOR PATTERN Adults are gray with bright, orange-yellow legs. They have a black head, a white cheek patch, and a yellow crown and head plumes. Immatures are brown with white spots on the back and wings and streaky underparts.

BEHAVIOR Yellow-crowned Night-Herons stalk prey in or near shallow water, usually alone, with a hunched posture. They perch on stumps and tree branches, often over water. The majority of their prey is crustaceans.

HABITAT These herons favor coastal wetlands, barrier islands, saltmarshes, and mangroves. They also occur inland along bottomland forests, swamps, and sometimes wet lawns or fields.

llow-crowned Night-Herons forage all day and night, stalking crustaceans in wetlands, wet fields, and en lawns. They catch crabs and crayfish with a lunge and shake them apart or swallow them whole. ey're most common in coastal marshes, barrier islands, and mangroves, but are also found in the interior.

ADULT

ADULT

IMMATURE (FIRST SUMMER)

JUVENILE

SIZE & SHAPE The White Ibis is a large wading bird with a football-shaped body. It has long legs, a long, curved bill, and a long neck held straight in flight. It is larger than a Cattle Egret, smaller than a Great Egret.

COLOR PATTERN Adults are almost entirely white, save for the black-tipped wings and brilliant reddish pink legs and bill. Reddish pink skin surrounds their blue eyes. Immatures are brown and white as they molt into adult plumage.

BEHAVIOR White Ibises forage in groups, walking slowly with their heads down, probing the mud for insects and crustaceans. In flight, their long necks are stretched out and their feet trail behind.

HABITAT White Ibises use freshwater marshes, coastal estuaries, mangroves, flooded pastures, mudflats, and swamps. They mostly forage in shallow areas, but also use lawns and parks, especially in southern Florida.

RANGE MAP

■ Breeding
■ Nonbreeding
■ Year-round

White Ibises gather in groups in shallow wetlands and estuaries in the southeastern United States, stepping through the water on bright red legs and probing the muddy surface below. They nest in colonie in trees and shrubs along the water's edge, changing locations nearly every year.

BREEDING ADULT

NONBREEDING ADULT

NONBREEDING ADULT / IMMATURE

JUVENILE

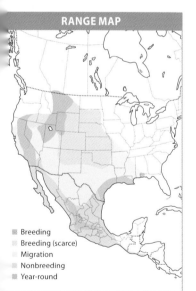

RANGE MAP

- Breeding
- Breeding (scarce)
- Migration
- Nonbreeding
- Year-round

SIZE & SHAPE The White-faced Ibis is a large wading bird with a football-shaped body, long legs, and a long, curved bill. It flies with its long neck outstretched and head slightly drooping.

COLOR PATTERN The breeding adult White-faced Ibis is maroon overall with reddish legs and a bare patch of pink skin in front of the eye which is bordered in white. In good light, wings are metallic green and bronze. Nonbreeding and immature birds look like adults but lack the bare skin patch and the white border around the eye. Juveniles have paler cheek patches and white feathers on the neck. Adults have red eyes.

BEHAVIOR Pairs of White-faced Ibises often preen each other during courtship, a behavior known as allopreening. Look for them perching in low trees and shrubs at the edge of wetlands.

HABITAT White-faced Ibises are found in freshwater and saltwater marshes, wetlands, and flooded fields. They often feed in large flocks.

e **White-faced Ibis** looks quite similar to its cousin, the Glossy Ibis. Often found in mixed flocks, imma-
e birds are nearly indistinguishable but may be paler underneath and have more green iridescence on
e back and wings. Breeding birds have more white on the face than the Glossy Ibis.

ADULT

ADULT

IMMATURE

JUVENILE

SIZE & SHAPE The Roseate Spoonbill is a large waterbird with a football-shaped body and long legs. The long bill is flattened into a spoon at the end and protrudes from a small head. They fly with long necks outstretched and often rest with it curled into an S.

COLOR PATTERN Adults are pale pink with deeper pink shoulders and rump. Their tails are orange. They have a white neck and a partially feathered, yellow-green head and red eyes. Juveniles are much duller and have a fully feathered head for three years until they attain adult plumage.

BEHAVIOR Roseate Spoonbills wade through shallow water swinging their head side to side with their bill under the water, feeling for prey. Spoonbills forage, roost, and nest in groups often with other ibises, herons, and egrets.

HABITAT Roseate Spoonbills forage in the shallows of fresh, brackish, and marine waters including bays, mangroves, forested swamps, and wetlands. They nest and roost in trees and shrubs along the water's edge.

RANGE MAP

■ Breeding
■ Year-round

The flamboyant **Roseate Spoonbill,** with its bright pink feathers, red eye staring out from a partly bald head, and giant spoon-shaped bill, looks like it came straight out of a Dr. Seuss book. Groups sweep their spoonbills through shallow fresh or salt waters snapping up crustaceans and fish.

ADULT

ADULT

ADULTS

ADULT (L) AND JUVENILE (R)

RANGE MAP

☐ Year-round
☐ Year-round (scarce)

SIZE & SHAPE In flight, the Black Vulture holds its broad, rounded wings flat and angled slightly forward. The tail is short and square-cornered. It has a small, bare head and a narrow but strongly hooked bill. Note splayed wingtips or "fingers" in flight.

COLOR PATTERN Black Vultures are uniformly blackish, except for white patches or "stars" on the underside of their wingtips (this can be hard to see in strong light or from far away). The bare skin of the head is gray in adults and blackish in juveniles, which also have some feathers on the head.

BEHAVIOR During the day, Black Vultures soar in flocks, often with Turkey Vultures and hawks. Look for them along highway margins eating roadkill, as well as picking through dumpsters. They roost in groups in trees and on transmission towers. In flight, note frequent, quick, snappy wingbeats.

HABITAT Look for Black Vultures in open areas within forested landscapes. They typically nest and roost in wooded areas and soar above open areas to seek their food. They have substantially increased their range northward in recent decades.

rkey Vultures have an excellent sense of smell, but **Black Vultures** aren't as accomplished as sniffers. To d food, they soar high in the sky, watching the lower-soaring Turkey Vultures. When a Turkey Vulture's se detects decaying flesh and descends on a carcass, the Black Vulture follows close behind.

ADULT

ADULT AND IMMATURES (FIRST YEAR)

IMMATURE

ADULT

SIZE & SHAPE Turkey Vultures are large, dark birds with long, broad wings. Bigger than other raptors, except eagles and condors, Turkey Vultures hold their wings slightly raised when soaring, making a V-shape when seen head-on.

COLOR PATTERN Turkey Vultures appear black from a distance but up close are dark brown with a featherless head and pale bill. While most of the body and forewings are dark, the undersides of the flight feathers and wingtips are paler. Adults' heads are red; juveniles' are grayish and become red over time.

BEHAVIOR Turkey Vultures are majestic but unsteady soarers. Their teetering flight with deep but few wingbeats is characteristic. Look for them gliding relatively low to the ground, sniffing for carrion, or riding thermals up to higher vantage points.

HABITAT Turkey Vultures are common around open areas such as roadsides, suburbs, farm fields, countryside, and food sources such as landfills, trash heaps, and construction sites.

RANGE MAP

■ Breeding
■ Year-round

If you see a large raptor soaring in wobbly circles with its wings raised in a V, it's likely a **Turkey Vulture**. These birds ride thermals in the sky and use their keen sense of smell to find fresh carcasses. A consummate scavenger, it cleans up the countryside one bite at a time, never mussing a feather on its bald head.

ADULT

ADULT

JUVENILE

ADULT

RANGE MAP

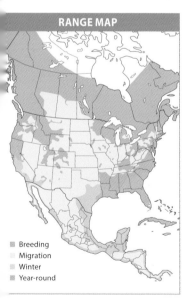

■ Breeding
  Migration
■ Winter
■ Year-round

SIZE & SHAPE Ospreys are very large, distinctively shaped hawks. Despite their size, their bodies are slender, with long, narrow wings and long legs. In flight, crooked wings combine with the body to make a distinctive M shape.

COLOR PATTERN Ospreys are brown above and white below, and overall, they are whiter than most raptors. From below, wings are mostly white with darker flight feathers and a prominent dark patch at the wrists. The head is white with a broad brown stripe through the eye. Juveniles have white spots on the back and buffy shading on the breast.

BEHAVIOR Ospreys search for fish by flying on steady wingbeats and bowed wings or circling high in the sky over relatively shallow water. They often hover briefly before diving, feet first, to grab a fish.

HABITAT Look for Ospreys around nearly any body of water: saltmarshes, rivers, ponds, reservoirs, estuaries, and even coral reefs.

vel among North American raptors for its diet of live fish and ability to dive into water to catch them, preys are common sights soaring over shorelines, patrolling waterways, and standing on their huge k nests, white heads gleaming. Their numbers have rebounded since the ban on the pesticide DDT.

ADULT

ADULT

JUVENILE

JUVENILE

SIZE & SHAPE The White-tailed Kite is a small to medium-sized raptor with narrow, pointed wings and a long tail. When perched, it looks rather big-headed with a long and skinny body.

COLOR PATTERN The White-tailed Kite is a largely pale raptor easily identified by its extensively white tail and black shoulder patches. Note the white head and red eyes (visible at close range). Sexes are similar. Juveniles are distinguished by a cinnamon wash on the breast and crown and a mottled brown back.

BEHAVIOR White-tailed Kites hover above open areas while hunting small mammals. They rapidly beat their wings while facing into the wind, with tail and head angled down. In the nonbreeding season, they gather in communal roosts.

HABITAT White-tailed Kites are found in savannas, open woodlands, marshes, desert grasslands, partially cleared lands, and cultivated fields. They tend to avoid heavily grazed areas.

RANGE MAP

Breeding
Year-round
Year-round (scarce)

Grasslands and savannas are great places to fly a kite, and that's exactly where you will find the **White-tailed Kite**. With its body turned toward the wind and wings gently flapping, it hovers above the ground, a behavior known as kiting. From above, it tips its head down to look for small mammals in the grass below.

ADULT

ADULT

JUVENILE (L) AND ADULT (R)

ADULT

RANGE MAP

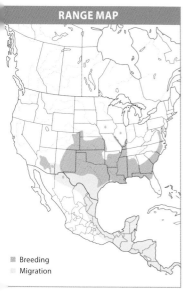

■ Breeding
■ Migration

SIZE & SHAPE Mississippi Kites are slender, fairly small raptors with long, pointed wings. The tail is fairly long and square-tipped. The strongly hooked bill is small and delicate.

COLOR PATTERN Mississippi Kites are an inky mix of gray and black, lightening to a pale grayish white on the head and on the upper secondaries in the wing. The wingtips and tail are black. Juveniles are streaky, with brownish chests and underwings, and banded tails.

BEHAVIOR These birds are excellent aerialists, spending much of their time aloft and sailing in the wind or flying with buoyant wingbeats. Their noticeable agility when flying is needed to catch large flying insects, such as dragonflies, which make up a large portion of their diet. They may form large flocks in late summer, and thousands travel together during spring and fall migration.

HABITAT Mississippi Kites live in bottomland hardwood forests of the Southeast and in tree-lined areas of the southern prairies, where they are found coursing over and nesting in windbreaks, parks, and even leafy urban backyards.

ississippi Kites** make a streamlined silhouette as they career through the sky hunting small prey, or ve-bombing intruders too close to the nest. These pearl-gray raptors often hunt together and nest colonially stands of trees, from windbreaks on southern prairies to old-growth bottomlands in the Southeast.

ADULT MALE

ADULT FEMALE

JUVENILE MALE

JUVENILE FEMALE

SIZE & SHAPE Northern Harriers are slender, medium-sized raptors with long, broad wings and a long, rounded tail. They have a flat, owl-like face and a small, sharply hooked bill. They often fly with their wings held in a V-shape.

COLOR PATTERN Males are gray above and whitish below with black wingtips, a dark edge to the wing, and a black-banded tail. Females and immatures are brown, with black bands on the tail. For both sexes, a white rump patch is obvious in flight.

BEHAVIOR Northern Harriers fly low over the ground when hunting, weaving back and forth over fields and marshes as they watch and listen for small animals. They eat on the ground, and they perch on low posts or trees. On the breeding grounds, males perform elaborate flying barrel rolls to court females.

HABITAT Northern Harriers are found in open areas such as grasslands, marshes, and fields. They like undisturbed tracts with low, thick vegetation.

RANGE MAP

■ Breeding
  Migration
  Nonbreeding
■ Year-round

The **Northern Harrier** is distinctive from a distance: a slim, long-tailed hawk gliding low over a marsh or grassland, wings held in a V-shape. Its owlish face helps it hear mice and voles beneath the vegetation. Each male may mate with several females. These unusual raptors are found across much of North America.

ADULT

ADULT

JUVENILE

JUVENILE

RANGE MAP

■ Breeding
■ Nonbreeding
■ Year-round

SIZE & SHAPE This is a medium-sized hawk with a slender body, vertical stance, rounded wingtips, and very long tail. In Cooper's Hawks, the head often appears large and square-shaped, the shoulders are broad, and the tail tip rounded. Females are significantly larger than males.

COLOR PATTERN Adults are steely blue gray above with warm reddish bars on the breast, a pale nape that contrasts with the dark cap, and thick, dark bands on the otherwise pale gray tail. Juveniles are brown above and crisply streaked with brown on the upper breast, giving them a somewhat hooded look compared with young Sharp-shinned Hawks' more diffuse streaking.

BEHAVIOR Cooper's Hawks fly with a flap-flap-glide pattern typical of the genus *Accipiter*. Even when crossing large open areas, they rarely flap continuously. They can also thread their way through tree branches at top speed.

HABITAT Cooper's Hawks are forest and woodland birds, but leafy suburbs are nearly as good. They are a regular sight in parks, quiet neighborhoods, over fields, and at backyard feeders.

Cooper's Hawks are common woodland hawks and skillful fliers that tear through cluttered tree canopies pursuit of other birds. Similar to their smaller lookalike, the Sharp-shinned Hawk, Cooper's Hawks can be wanted guests at bird feeders, looking for an easy meal (but not one of sunflower seeds).

ADULT

IMMATURE

JUVENILE

JUVENILE

SIZE & SHAPE The Bald Eagle dwarfs most other raptors. It has a heavy body, large head, and long, hooked bill. In flight, a Bald Eagle holds its broad wings flat like a board.

COLOR PATTERN Adults have white heads and tails with dark brown bodies and wings. Legs and bills are bright yellow. Immature birds have dark heads and tails and are mottled in white in varying amounts before they reach maturity at five years of age.

BEHAVIOR You'll find Bald Eagles soaring high in the sky, flapping low over treetops with slow wingbeats, perched in trees, or on the ground. They scavenge many meals by harassing other birds or by eating carrion or garbage. They eat mainly fish but also hunt mammals, gulls, and waterfowl.

HABITAT Look for Bald Eagles near lakes, reservoirs, rivers, marshes, and coasts. To see large Bald Eagle congregations, check out wildlife refuges or large bodies of water in winter over much of the continent, or fish processing plants and dumpsters year-round in the Pacific Northwest.

RANGE MAP

■ Breeding
  Migration
  Nonbreeding
■ Year-round

The **Bald Eagle** has been the U.S. national emblem since 1782 and a spiritual symbol for native people for far longer. Look for these regal birds soaring in solitude, chasing other birds for their food, or gathering in droves in winter. Once endangered by hunting and pesticides, Bald Eagles now thrive under protection.

ADULT

ADULT

IMMATURE

IMMATURE

RANGE MAP

■ Year-round

SIZE & SHAPE Harris's Hawks are medium-sized, lanky raptors with long legs and fairly long tails. They fly on broad, rounded wings. Females weigh nearly twice as much as males. It is larger than a Cooper's Hawk and slightly smaller than a Red-tailed Hawk.

COLOR PATTERN Adults are dark brown overall with reddish brown feathers on the wings and thighs. The tail is dark with a white rump and terminal band. Immature birds have white streaking below, a narrower tail band, and white wing patches.

BEHAVIOR Harris's Hawks perch upright on telephone poles, cactuses, or posts for a view of the surroundings. They hunt and travel in groups and may even walk or run along the ground when hunting. They soar on rounded wings, frequently fanning their tails.

HABITAT Harris's Hawks occur in semiopen desert lowlands—often among mesquite, paloverde, saguaro, and organ pipe cactus. They also frequent urban and suburban areas, which offer easy access to water and food (pigeons).

mong the most social of North American raptors, **Harris's Hawks** cooperate at nests and hunt as a team. group of hawks surrounds its prey, flushes it for another to catch, or takes turns chasing it. Their social ture and relative ease with humans make them popular among falconers and in education programs.

ADULT

ADULT

JUVENILE

JUVENILE

SIZE & SHAPE Red-shouldered Hawks are medium sized, with broad, rounded wings and medium-length tails that they fan when soaring. They glide or soar with their wingtips pushed slightly forward, giving them a distinctive "reaching" posture.

COLOR PATTERN Adults are colorful hawks with dark-and-white checkered wings and warm reddish barring on the breast. The tail is black with narrow white bands. Immatures are brown above and white, streaked with brown, below. All ages show narrow, pale crescents near the wingtips in flight.

BEHAVIOR Red-shouldered Hawks soar over forests or perch on tree branches or utility wires. Their whistled *kee-rah* is a distinctive sound of the forest. They hunt small mammals, amphibians, and reptiles from perches or in flight.

HABITAT Look for Red-shouldered Hawks in broadleaf woodlands, often near rivers and swamps. During migration, they often move high overhead along ridges or coastlines. They may be abundant at some hawk-watching overlooks.

RANGE MAP

■ Breeding
■ Nonbreeding
■ Year-round

Whether wheeling over a swamp forest or whistling from a riverine park, a **Red-shouldered Hawk** is a sign of tall woods and water. It's one of our most distinctively marked common hawks, with barred, reddish peac underparts and a strongly banded tail. They hunt prey ranging from mice to frogs and snakes.

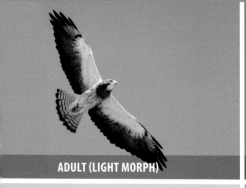

ADULT (LIGHT MORPH)

ADULT (DARK MORPH)

JUVENILE (LIGHT MORPH)

JUVENILE (DARK MORPH)

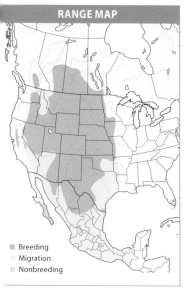

RANGE MAP

Breeding
Migration
Nonbreeding

SIZE & SHAPE Swainson's Hawks are large with fairly narrow wings and short tails. However, they are less hefty than many other *Buteo* hawks. They are slimmer, have longer wings, and hold their wings in a shallow V when soaring.

COLOR PATTERN Though quite variable, most Swainson's Hawks are light-bellied birds with a dark or reddish brown chest and brown or gray upperparts. Underwings have distinct white wing linings that contrast strongly with blackish flight feathers. Most males have gray heads; females tend to have brown heads. Dark morphs are dark brown and rusty below.

BEHAVIOR Swainson's Hawks are social raptors, nearly always found in groups outside the breeding season. Look for them soaring with other migrating birds, foraging for grasshoppers, or chasing swarms of dragonflies on winter grounds.

HABITAT These hawks summer in open areas of the Great Plains and further west. They nest in grasslands, but also use sage flats and even swaths of agriculture intermixed with native habitat. Nests are placed in trees, often in the only tree visible for miles.

vainson's Hawks soar on narrow wings or perch on fence posts and irrigation spouts. They hunt rodents flight or run after insects on the ground. In fall, they take off for Argentine wintering grounds—one of the 1gest migrations of any American raptor—forming flocks of hundreds or thousands as they travel.

ADULT (LIGHT MORPH)

ADULT (INTERMEDIATE MORPH)

JUVENILE (LIGHT MORPH)

JUVENILE (LIGHT MORPH)

SIZE & SHAPE Red-tailed Hawks are fairly large and have proportions typical of the genus *Buteo*: very broad, rounded wings and a short, wide tail. Females seen from a distance might fool you into thinking you're seeing an eagle—until an actual eagle comes along.

COLOR PATTERN Red-tailed Hawks have extremely variable plumage, and some of this variation is regional. Most are rich brown above and pale below with a streaked belly. The tail is usually pale below and cinnamon red above, though in young birds it's brown and banded. Dark-morph and intermediate-morph birds are variably dark brown and rusty below.

BEHAVIOR Red-tailed Hawks soar in wide circles high over a field. In high winds, they may hover without flapping, eyes fixed on the ground. Unlike a falcon's stoop, they attack in a slow, controlled dive with legs outstretched.

HABITAT The Red-tailed Hawk is a bird of open country. Look for it along fields and perched on telephone poles, fenceposts, or trees standing alone or along edges of fields.

RANGE MAP

■ Breeding
■ Year-round

Probably the most common hawk in North America, the **Red-tailed Hawk** soars above open fields, turning circles on its broad, rounded wings. Find it atop telephone poles, eyes fixed on the ground to catch prey movements, or simply waiting out cold weather before climbing a thermal updraft into the sky.

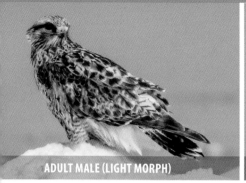
ADULT MALE (LIGHT MORPH)

ADULT FEMALE (LIGHT MORPH)

IMMATURE (LIGHT MORPH)

ADULT FEMALE (DARK MORPH)

RANGE MAP

▪ Breeding
▪ Migration
▪ Nonbreeding

SIZE & SHAPE Rough-legged Hawks are fairly large with broad wings. Proportionately, their wings are longer and narrower and their tails longer than in most members of the genus *Buteo*. Wingtips are swept back slightly from the wrist, giving a hint of an M shape to wings in flight. Bill is fairly small.

COLOR PATTERN The Rough-legged Hawk is boldly patterned in brown and white. The tail is dark at the tip and pale at the base. Light morphs have pale underwings with dark patches at the bend of the wing. Dark morphs are mostly dark brown with pale trailing edges to the underwing.

BEHAVIOR When hunting, these hawks often face into the wind and hover, scanning the ground below for small mammal prey. They perch on fence posts and utility poles, and sometimes on slender branches at the very tops of trees.

HABITAT Rough-legged Hawks breed in the Arctic. In winter, they migrate to open habitats such as fields, prairies, deserts, and airports in the U.S. and southern Canada.

e **Rough-legged Hawk** spends the summer capturing lemmings on the Arctic tundra, tending a cliffside st under a sun that never sets. In winter, look for this large, open-country hawk in southern Canada and e U.S. perched on a pole or hovering over a marsh or pasture while it hunts small rodents.

ADULT (GRAY)

ADULT (BROWN)

JUVENILE

ADULT (RED)

SIZE & SHAPE The Eastern Screech-Owl is a short, stocky, pigeon-sized bird with a large head and almost no neck. Its wings are rounded; its tail is short and square. Pointed ear tufts are often raised, giving this owl a distinctive silhouette.

COLOR PATTERN Eastern Screech-Owls can be either mostly gray or mostly reddish brown. Whatever the overall color, they are patterned with complex bands and spots that give the bird excellent camouflage against tree bark. Eyes are yellow.

BEHAVIOR Eastern Screech-Owls are active at night and more often heard than seen. This cavity-roosting owl can be attracted to nest boxes or spotted in daylight at the entrance to its home in a tree cavity.

HABITAT Trees define the Eastern Screech-Owl's habitat. This owl is fairly common in most types of woods (coniferous or broadleaf; urban or rural), particularly near water. It shuns treeless expanses of mountains or plains.

RANGE MAP

■ Year-round

The **Eastern Screech-Owl**, no bigger than a pint glass, is found wherever there are trees. It is quite willing to nest in backyard nest boxes. These camouflaged birds hide out in nooks and tree crannies in the day, s⟨ listen for their hollow trills and descending whinnies at night.

ADULT

ADULT

JUVENILE

ADULT

RANGE MAP

■ Year-round
■ Year-round (scarce)

SIZE & SHAPE Great Horned Owls are large and thick-bodied with two prominent feathered tufts on the head. The wings are broad and rounded. In flight, the rounded face and short bill combine to create a blunt-headed appearance.

COLOR PATTERN Great Horned Owls are mottled grayish brown, with reddish brown faces and a neat white patch on the throat. Their overall color tone varies regionally from sooty to pale. The color of the facial disc also varies regionally from grayish to cinnamon.

BEHAVIOR You may see Great Horned Owls at dusk on fence posts or tree limbs at the edge of open areas, or flying across roads or fields with stiff, deep beats of their rounded wings. Their call is a stuttering series of mellow hoots.

HABITAT Look for this widespread owl in young woods interspersed with fields or other open areas. The broad range of habitats they use includes forests, swamps, desert, and tundra edges, as well as cities, suburbs, and parks.

:h its long earlike tufts, yellow eyes, and deep hooting voice, the **Great Horned Owl** is the quintessential
l of storybooks. This powerful predator can take down birds and mammals larger than itself, but it also
es on daintier fare such as mice, and frogs. It's one of the most common owls in North America.

ADULT

ADULT

JUVENILE

ADULTS

SIZE & SHAPE Burrowing Owls are small with long legs and short tails. The head is rounded and does not have ear tufts. It is about the same length/height as an American Robin but much bulkier.

COLOR PATTERN Adult Burrowing Owls are brown birds mottled with sand-colored pale spots on the upperparts. The breast is spotted, grading to dark brown bars on the belly. They have a bold white throat and eyebrows, and yellow eyes. Juveniles are unpatterned buffy below with a brown chest.

BEHAVIOR Burrowing Owls spend most of their time on the ground or low perches. They hunt close to the ground catching insects and small animals. When alarmed, they jerk their bodies quickly up and down. They are active during the day.

HABITAT Burrowing Owls live in open habitats with sparse vegetation such as prairies, pastures, desert or shrub-steppe, and airports. In parts of their range, they nest in the burrows of prairie dogs and ground squirrels.

RANGE MAP

■ Breeding
■ Nonbreeding
■ Year-round

Owls are unmistakable, and that goes double for a long-legged owl that hunts on the ground during the day. Petite **Burrowing Owls** live underground in burrows they've dug themselves or taken over from a prairie dog or ground squirrel. Their numbers have declined sharply with human alteration of their habitat

ADULT

ADULT

ADULT

JUVENILE

RANGE MAP

Year-round

SIZE & SHAPE Barred Owls are large, stocky owls with rounded heads, no ear tufts, and medium-length, rounded tails.

COLOR PATTERN Barred Owls are mottled brown and white overall, with dark brown, almost black, eyes. The underparts are mostly marked with vertical brown bars on a white background, while the upper breast is crossed with horizontal brown bars. The wings and tail are barred brown and white.

BEHAVIOR Barred Owls are mostly nocturnal and roost quietly in forest trees during the day. At night they hunt small animals, especially rodents, and give an instantly recognizable *Who cooks for you?* call.

HABITAT Barred Owls live in large, mature forests made up of both broadleaf trees and conifers, often near water. They nest in tree cavities. In the Northwest, Barred Owls have moved into old-growth coniferous forest, where they compete with the threatened Spotted Owl.

e **Barred Owl's** hooting call, *Who cooks for you? Who cooks for you-all?*, is a classic sound of old forests and amps. But this attractive owl with soulful brown eyes and brown-and-white striped plumage, can pass mpletely unnoticed as it flies noiselessly through the dense canopy or snoozes on a tree limb.

ADULT MALE

ADULT

ADULT FEMALE

ADULT FEMALE

SIZE & SHAPE Belted Kingfishers are stocky, large-headed birds with a shaggy crest on the top and back of the head and a straight, thick, pointed bill. Their legs are short and their tails are medium length and square-tipped.

COLOR PATTERN These ragged-crested birds are a powdery blue gray with white spotting on the wings and tail. Males have one blue band across the white breast, while females also have a broad rusty band on their bellies. Juveniles show irregular rusty spotting in the breast band.

BEHAVIOR Belted Kingfishers often perch alone along the edges of streams, lakes, and estuaries, searching for small fish. They fly quickly up and down rivers and shorelines giving loud rattling calls. They hunt by plunging directly from a perch, or by hovering over the water, bill downward, before diving after a fish they've spotted.

HABITAT Kingfishers live near streams, rivers, ponds, lakes, and estuaries. They spend winters in areas where the water doesn't freeze so they have continual access to their aquatic foods.

RANGE MAP

- Breeding
- Nonbreeding
- Year-round

With its top-heavy physique, energetic flight, and piercing, rattled call, the **Belted Kingfisher** seems to have an air of self-importance as it patrols up and down rivers and shorelines. The Belted Kingfisher is one of the few bird species in which the female is more brightly colored than the male.

ADULT MALE

ADULT FEMALE (BLACK-CROWNED VARIANT)

ADULT FEMALE

JUVENILE

RANGE MAP

Breeding
Migration
Nonbreeding

SIZE & SHAPE Yellow-bellied Sapsuckers are fairly small with stout, straight bills. The long wings extend about halfway to the tip of the stiff, pointed tail at rest. They often hold their crown feathers up to form a peak at the back of the head.

COLOR PATTERN Both sexes are mostly black and white with red foreheads, but males also have red throats. Look for a white stripe along the folded wing and black-and-white face stripes, a black chest shield, and white or yellowish underparts. Occasionally, females have a black crown.

BEHAVIOR Yellow-belled Sapsuckers perch upright, leaning on their tails like other woodpeckers. They feed at sap wells—neat rows of shallow holes they drill in tree bark—and drum on trees in a distinctive stuttering pattern. Listen for their loud mewing calls.

HABITAT Yellow-bellied Sapsuckers live in both hardwood and conifer forests. They often nest in groves of small trees such as aspens, and spend winters in open woodlands.

orests, look for rows of shallow holes in tree bark. If you live in the East, this is the work of the **Yellow-bel-** **Sapsucker,** an enterprising woodpecker that laps up the leaking sap and any trapped insects with its cialized, brush-tipped tongue. They often sit still on tree trunks for long intervals while feeding.

SIZE & SHAPE Red-headed Woodpeckers are medium-sized woodpeckers with fairly large, rounded heads, short, stiff tails, and powerful, straight bills.

COLOR PATTERN Adults have bright red heads, white underparts, and black backs with large, white patches in the wings, making the lower back appear all white when perched. Juveniles have a brown head, a dingy belly, and a blackish brown back with white wing patches.

BEHAVIOR Red-headed Woodpeckers hammer into wood for insects, but also catch insects in flight and on the ground, and eat considerable amounts of fruit and seeds. Their raspy calls are shriller and scratchier than Red-bellied Woodpeckers.

HABITAT Red-headed Woodpeckers live in pine and oak savannas and open forests with clear understories. They like pine plantations, tree rows in agricultural areas, standing timber in beaver swamps, and other wetlands.

RANGE MAP

■ Breeding
  Migration
■ Nonbreeding
■ Year-round

The **Red-headed Woodpecker's** bold pattern has earned it the description of a "flying checkerboard." Th catch insects in the air and eat lots of acorns and beech nuts, often storing food in tree crevices for later. the past half-century, habitat loss and changes in food supply have led to severe population decline.

ADULT MALE

ADULT FEMALE

ADULT FEMALE

IMMATURE MALE

RANGE MAP

■ Year-round

SIZE & SHAPE Acorn Woodpeckers are medium-sized woodpeckers with straight, spikelike bills and stiff, wedge-shaped tails used for support as the birds cling to tree trunks.

COLOR PATTERN A clown-faced woodpecker with a black back, red cap, creamy white face, and black patch around the bill. Females have less red on the crown than males. In flight, they show three patches of white: one on each wing and one on the rump. Immature birds often have darker eyes.

BEHAVIOR Acorn Woodpeckers are unusual woodpeckers that live in large groups, hoard acorns, and breed cooperatively. Group members gather acorns by the hundreds and wedge them into holes they've made in a tree trunk or telephone pole. They give raucous, scratchy *waka-waka* calls frequently.

HABITAT These woodpeckers live in oak and mixed oak-conifer forests on slopes and mountains. Telephone poles and wood siding in urban areas also make for good granaries.

orn Woodpeckers live in large groups, and their social lives are endlessly fascinating. Every year they ore thousands of acorns in specially made holes in trees, and a group member guards the hoard from eves. Many males and females also combine efforts to raise young in a single nest.

ADULT MALE

ADULT FEMALE

ADULT FEMALE

IMMATURE MALE

SIZE & SHAPE The Golden-fronted Woodpecker is a medium- to large-sized woodpecker.

COLOR PATTERN The Golden-fronted Woodpecker has a barred black-and-white back and a tan breast. Both sexes have brown eyes, and a yellow-orange patch in front of the eyes and at the nape. Males have a red crown. Juveniles are similar to adults, but duller, with fine streaking on the crown and breast, and only faint color on the nape and nasal tufts. Eyes are brown.

BEHAVIOR Golden-fronted Woodpeckers glean insects from bark, probe into holes and dead wood, scale bark, and hawk for flying insects. They also eat fruits and nuts. They will occasionally eat lizards and other birds' eggs.

HABITAT Look for Golden-fronted Woodpeckers in open to semiopen woodlands, second-growth forests, and brushlands.

RANGE MAP

■ Year-round

The **Golden-fronted Woodpecker** consumes about as much fruit and nuts as it does insects. In summertime, the faces of some woodpeckers become stained purple from eating the fruit of the prickly pear cactus.

ADULT MALE

ADULT MALE

ADULT FEMALE

JUVENILE

RANGE MAP

■ Year-round

SIZE & SHAPE The Red-bellied Woodpecker is a sleek, round-headed woodpecker, about the same size as a Hairy Woodpecker but without the blocky outlines.

COLOR PATTERN The Red-bellied Woodpecker may appear pale overall, even with a bold black-and-white barred back and flashy red forehead and nape. Look for white patches near the wingtips. The red belly is subtle and hard to see. The rump and central tail feathers are white with black spots. Females lack the male's red crown.

BEHAVIOR Look for Red-bellied Woodpeckers hitching along branches and trunks of medium to large trees, picking at the surface more often than drilling into it. Like most woodpeckers, they have an undulating flight pattern.

HABITAT Red-bellied Woodpeckers are common in many eastern woodlands and forests, from old stands of oak and hickory to young hardwoods and pines. They will also venture from forests to appear at backyard feeders.

d-bellied Woodpeckers** are common in forests of the East. Their gleaming red napes make them an forgettable sight; just resist the temptation to call them Red-headed Woodpeckers, a somewhat rarer cies with a completely red head. Learn this bird's rolling call, and you'll notice them everywhere.

ADULT MALE

ADULT FEMALE

ADULT FEMALE

JUVENILE

SIZE & SHAPE The tiny, sparrow-sized Downy Woodpecker has a straight, chisel-like bill, blocky head, wide shoulders, and straight-backed posture as it leans away from tree limbs braced by its tail feathers. The bill is short for a woodpecker.

COLOR PATTERN Downy Woodpeckers have black upperparts checked with white on the wings, bold white stripes on the head, and the back has a broad white stripe down the center. Males have a small red patch on the head; it's on the nape in adults and on the crown in juveniles.

BEHAVIOR Downy Woodpeckers hitch around tree trunks and even small weed stalks, moving more acrobatically than larger woodpeckers. In spring and summer, they are noisy, making shrill whinnying calls and drumming on trees.

HABITAT You'll find Downy Woodpeckers in open woodlands, particularly among broadleaf trees, and brushy or weedy edges. They're also at home in orchards, city parks, backyards, and vacant lots.

RANGE MAP

■ Year-round

This active little black-and-white woodpecker, the **Downy Woodpecker**, is a familiar sight. An acrobatic forager, it's at home on tiny branches or balancing on seed balls and suet feeders. Downies and their larg lookalike, the Hairy Woodpecker, are one of the first ID challenges for beginner birdwatchers.

ADULT MALE

ADULT MALE / IMMATURE MALE

ADULT FEMALE

ADULT FEMALE

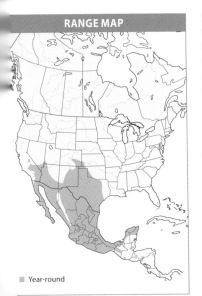

RANGE MAP

■ Year-round

SIZE & SHAPE Ladder-backed Woodpeckers are small woodpeckers with a square head, short neck, and stiff tail that they lean against for support. The bill is small but straight and chisel-like.

COLOR PATTERN Ladder-backed Woodpeckers are black and white above, with neat bars like ladder rungs on the back, and a checkered pattern on the wings. The underparts are buffy white or grayish, stippled with black. The buffy white face is broken by black lines that extend from the bill and eye and join at the neck. Males have mostly red crowns; females have blackish crowns. Immature males have less red on the crown.

BEHAVIOR Ladder-backed Woodpeckers forage by hitching around branches, pecking at bark or other spots that might hold insects or larvae. They hide in vegetation as they forage, usually detected by their calls or by their rapid drumming on trees.

HABITAT Ladder-backed Woodpeckers live in very dry habitats such as deserts, desert scrub, thorn forests, and pinyon-juniper woodlands, as well as adjacent towns and cities.

hen traveling through the scattered cactus and brush of the arid Southwest, it's difficult to believe that ese almost treeless habitats are home to woodpeckers, but this is one of the places the **Ladder-backed oodpecker** lives. They can be inconspicuous and quiet, requiring a bit of time and patience to find.

ADULT MALE (INTERIOR WEST)

IMMATURE MALE (EASTERN)

ADULT FEMALE (EASTERN)

SIZE & SHAPE The Hairy Woodpecker is a medium-sized woodpecker with a fairly square head, a long, straight, chisel-like bill, and stiff, long tail feathers it braces against tree trunks. The bill is nearly the same length as the head. It is about the same size as Red-bellied and Golden-fronted woodpeckers.

COLOR PATTERN Hairy Woodpeckers in Texas and Oklahoma have wings that range from mostly black to being checkered with white. The head has two white stripes, and in males, a red spot, which is on the nape in adults and on the crown in juveniles. The back is gleaming white between folded black, dark brown, or black-and-white wings.

BEHAVIOR Hairy Woodpeckers hitch up tree trunks and along main branches. They sometimes feed at the bases of trees, along fallen logs, and, rarely, on the ground. They have the slowly-undulating flight pattern of woodpeckers.

HABITAT You can find Hairy Woodpeckers in mature forests, woodlots, suburbs, parks, and cemeteries, as well as forest edges, open woodlands of oak and pine, recently burned forests, and stands infested by bark beetles.

RANGE MAP

■ Year-round

The larger of two lookalikes, **Hairy Woodpeckers** are powerful, medium-sized birds that forage along trunk and branches of large trees. They have a much longer bill than the Downy Woodpecker's smaller thornlike b and have a soldierly look, with an erect, straight-backed posture on tree trunks and cleanly striped heads.

ADULT MALE (L) AND IMMATURES

ADULT FEMALE

ADULT

ADULT MALE

RANGE MAP

◼ Year-round
◻ Year-round (scarce)

SIZE & SHAPE The Pileated Woodpecker is a very large woodpecker with a long neck and a triangular crest that sweeps off the back of the head. The bill is long and chisel-like and is about the length of the head. In flight, wings are broad.

COLOR PATTERN Pileated Woodpeckers are mostly black with white stripes on the face and neck and a flaming red crest. Males have a red stripe on the cheek. In flight, the bird reveals extensive white underwings and small white crescents on the upper side at the base of the primary feathers.

BEHAVIOR Pileated Woodpeckers drill distinctive rectangular-shaped holes in rotten wood to get at carpenter ants and other insects. They are loud birds with strident calls.

HABITAT Pileated Woodpeckers require forests with large, standing dead trees and downed wood. Such forests are often old, particularly in the West. In the East, they live in young forests as well and may be seen in wooded suburbs.

ack with a flaming red crest, the **Pileated Woodpecker** is one of the biggest, most striking forest birds the continent. Look for them whacking at dead trees and fallen logs in search of carpenter ants, leaving ique rectangular holes in the wood. These holes are crucial shelters for birds and other animals of the forest.

ADULT MALE (YELLOW-SHAFTED)

ADULT FEMALE (RED-SHAFTED)

ADULT MALE (YELLOW-SHAFTED)

ADULT MALE (RED-SHAFTED)

SIZE & SHAPE Flickers are fairly large woodpeckers with a slim, rounded head, long, slightly curved bill, and long, flared tail that tapers to a point.

COLOR PATTERN Flickers in this region can be either yellow-shafted or red-shafted, or have a mixture of plumage markings. The undersides of the wing and tail feathers may be bright yellow or red. Up close, the brown or gray-brown plumage is richly patterned with black spots, bars, and crescents. Males may have a black or red whisker and may have a red patch on the nape. Female flickers do not have a mustache.

BEHAVIOR Unlike most woodpeckers, Northern Flickers spend lots of time on the ground. Ants and beetles are its main food, and the flicker often digs in the dirt to find them. When in trees, they usually perch upright on horizontal branches instead of leaning against their tails on a trunk.

HABITAT Look for Northern Flickers in woodlands, forest edges, and open fields with scattered trees, as well as city parks and suburbs. You can also find them in wet areas such as flooded swamps and marsh edges.

RANGE MAP

- Breeding
- Winter
- Year-round

Northern Flickers are large, brown woodpeckers with a gentle expression and handsome black-scalloped plumage. On walks, don't be surprised if you scare one up from the ground. It's not where you'd expect to find a woodpecker, but flickers eat ants and beetles, digging for them with their slightly curved bill.

ADULT

ADULT

JUVENILE

ADULT

RANGE MAP

▨ Year-round
▨ Year-round (scarce)

SIZE & SHAPE The Crested Caracara is a medium-sized, bulky raptor with long legs. Its flat head is topped with a shaggy crest. In flight, note its long, straight wings and rather long tail. The bill is heavy and hooked with a sharp tip.

COLOR PATTERN Adults are black and white with yellow-orange legs and red-orange skin around the pale blue bill. Their black cap contrasts with their white neck and cheeks. Juveniles are brown and white with pale pink legs and facial skin.

BEHAVIOR Crested Caracaras fly close to the ground with slow and powerful wingbeats. They are equally adept at walking on the ground as they are in the air. Crested Caracaras often join vultures to feed on carrion.

HABITAT Crested Caracaras inhabit open country including pastures, cultivated areas, deserts, scrub, and savannas. They perch on scattered trees, poles, and fences that offer a good view of the surroundings.

ₑ **Crested Caracara** looks like a hawk with its sharp beak and talons, but it behaves like a vulture, and it is ₜhnically a large tropical black-and-white falcon. A common subject of folklore and legends throughout ₌ddle and South America, the Crested Caracara is sometimes erroneously called the "Mexican eagle."

ADULT MALE

ADULT MALE

ADULT FEMALE

ADULT FEMALE

SIZE & SHAPE The slender American Kestrel is roughly the size and shape of a Mourning Dove, although it has a larger head; longer, narrow wings; and a long, square-tipped tail. In flight, the wings are often bent and the wingtips swept back.

COLOR PATTERN American Kestrels are pale when seen from below and a warm, rusty brown, spotted with black, above. The tail has a black band near the tip. Males have slate-blue wings; females' wings are reddish brown. Both sexes have pairs of black vertical slashes on the sides of their pale faces—sometimes called "mustaches" or "sideburns."

BEHAVIOR American Kestrels snatch their victims from the ground, though some catch quarry on the wing. They are gracefully buoyant in flight and small enough to get tossed around in the wind. When perched, kestrels often pump their tails as if they are trying to balance.

HABITAT You'll find kestrels in habitats ranging from deserts and grasslands to alpine meadows. You're most likely to see them perching on telephone wires along roadsides in open country with short vegetation and few trees.

RANGE MAP

- Breeding
- Nonbreeding
- Year-round

The **American Kestrel**, North America's smallest falcon, packs a predator's fierce intensity into its small body. They hunt for insects and small prey in open territory, perch on wires, or hover in the wind, flapping and adjusting their long tails to stay in place. Kestrels are declining; you can help them by putting up nest boxes.

ADULT

ADULT

JUVENILE

JUVENILE

RANGE MAP

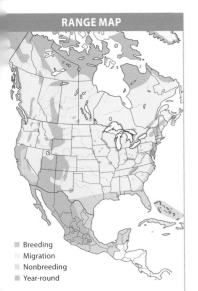

- Breeding
- Migration
- Nonbreeding
- Year-round

SIZE & SHAPE The largest falcon over most of the continent, the Peregrine Falcon has long, pointed wings and a long tail. The bill is strongly hooked. Males are smaller than females, so size can overlap with large female Merlins or small male Gyrfalcons.

COLOR PATTERN Adults are dark gray above with a blackish helmet and yellow eyering. The cere (a fleshy covering at the base of the upper bill) is also vivid yellow. Pale whitish underparts have fine, dark barring. Juveniles are heavily marked, with vertical streaks on the breast, and a gray bill. They lack the yellow eyering and cere.

BEHAVIOR Peregrine Falcons catch medium-sized birds in the air with swift, spectacular dives, called stoops. In cities, they are masterful at catching pigeons. Elsewhere, they feed especially on shorebirds and ducks. They often sit on high perches, waiting for the right opportunity to make their aerial assault.

HABITAT If a mudflat full of shorebirds suddenly erupts, scan the skies for a Peregrine Falcon. Also, look on skyscrapers, cliffs, and other tall structures. They are seen all over North America but are more common along coasts.

werful and fast flying, the **Peregrine Falcon** drops down on prey from high above in a spectacular stoop.
tually eradicated from eastern North America by pesticide poisoning in the middle 20th century, they
e now thriving in many large cities and coastal areas thanks to recovery efforts.

ADULT

ADULT

ADULT

ADULTS

SIZE & SHAPE Monk Parakeets are small with a long, pointed tail and fairly narrow, pointed wings. Like other parakeets, they have large heads and large, hooked bills. They are larger than a European Starling, smaller than a Rock Pigeon.

COLOR PATTERN Monk Parakeets are green with a gray face and breast. The bill is a pale peachy color. In flight, the wings' primary and outer secondary flight feathers flash blue.

BEHAVIOR These noisy birds are often seen and heard traveling between their nests and feeding sites. Adults forage for seeds, nuts, fruits, and greens. Look for them in small flocks in trees, where they can be hard to pick out against the green leaves. They sometimes also feed on the ground.

HABITAT In their native South America, Monk Parakeets live in dry, open habitats. In the U.S., they live in urban and suburban settings, where they feed on ornamental fruit trees and often nest on human structures such as power transformers.

RANGE MAP

■ Year-round

The noisy, green-and-gray **Monk Parakeet**, native to South America but popular in the pet trade, formed wild populations in U.S. cities in the 1960s. They nest communally, living together year-round in multifamily stick nests in trees and on power poles; these large communal nests may help in surviving the cold northern winters.

ADULT

ADULT

JUVENILE

ADULT

RANGE MAP

Breeding
Migration

SIZE & SHAPE The Western Wood-Pewee is a medium-sized flycatcher with a long tail and wings, short legs, an upright posture, and a peaked crown that tends to give the head a triangular shape. The long wings help separate it from many other flycatchers.

COLOR PATTERN Western Wood-Pewees are grayish brown overall, with two pale wingbars. The underparts are whitish with smudgy gray on the breast and sides that can make them look like they are wearing a partially buttoned vest. The face is dark grayish brown with little to no eyering. The bill is mostly dark with yellow at the base of the lower mandible. Juveniles are similar to adults but have buffy wingbars.

BEHAVIOR Pewees sit on exposed perches and fly out to grab flying insects, repeatedly returning to the same or a nearby perch. The song, a harsh, burry *pee-eer*, is quite unlike that of the Eastern Wood-Pewee and the best way to tell the two apart.

HABITAT Western Wood-Pewees breed in open forests up to 10,000 feet. Look for them in cottonwoods and sycamores along rivers, or in stands of pine, oak, or aspen. They spend winters in mature tropical forests of South America.

summer, open woodlands throughout the West come alive with returning **Western Wood-Pewees**. ese flycatchers use exposed branches as their stage, flying to and fro to nab flying insects with stunning ecision. They sit tall when perched, singing a burry and nasal version of their name all summer long.

SIZE & SHAPE Eastern Wood-Pewees are medium-sized flycatchers with long wings and tails. Like other pewee species, they have short legs, an upright posture, and a peaked crown that tends to give the head a triangular shape. Their long wings are an important clue to separate them from *Empidonax* flycatcher species.

COLOR PATTERN Eastern Wood-Pewees are olive gray with dark wings and little or no yellow on the underparts. The sides of the breast are dark with an off-white throat and belly, giving them a vested look. They have little or no eyering.

BEHAVIOR Eastern Wood-Pewees are sit-and-wait predators that fly out from perches after insects and return to the same or a nearby perch. They often perch high in trees in exposed places with good viewpoints.

HABITAT Eastern Wood-Pewees are most common in broadleaf forest, but they breed in nearly any forested habitat, even smaller woodlots, as long as it is fairly open. On migration, they can occur in nearly any spot with trees.

RANGE MAP

■ Breeding
■ Migration

The **Eastern Wood-Pewee** is inconspicuous until it gives its unmistakable slurred *pee-a-wee!* song, a characteristic sound of summers in the East. The Eastern Wood-Pewee's lichen-covered nest is so inconspicuous that it often looks like a knot on a branch.

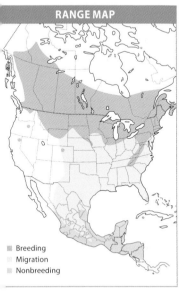

RANGE MAP

- Breeding
- Migration
- Nonbreeding

SIZE & SHAPE Least Flycatchers are the smallest *Empidonax* flycatchers in the East. They tend to perch upright, but they appear a little more compact than most. The head is proportionally large and is round to square in shape. Note their short wings.

COLOR PATTERN Least Flycatchers are grayish olive above with a dusky breast. Their head is grayish olive as well, with a bold, white eyering. They have a very faint yellow wash to the belly and two white wingbars. Adult and immature birds look similar.

BEHAVIOR Least Flycatchers congregate in clusters in broadleaf forests during the breeding season. They sing incessantly in summer, tossing their head back with each *chebec*. They flit from perch to perch on dead branches in the middle to upper level of the forest canopy.

HABITAT These birds breed in broadleaf and mixed forests of all ages, including second-growth and mature forests. These forests tend to have a few shrubs or small saplings in the understory and a well-developed canopy.

ast Flycatchers are fairly easy to identify due to their small size, white eyering, and *chebec* song. In mmer, look for them singing in broadleaf forests. These little birds don't let others push them around and ay chase species as large as Blue Jays. Over half of their population has been lost since 1970.

ADULT

ADULT

ADULT

JUVENILE

SIZE & SHAPE Black Phoebes are small, plump songbirds with large heads and medium-long, squared tails. They often show a slight peak at the rear of the crown. The bill is straight and thin.

COLOR PATTERN Black Phoebes are mostly sooty gray on the upperparts and chest, with a slightly darker black head. The belly is clean white, and the wing feathers are edged with pale gray. Juveniles are similar to adults but have buffy wingbars.

BEHAVIOR Black Phoebes sit upright on low perches near water and make short flights to catch insects. Although they mostly eat insects, they may snatch minnows from the surface of ponds. They pump their tails up and down incessantly when perched. They often keep up a string of sharp *chip* calls.

HABITAT Black Phoebes live along streams, rivers, lakes, and the Pacific Ocean. As long as there is water present and some kind of ledge, Black Phoebes could be around.

RANGE MAP

■ Breeding
■ Nonbreeding
■ Year-round

The **Black Phoebe** is a dapper flycatcher of the western U.S. They sit in the open on low perches to scan for insects, giving a series of shrill chirps. They use mud to build cup-shaped nests against walls, overhangs, culverts, and bridges. Look for them near any water source, from small streams to the Pacific Ocean.

ADULT / IMMATURE

ADULT / IMMATURE

JUVENILE

ADULT / IMMATURE

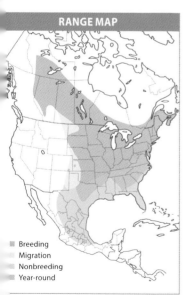

RANGE MAP

■ Breeding
■ Migration
■ Nonbreeding
■ Year-round

SIZE & SHAPE The Eastern Phoebe is a plump flycatcher with a long tail and short wings. The head appears large for its size and can look flat, but the crown feathers may be raised into a peak. Short, wide bills are useful for snatching insects on the wing.

COLOR PATTERN The Eastern Phoebe is brownish gray above and off-white below, with a dusky wash to the sides of the breast and a darker head. Birds in fresh fall plumage show faint yellow on the belly and whitish edging on wing feathers. Juveniles resemble adults but may have cinnamon wingbars.

BEHAVIOR The Eastern Phoebe perches low in trees or on fencelines. They are very active, making short flights to capture insects, often returning to the same perch. They make sharp *peep* calls in addition to their familiar *phoebe* vocalizations. When perched, Eastern Phoebes wag their tails down and up frequently.

HABITAT These birds favor open woods such as yards, parks, woodlands, and woodland edges. Phoebes usually breed around buildings or bridges, constructing their nests under the protection of an eave or ledge.

ten for the **Eastern Phoebe's** raspy *phoebe* song around yards and farms in spring and summer. Their d-and-grass nests can be found in nooks on bridges, barns, and houses, adding to the species' familiarity numans. They winter farther north than most other flycatchers and return north early in spring.

ADULT

ADULT

JUVENILE

ADULT

SIZE & SHAPE This slender, long-tailed flycatcher appears large-headed for a bird of its size. The head often looks flat on top, but they sometimes raise their head feathers into a small peak at the back.

COLOR PATTERN Say's Phoebes are pale brownish gray above with a cinnamon belly, blackish tail, and gray breast. The immature bird is similar to the adult but browner and may have a buffy wingbar. Juveniles have a pink gape and cinnamon wingbars.

BEHAVIOR Like other phoebes, the Say's Phoebe wags or pumps its tail when perched. When foraging, they often perch around eye level on exposed twigs, jumping up to snatch a flying insect and returning to the same or a nearby perch.

HABITAT Say's Phoebes live in open country, sagebrush, badlands, dry barren foothills, canyons, and desert borders; they avoid forests. They often gravitate to buildings and aren't closely tied to watercourses like other phoebes.

RANGE MAP

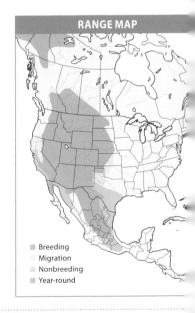

- Breeding
- Migration
- Nonbreeding
- Year-round

Like other phoebes, the **Say's Phoebe** is seemingly undaunted by people and often nests on buildings. They breed farther north than any other flycatcher and are seemingly limited only by the lack of nest site Its breeding range extends from central Mexico all the way to the Arctic tundra.

ADULT MALE

IMMATURE MALE (FIRST YEAR)

ADULT FEMALE

IMMATURE FEMALE (FIRST YEAR)

RANGE MAP

- Breeding
- Breeding (scarce)
- Nonbreeding
- Nonbreeding (scarce)
- Year-round

SIZE & SHAPE The Vermilion Flycatcher is a small, compact flycatcher with a short tail.

COLOR PATTERN Adult male Vermilion Flycatchers are a brilliant red or red orange and blackish brown. Immature males have variable patches of red feathers on the head and breast. Females are dark grayish brown above, with white near the throat becoming pale salmon or orangish under the tail. Breast, sides, and flanks are streaked with grayish brown. Immature females are duller than adults with a yellow or peachy belly and streaked breast.

BEHAVIOR During breeding season, males display high above the canopy, puffing up and singing in flight. They may also deliver a butterfly or other insect to the female. These birds sit low on exposed perches, scanning for insects, which they often take on the wing.

HABITAT Look for Vermilion Flycatchers in open habitats, including scrub, deserts, weedy fields, cultivated lands, mowed parks, and riparian woodlands.

A feathered ember in a desert landscape, the male **Vermilion Flycatcher** is exactly what its name says: a brilliant red bird that hawks flying insects from conspicuous perches on shrub tops and fences. Watch for the male's high, fluttering flight display and listen for his twittering display song.

SIZE & SHAPE This medium-sized flycatcher is long and slender with a long tail. Its head is slightly peaked at the back, making it look large-headed for its size. It has a medium-sized bill that is fairly thick.

COLOR PATTERN Both sexes are grayish brown overall with a pale yellow belly and two whitish wingbars. The head and face are ashy gray, and the throat is whitish. The underside of the tail has a broad cinnamon stripe down the center. Immature birds look like adults.

BEHAVIOR These flycatchers tend to lean forward on perches and move their heads up and down, especially when agitated. They also tip their heads side to side while looking around from a perch. Ash-throated Flycatchers spend most of their time at eye level, flying out from low perches to nab an insect or two.

HABITAT The Ash-throated Flycatcher occupies dry scrub, open woodlands, and deserts in the West. They usually avoid humid forested areas, but do occur in woodlands along streams in dry regions.

RANGE MAP

■ Breeding
■ Migration
■ Nonbreeding
■ Year-round

The **Ash-throated Flycatcher's** subtle hues are reminiscent of a desert just before sunset. This genteel flycatcher tips its head side to side with seeming curiosity while perched among low oaks and mesquite trees. A bird of dry places, it gets all the water it needs from the insects and spiders it eats.

RANGE MAP

- Breeding
- Migration
- Nonbreeding
- Year-round

SIZE & SHAPE Great Crested Flycatchers are large flycatchers with fairly long and lean proportions. They have a large head, broad shoulders, and a fairly long tail. The crest is not especially prominent. The bill is fairly wide at the base and straight.

COLOR PATTERN Great Crested Flycatchers are reddish brown above, with a brownish gray head, gray throat and breast, and bright lemon-yellow belly. Brown upperparts are highlighted by rufous-orange flashes in the primaries and in the tail feathers. Adult and immature birds look alike.

BEHAVIOR Great Crested Flycatchers fly out from high perches near the top of a tree after large insects, returning to the same or a nearby perch. Their clear, rising *reep!* calls are a very common sound in summer.

HABITAT Great Crested Flycatchers nest in open woodlands and edges with dead and dying trees. They tolerate humans and sometimes choose old orchards and woody urban areas such as parks, cemeteries, and golf courses.

ommon in eastern woodlands, the **Great Crested Flycatcher** hunts high in the canopy, giving an emphatic ing whistle. They swoop after flying insects and may crash into foliage in pursuit of leaf-crawling prey. The ly eastern flycatchers that nest in cavities, they sometimes make use of nest boxes.

SIZE & SHAPE Great Kiskadees are large, blocky flycatchers. They have a large head, thick neck, and straight, stout bill. Their wings are broad and rounded, and their tails are medium length and square-tipped.

COLOR PATTERN Kiskadees are an eye-catching mix of black, white, yellow, and reddish brown. The black head is set off by a white eyebrow and throat; the underparts are yellow. The wings and tail are a warm reddish brown that is particularly noticeable in flight. Adult and immature birds look similar.

BEHAVIOR Kiskadees sit on exposed branches near the tops of trees, often above water, where they give a piercing *kis-ka-dee* call and dart out to catch flying insects or pluck small fish from the water.

HABITAT In the U.S., Great Kiskadees live in thorn-scrub and riverine forests of southern Texas, along scrubby irrigation channels, in open or second-growth woodlots, and suburbs.

RANGE MAP

■ Year-round

Look for **Great Kiskadees** when visiting south Texas—these boisterous birds won't keep you waiting. Kiskadees sit in the open and attract attention with incessant *kis-ka-dee* calls and short flights. Despite the small U.S. range, this is one of the most widespread flycatchers in the Western Hemisphere.

ADULT

ADULT

ADULT

ADULT

RANGE MAP

- Breeding
- Breeding (scarce)
- Migration
- Nonbreeding

SIZE & SHAPE Western Kingbirds are fairly large flycatchers with large heads and broad shoulders. They have heavy, straight bills, long wings, and medium-length, square-tipped tails.

COLOR PATTERN Western Kingbirds are gray-headed birds with a yellow belly, pale gray chest, and a whitish throat. The tail is black with white outer edges that are especially conspicuous in flight. Juvenile birds are not as brightly colored.

BEHAVIOR Easily found perched upright on fences and utility lines, Western Kingbirds hawk insects from the air or fly out to pick prey from the ground. They ferociously defend their territories with wing-fluttering, highly vocal attacks. Vocalizations include a long series of squeaky, bubbling calls as well as single, accented *kip* notes.

HABITAT Western Kingbirds live in open valleys and lowlands up to about 7,000 feet elevation. They perch on utility lines, fences, and trees in cities, grasslands, deserts, sagebrush, agricultural fields, and open woodlands.

eye-catching bird, the **Western Kingbird** is a familiar summertime sight in open habitats across much of stern North America. They are aggressive and will scold and chase intruders (including Red-tailed Hawks d American Kestrels) with a snapping bill and flared crimson crown feathers that are normally hidden.

ADULT

ADULT

JUVENILE

ADULT

SIZE & SHAPE The Eastern Kingbird is a large, sturdy flycatcher with a large head, upright posture, square-tipped tail, and a relatively short, wide, straight bill.

COLOR PATTERN Eastern Kingbirds are blackish above and white below, with a darker head than the wings and back. The black tail has a white tip. Look for red feathers on the crown of an agitated male, though he usually keeps these hidden.

BEHAVIOR Eastern Kingbirds often perch in the open atop trees or along utility lines or fences. They fly with very shallow, rowing wingbeats and a raised head, usually accompanied by metallic, sputtering calls. Eastern Kingbirds are visual hunters, flying out from perches to snatch flying insects.

HABITAT Eastern Kingbirds breed in open habitats such as yards, fields, pastures, grasslands, or wetlands, and are especially abundant in open places along forest edges or water. They spend winters in forests of South America.

RANGE MAP

■ Breeding
Migration

With dark-gray upperparts and a neat white tip to the tail, the **Eastern Kingbird** looks like it's wearing a business suit. And this big-headed, broad-shouldered bird does mean business—just watch one harassing crows, Red-tailed Hawks, Great Blue Herons, and other birds that pass over its territory.

ADULT

ADULT

ADULT

ADULT / JUVENILE

RANGE MAP

Breeding
Migration
Nonbreeding

SIZE & SHAPE Scissor-tailed Flycatchers are slender and stout-billed with very long, stiff, deeply forked tails. Adult males have longer tail feathers than females and immatures. It is smaller and more slender than an American Robin.

COLOR PATTERN These are pale gray birds with blackish wings and black tails with white edges. Adults have salmon-pink flanks that extend to underwing patches. Males are more intensely colored than females, and their tails are longer.

BEHAVIOR These birds perch on utility lines, treetops, and fences to watch for insect prey. They are agile fliers, thanks to their long tails. They are highly territorial, and will chase other birds out of their territories accompanied by loud, squeaky calls.

HABITAT Scissor-tailed Flycatchers breed in open habitats in the southern Great Plains and south Texas, especially around scattered trees or utility lines. They tolerate human presence well and frequently breed in towns.

elegant gray-and-salmon-pink flycatcher festooned with an absurdly long tail, the **Scissor-tailed** **catcher** is the bird to look for on fence wires in the south-central United States. Their long, forked tails ⸱ve useful as they expertly catch insects on the wing with sharp midair twists and turns.

ADULT

ADULT

JUVENILE

ADULT

SIZE & SHAPE Yellow-throated Vireos are small songbirds, but they are chunky, with a big head, thick bill, and short tail.

COLOR PATTERN Male and female Yellow-throated Vireos look as if they are wearing bright-yellow spectacles on their olive-green heads. The throat and chest match the spectacles, but the lower belly is bright white. Two white bars mark the gray wings.

BEHAVIOR Yellow-throated Vireos forage in middle and upper stories of forests, gleaning insects off trunks, branches, and leaves. They tend to forage in the interior parts of trees, particularly on bare branches. They move slowly from place to place and search for a relatively long time from one spot.

HABITAT Yellow-throated Vireos breed in broadleaf forests and prefer forest edges with an open understory. They winter in a range of habitats, from dry tropical forest to rainforest up to 6,000 feet.

RANGE MAP

■ Breeding
  Migration
■ Nonbreeding

The **Yellow-throated Vireo's** bright throat and bespectacled eyes make it one of the most colorful members of its family. Hopping through the broadleaf forest canopy, it picks insects off branches and twigs. Males sing a burry *three-eight* throughout the day, joined by chattering females during aggressive encounters.

RANGE MAP

Breeding
Migration
Nonbreeding
Year-round

SIZE & SHAPE Warbling Vireos are small, chunky songbirds with thick, straight, slightly hooked bills. They are medium sized for vireos, with a fairly round head and medium-length bill and tail.

COLOR PATTERN These birds are grayish olive above and whitish below, washed on the sides and vent with yellow. They have a dark line through the eye and a white line over the eye. The space between the eye and the bill is usually white. Adult and immature birds look similar.

BEHAVIOR Warbling Vireos forage sluggishly, intently peering at leaf surfaces from a single perch before pouncing or moving on. They eat mostly caterpillars. They give their loud, rollicking, finchlike song frequently on summer territories.

HABITAT Open, broadleaf woodlands, forest edges, and riverside woodlands are the preferred habitats of Warbling Vireos throughout the year, though they also use some mixed coniferous-broadleaf habitats. Even on migration, they typically occur in areas with taller trees.

he rich, rollicking song of the **Warbling Vireo** is a common sound in many parts of central and northern orth America during summer, making it a great bird to learn by ear. Warbling Vireos are otherwise fairly ain birds that stay high in broadleaf treetops, hunting methodically among the leaves for caterpillars.

ADULT ADULT

IMMATURE ADULT

SIZE & SHAPE Red-eyed Vireos are chunky songbirds, a bit bigger than most warblers, with a long, angular head, thick neck, and a strong, long bill with a small but noticeable hook at the tip. The body is stocky and the tail fairly short.

COLOR PATTERN Red-eyed Vireos are olive green above and clean white below with a gray crown and white eyebrow stripe bordered above and below by blackish lines. Flanks and under the tail have a green-yellow wash. Adults have red eyes; immature birds have dark eyes.

BEHAVIOR These vireos forage in broadleaf canopies, moving slowly and methodically, carefully scanning leaves for caterpillars and other prey. They sing incessantly in summer, even in the afternoon heat.

HABITAT Red-eyed Vireos breed in broadleaf and mixed forests with shrubby understories. They are also found in neighborhoods with large trees. During migration, look for them in more varied habitats.

RANGE MAP

■ Breeding
■ Breeding (scarce)
■ Migration

A tireless songster, the **Red-eyed Vireo's** brief but incessant songs—sometimes more than 20,000 per day by a single male—contribute to the characteristic sound of summer in eastern and northern forests. When fall arrives, they head for the Amazon basin, fueled by a summer of plucking caterpillars from leaves in the treetop

ADULT

ADULT

ADULT

ADULT

RANGE MAP

Breeding
Breeding (scarce)
Nonbreeding
Year-round

SIZE & SHAPE The Loggerhead Shrike is a thick-bodied songbird with a large, blocky head. The thick bill has a small hook. The tail is fairly long and rounded.

COLOR PATTERN The Loggerhead Shrike is a gray bird with a wide black mask contrasting a white throat. The tail is black with white corners; the wings are black with white at the base of the primaries that form a small "handkerchief" spot when the wing is closed and larger white patches in flight. Juveniles have darker barring above and below.

BEHAVIOR Loggerhead Shrikes sit on low, exposed perches and scan for rodents, lizards, birds, and insects. They eat smaller prey right away, but they are famous for impaling larger items on thorns or barbed wire to be eaten later.

HABITAT Open country with scattered shrubs and trees is the typical habitat of Loggerhead Shrike, but the species can also be found in more heavily wooded habitats with large openings, and in very short habitats with few or no trees.

e **Loggerhead Shrike** is a songbird with a raptor's habits, hunting small prey from conspicuous perches. ese masked predators lack a raptor's talons, so they skewer their kills on thorns or barbed wire or wedge m into tight places for easy eating. Their numbers have dropped sharply in the last half-century.

SIZE & SHAPE Large and unmistakable, the sturdy Green Jay has a thick, straight bill, a long, rounded tail, and fairly long legs. It has no crest. In flight, the wings are broad and rounded.

COLOR PATTERN Green Jays are a rich green above and pale yellow green below, with a vivid blue crown, black throat and eyepatch. It flashes yellow outer tail feathers in flight. Adult and immature birds look alike.

BEHAVIOR Green Jays forage together in family flocks that rove woodlands and thickets, searching all levels of the vegetation for insects, fruit, and small vertebrates, maintaining contact with noisy calls. Highly social and territorial year-round, they drive away rival Green Jays and mob predators such as owls or snakes.

HABITAT Green Jays inhabit woodlands, thickets, and parks, especially sites with native trees. They also favor citrus orchards and parks.

RANGE MAP

■ Year-round

The noisy, colorful **Green Jay** of the tropics travels in conspicuous family flocks through brushlands and forests, seeking small prey and fruit. They are versatile foragers, equally comfortable at picking, gleaning, pouncing, and even flycatching. In the breeding season, these garrulous birds become a bit quieter.

ADULT

ADULT

ADULT

ADULT

RANGE MAP

RANGE MAP

Nonbreeding (scarce)
Year-round

SIZE & SHAPE Blue Jays are large crested songbirds with broad, rounded tails. They are smaller than crows, but larger than robins.

COLOR PATTERN Blue Jays are a brilliant blue above and white or light gray below, with a prominent crest and a bold black necklace. The wings and tail are barred with black, and the wings are spangled with white. Large white tail corners are prominent in flight.

BEHAVIOR Blue Jays make a large variety of calls that carry long distances. Most calls are produced while the jay is perched in a tree. It flies across open areas silently, especially during migration. Blue Jays stuff food items in a throat pouch to cache elsewhere. When eating, it will hold a seed or nut securely in its feet and peck it open.

HABITAT Blue Jays are birds of forest edges. A favorite food is acorns, and they are often found near oaks, in forests, woodlots, towns, cities, and parks.

e common, large **Blue Jay** is familiar to many people, with its perky crest; blue, white, and black plumage; d noisy calls. This songbird is known for its intelligence and complex social systems with tight family nds. Its fondness for acorns is credited with helping spread oak trees after the last glacial period.

ADULT · ADULT · JUVENILE · ADULT

SIZE & SHAPE The Woodhouse's Scrub-Jay is a fairly large, lanky songbird with a long, floppy tail and an often hunched-over posture. The bill is fairly long and straight, with a pointed tip.

COLOR PATTERN Woodhouse's Scrub-Jays are light blue and gray above, with a whitish throat and gray belly separated by a partial breast band of blue. In birds, the color blue depends on lighting, so Woodhouse's Scrub-Jays can look simply dark. Juveniles have a grayer head and throat than adults, but otherwise look similar.

BEHAVIOR Woodhouse's Scrub-Jays are assertive, vocal, and inquisitive. You'll often notice them silhouetted high in trees, on wires, or on posts, where they act as lookouts. Their flight is slow, with bouts of fluttering alternating with glides. Listen for the raspy scolds and *weep* calls these birds use to communicate.

HABITAT Look for these scrub-jays in open habitats and pinyon-juniper woodlands of the intermountain West; also backyards and pastures. They are typically found in lower and drier habitats than Steller's Jay.

RANGE MAP

■ Year-round
  Year-round (scarce)

Woodhouse's Scrub-Jays have a mischievous streak, and they're not above outright theft. They've been caught stealing acorns, seeds, and pine cones from Clark's Nutcrackers. You might see one standing on the back of a mule deer—they're picking off and eating ticks and other parasites.

RANGE MAP

■ Breeding
■ Nonbreeding
■ Year-round

SIZE & SHAPE American Crows are long-legged, thick-necked, oversized songbirds with a heavy, straight bill. In flight, the wings are fairly broad and rounded with the wingtip feathers spread like fingers. The short tail is rounded or squared off at the end.

COLOR PATTERN American Crows are all black, including the legs and bill and eyes. As they molt, old feathers can appear brownish or scaly compared to glossy new feathers. Adult and immature birds look similar.

BEHAVIOR American Crows are very social, sometimes forming flocks in the thousands. Inquisitive and sometimes mischievous, crows are good learners and problem solvers, often raiding garbage cans and picking over discarded food containers. They're also aggressive and chase away larger birds including hawks, owls, and herons.

HABITAT American Crows are common birds of fields, open woodlands, and forests. They thrive around people, and you'll often find them in farm fields, lawns, parking lots, athletic fields, roadsides, towns, and garbage dumps.

American Crows are familiar over much of the continent: large, intelligent, all-black birds with hoarse, cawing voices. They are a common sight in treetops, fields, and on roadsides, and in habitats ranging from open woods and empty beaches to town centers. They usually feed on the ground and eat almost anything.

SIZE & SHAPE Fish Crows fit the standard crow shape: hefty, well-proportioned birds with heavy bills, sturdy legs, and broad wings. At rest, Fish Crows' wings fall short of their medium-length, square tails.

COLOR PATTERN Fish Crows are all black. Immatures are less glossy and can become brownish as their feathers wear in their first year, but adult and immature birds look quite similar.

BEHAVIOR Fish Crows are very social birds; look for them in pairs in the breeding season and in groups of up to several hundred or more during migration or winter. When they give their distinctive nasal calls from the ground, they often puff out their neck and body feathers, forming a ragged throat ruff.

HABITAT Fish Crows live along the coasts and inland along major freshwater rivers and lakes. You may find Fish Crows in a wide variety of habitats near water, often in towns and cities near parks, docks, and landfills. They share many habitats with American Crows.

RANGE MAP

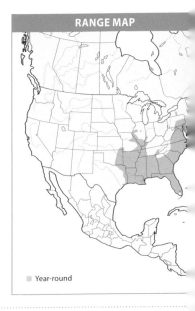

■ Year-round

Not everyone realizes it, but there are two kinds of crows across much of the eastern United States. Lookir almost identical to the American Crow, **Fish Crows** are tough to identify until you learn their nasal *uh-uh* call. Look for them around bodies of water, usually in flocks and sometimes with American Crows.

RANGE MAP

■ Year-round

SIZE & SHAPE The Common Raven is not just large but massive, with a thick neck, shaggy throat feathers, and a Bowie knife of a beak. In flight, ravens have long, wedge-shaped tails. They're more slender than crows, with longer, narrower wings, and longer, thinner "fingers" at the wingtips.

COLOR PATTERN Common Ravens are entirely black, right down to the legs, eyes, and beak. Adult and immature birds look similar.

BEHAVIOR Common Ravens aren't as social as crows and tend to be alone or in pairs, except at food sources like landfills. They're confident, inquisitive birds that strut around or bound forward with light, two-footed hops. In flight, they are buoyant and graceful, interspersing soaring, gliding, and slow flaps.

HABITAT Look for the Common Raven in open and forest habitats across western and northern North America, as well as high desert, seacoast, and grasslands. It also does well in rural settlements, towns, and cities.

e **Common Raven** has accompanied people around the Northern Hemisphere for centuries, following em in hopes of a quick meal. Ravens are among the smartest of all birds, gaining a reputation for solving er more complicated problems invented by ever more creative scientists.

ADULT

ADULT

ADULT

ADULT

SIZE & SHAPE This tiny, approachable songbird has a short neck and large head, giving it a distinctive round body shape. Its tail is fairly long and narrow, and its short bill is thicker than a warbler's but thinner than a finch's.

COLOR PATTERN Carolina Chickadees have a black cap and bib separated by stark white cheeks. The back, wings, and tail are soft gray. Compared to Black-capped Chickadees, their black bib is smaller and looks cleaner at the edge. Secondary feathers are edged in pale gray, not white like Black-capped Chickadees.

BEHAVIOR Inquisitive and acrobatic, this sociable bird forms mixed feeding flocks with other small birds, roaming within a fairly large area, except during the breeding season.

HABITAT Carolina Chickadees live in broadleaf and coniferous forests, swamps, wet woods, open woods, parks, and urban and suburban yards.

RANGE MAP

■ Year-round

Named by John James Audubon, the curious **Carolina Chickadee** looks very much like a Black-capped Chickadee, with a black cap, black bib, gray wings and back, and whitish underside. The two species hybridize in the area where their ranges overlap but probably diverged more than 2.5 million years ago.

ADULT ADULT ADULT ADULT

RANGE MAP

Year-round

SIZE & SHAPE The Tufted Titmouse looks large among the small birds that come to feeders, an impression that comes from its large head and eye, thick neck, and full body. The pointed crest and stout bill help identify them even in silhouette.

COLOR PATTERN The Tufted Titmouse is soft, silvery gray above and white below, with a rusty or peach-colored wash down the flanks. A black patch just above the bill makes the bird look stub-nosed.

BEHAVIOR These acrobatic foragers often join flocks of chickadees and other small birds as the group passes through the titmouse's territory. Their flight tends to be fluttery but level. When a titmouse finds a large seed, you'll see it carry the prize to a perch and crack it with sharp whacks of its stout bill.

HABITAT The Tufted Titmouse lives in broadleaf or mixed coniferous-broadleaf woods with dense canopies, typically at elevations up to about 2,000 feet. They're also common in orchards, parks, and suburbs.

little gray bird with an echoing voice, the **Tufted Titmouse** is common in eastern broadleaf forests. Large ack eyes, a small, round bill, and a brushy crest give these birds a quiet but eager expression that matches e way they flit through canopies, hang from twig-ends, and frequently drop in to feeders.

ADULT

ADULT

JUVENILE

ADULT BLACK-CRESTED × TUFTED TITMOUSE HYBF

SIZE & SHAPE The Black-crested Titmouse is a small songbird that appears larger than it is due to its crest and long tail. It has a rounded, stubby bill.

COLOR PATTERN The Black-crested Titmouse is gray above and whitish below with peach-colored flanks. Note the white forehead and bold black crest. Juveniles lack the black crest and have less peach on their sides. They commonly hybridize with the Tufted Titmouse where their ranges overlap in southern Oklahoma and north and central Texas. Hybrids have dark gray crests and rusty foreheads.

BEHAVIOR The Black-crested Titmouse gleans insects from bark and foliage, hanging upside down to reach them. They also eat seeds. They hold food under their feet to peck it.

HABITAT The Black-crested Titmouse is commonly found in forests, woodlands, oak-juniper scrub, mesquite, thorn scrub, riparian woodlands, and in towns in Texas, southern Oklahoma, and northeastern Mexico.

RANGE MAP

■ Year-round

A bird of Texas, Oklahoma, and northeastern Mexico, the **Black-crested Titmouse** is common in oak woo and towns. It was once considered a subspecies of the Tufted Titmouse, and the two species hybridize an are very similar in appearance, voice, and habits, but they are distinct genetically and vocally.

ADULT

ADULT

JUVENILE

IMMATURE

RANGE MAP

◼ Year-round

SIZE & SHAPE The Verdin is a small, delicate songbird with a small, sharply pointed bill. It has a moderately long tail and a small head.

COLOR PATTERN Adult Verdins have a gray body, a yellow head, and a black bill. Their unique chestnut shoulder patches are not always visible. Immatures are pale gray overall and lack the yellow head and chestnut shoulder patches. Juveniles have a yellow bill, especially when very young.

BEHAVIOR Verdins move actively and nimbly among limbs of scrub vegetation, in a manner resembling that of chickadees. They often hold blossoms with the feet while looking and picking at prey with the bill. Verdins sometimes visit hummingbird feeders and flowering shrubs.

HABITAT Verdins are permanent residents of arid habitats in Mexico and the desert Southwest of the United States. They prefer desert scrub or chaparral with thorny trees and avoid both open flats with low vegetation and dense forest. They often occur along washes (arroyos) where trees and shrubs are present.

the heat of desert arroyos and scrublands, tiny gray **Verdins** flash bright colors: a yellow head and
estnut shoulder patches. More slender than a chickadee, these restless birds comb the foliage of trees
r insects and spiders, sometimes hanging upside down to investigate hard-to-reach places.

BREEDING MALE

NONBREEDING MALE

JUVENILE

ADULT FEMALE

SIZE & SHAPE Horned Larks are small, long-bodied songbirds that usually adopt a horizontal posture. They have short, thin bills, short necks, and rounded heads that sometimes show two small "horns" of feathers sticking up toward the back.

COLOR PATTERN Males are sandy brown above and white beneath, with a black chest band, mask, and head stripes which are sometimes raised like tiny "horns." The face and throat are yellow or white. Females have less defined markings. Juveniles are brown overall with white-edged feathers and a brown breast band.

BEHAVIOR Horned Larks are usually found in flocks except during the breeding season. They creep along bare ground, searching for small seeds and insects. They often join in winter flocks with other open-country species.

HABITAT Horned Larks favor starkly open habitats with bare earth: deserts, tundra, beaches, dunes, grazed pastures, plowed fields, roadsides, and feedlots. They are drawn to fields spread with waste grain and manure. In winter, they mostly feed in areas free of snow.

RANGE MAP

■ Breeding
  Migration
  Nonbreeding
  Nonbreeding (scarce)
■ Year-round

Look carefully at a bare field, especially in winter, and you may see it crawling with little **Horned Larks**. These songbirds are widespread in fields, deserts, and tundra, where they forage for seeds and insects, and sing a high, tinkling song. Though still common, they have declined sharply in the last half-century.

ADULT MALE

ADULT MALE

IMMATURE MALE (L) AND ADULT FEMALE (R)

ADULT FEMALE

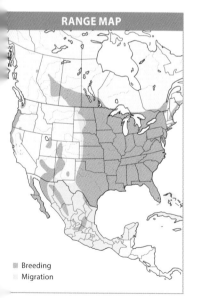

RANGE MAP

◼ Breeding
◻ Migration

SIZE & SHAPE Purple Martins are very large, broad-chested swallows. They have stout, slightly hooked bills, short, forked tails, and long, tapered wings.

COLOR PATTERN Adult males are an iridescent, dark bluish purple overall with brown-black wings and tail. Females and immatures are duller, with variable amounts of gray on the head and chest and a whitish lower belly.

BEHAVIOR Purple Martins fly rapidly with a mix of flapping and gliding. They feed in midair, catching large, aerial insects such as dragonflies. Martins feed and roost in flocks, often mixed with other species of swallows. They often feed higher in the air than other swallows, which can make them tough to spot.

HABITAT Purple Martins are colonial, with dozens nesting in the same spot. They feed in open areas, especially near water. In the East, they nest almost exclusively in nest boxes and martin houses; in the West, they nest in natural cavities.

tting up a **Purple Martin** house is like installing a miniature neighborhood in your backyard. In the East, ey will peer from the entrances and chirp from the rooftops all summer. In the West, martins mainly nest woodpecker holes. North America's largest swallow, it performs aerial acrobatics to snap up flying insects.

ADULT MALE

ADULT MALE

JUVENILES

ADULT FEMALE

SIZE & SHAPE Tree Swallows are small streamlined songbirds with long, pointed wings and a short, squared or slightly notched tail. Their bills are very short and flat.

COLOR PATTERN Adult males are blue green above and white below with blackish flight feathers and a thin black eye mask. Females are duller with more brown in their upperparts, and juveniles are completely brown above. Juveniles and some females can show a weak, blurry gray-brown breast band.

BEHAVIOR Tree Swallows feed on small, aerial insects that they catch during acrobatic flight. After breeding, they will gather in large flocks to molt and migrate. In the nonbreeding season, they form huge communal roosts.

HABITAT Tree Swallows feed on small, aerial insects that they catch in their mouths during acrobatic flight. After breeding, Tree Swallows gather in large flocks to molt and migrate. In the nonbreeding season, they form huge communal roosts.

RANGE MAP

- Breeding
- Migration
- Winter
- Year-round

Handsome aerialists with deep, iridescent blue backs and clean white fronts, **Tree Swallows** are a familiar sight in summer fields and wetlands across northern North America. They chase after flying insects with acrobatic twists and turns, their steely blue-green feathers flashing in the sunlight.

ADULT MALE

ADULT MALE

ADULT FEMALE

JUVENILES

RANGE MAP

- Breeding
- Migration
- Nonbreeding
- Year-round

SIZE & SHAPE When perched, the sparrow-sized Barn Swallow appears cone shaped, with a slightly flattened head, no visible neck, and broad shoulders that taper to long, pointed wings. The tail extends well beyond the wingtips and the long outer feathers give the tail a deep fork.

COLOR PATTERN Barn Swallows have a steely blue back, wings, and tail, and rufous to tawny underparts. The blue crown and face contrast with the cinnamon-colored forehead and throat. White spots under the tail can be difficult to see except in flight. Males are more boldly colored than females. Juveniles are dark above and pale cinnamon below with a rich rusty throat and forehead.

BEHAVIOR Watch for the Barn Swallow's smooth, fluid wingbeats. They often follow farm implements, cattle herds, and humans to snag flushed insects.

HABITAT You can find the adaptable Barn Swallow feeding in open habitats from fields, parks, and roadway edges to marshes, meadows, ponds, and coastal waters.

...stening cobalt blue above and tawny below, **Barn Swallows** dart gracefully over fields, barnyards, and ...en water in search of flying insects. They often cruise low, flying just a few inches above the ground or ...ter. The Barn Swallow is the most abundant and widely distributed swallow species in the world.

ADULT | JUVENILE

ADULT | ADULT

SIZE & SHAPE These compact swallows have rounded, broad-based wings, a small head, and a medium-length, squared tail. They are sparrow-sized.

COLOR PATTERN In poor light, Cliff Swallows look brown with dark throats and white underparts. In good light, you'll see their metallic, dark-blue backs and pale, buff-colored rumps. They have rich, brick-red faces and a bright buff-white forehead patch like a headlamp. In the Southwest, some birds have a rust colored forehead instead. Some juveniles show whitish throats in summer and fall.

BEHAVIOR Cliff Swallows zoom around in intricate aerial patterns catching insects on the wing. When feeding with other species of swallows, they often stay higher in the air.

HABITAT Cliff Swallows traditionally built their nests on cliff faces but now have adopted bridges, overpasses, and culverts as colonial nesting sites. They feed near and over water, frequently mixing with other species of swallows.

RANGE MAP

■ Breeding
■ Migration

In summer, flocks of **Cliff Swallows** swarm around bridges and overpasses, where clusters of their intricate mud nests cling to vertical walls. These sociable swallows are nearly always found in large groups, chasing insects high above the ground, preening on perches, or dipping into a river for a bath.

ADULTS

ADULT

PHOTO 3

ADULT

RANGE MAP

Breeding
Year-round

SIZE & SHAPE Cave Swallows have a cylindrical body with long, pointed wings and a square-tipped tail that sometimes shows a slight notch. The bill is very short and the feet very small. They are sparrow-sized.

COLOR PATTERN Cave Swallows are dark above and pale below. Their most notable features include the rusty rump, forehead, and cheeks, and the pale rusty throat.

BEHAVIOR Cave Swallows are aerial insectivores that eat insects on the wing. They nest colonially and forage in groups, often with other swallows. They build nests with bits of mud and bat guano that they collect with their bill.

HABITAT Cave Swallows nest in natural or human-made structures including caves, sinkholes, buildings, silos, bridges, and culverts. During the day they forage over open areas, often near water.

e **Cave Swallow** devours flying insects with airborne twists and turns that show off its chestnut rump ch and forehead. It often roosts and nests inside the entrances to caves, sharing the space with bats. ently, Cave Swallows started nesting under bridges and culverts and expanding their range northward.

MALE | FEMALE

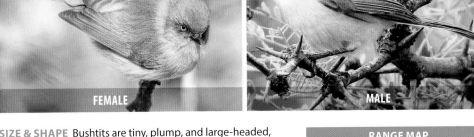

FEMALE | MALE

SIZE & SHAPE Bushtits are tiny, plump, and large-headed, with long tails and short, stubby bills. They are slightly smaller than a chickadee; about the size of a kinglet.

COLOR PATTERN Bushtits are fairly plain brown and gray. Slightly darker above than below, they have brown-gray heads, gray wings, and tan-gray underparts. Some males in Texas, especially immature males, have black on the cheeks. Females have light eyes, males have dark eyes. Plumage varies little by age.

BEHAVIOR Bushtits move quickly through vegetation, almost always in flocks, and continuously make soft chips and twitters. They forage much as chickadees do, frequently hanging upside down to grab small insects and spiders from leaves.

HABITAT Bushtits live in oak forest, coniferous woodlands, dry scrublands, streamsides, and suburbs. You can find them at elevations from sea level to over 10,000 feet.

RANGE MAP

■ Year-round

Bushtits are sprightly, social songbirds that twitter as they fly between shrubs and thickets. Found in lively flocks, they move constantly, often hanging upside down to pick at insects underneath leaves. Bushtits weave an unusual hanging nest, shaped like a pouch or sock, from moss, spiderwebs, and grasses.

ADULT

ADULT MALE

JUVENILE

ADULT FEMALE

RANGE MAP

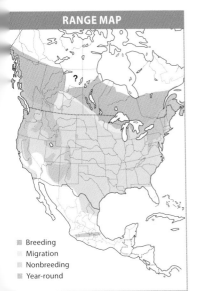

■ Breeding
■ Migration
■ Nonbreeding
■ Year-round

SIZE & SHAPE Golden-crowned Kinglets are tiny songbirds with a rounded body, short wings, and skinny tail. They have relatively large heads, and their bills are short and thin—perfect for gleaning small insects.

COLOR PATTERN Golden-crowned Kinglets are pale olive above and gray below, with a black-and-white striped face and a bright yellow crown patch. In males, the crown patch is accented with a red-orange stripe down the middle. Both sexes have a thin white wingbar and yellow edges to their black flight feathers.

BEHAVIOR Golden-crowned Kinglets stay concealed high in dense trees, giving thin, very high-pitched calls. They pluck small insects from conifer needles, hovering to reach them. In migration and winter, they join other insectivorous songbirds in mixed flocks.

HABITAT These birds live mainly in coniferous forests, breeding in boreal or montane forests, and conifer plantations. In winter, look for them in broadleaf forests, suburbs, swamps, bottomlands, and scrubby habitat.

hough the **Golden-crowned Kinglet** is barely larger than a hummingbird, this frenetically active bird n survive −40° nights, sometimes huddling together for warmth. A good look can require some patience, they spend much of their time high up in dense spruce or fir foliage.

ADULT MALE

ADULT MALE

ADULT / IMMATURE

ADULT / IMMATURE

SIZE & SHAPE Ruby-crowned Kinglets are tiny songbirds with relatively large heads, almost no neck, and thin tails. They have very small, thin, straight bills.

COLOR PATTERN Ruby-crowned Kinglets are olive green with a prominent broken white eyering and white wingbar. This wingbar contrasts with an adjacent blackish bar in the wing. The brilliant ruby crown of the male is only occasionally visible, usually in spring and summer.

BEHAVIOR These are restless, acrobatic birds that move quickly through foliage, typically at lower and middle levels. They flick their wings almost constantly as they go.

HABITAT Ruby-crowned Kinglets breed in tall, dense conifer forests such as spruce, fir, and tamarack. In winter and during migration, also look for them in shrubby habitats, broadleaf forests, parks, and suburbs.

RANGE MAP

■ Breeding
■ Migration
■ Nonbreeding
■ Year-round

A tiny bird overflowing with energy, the **Ruby-crowned Kinglet** forages frantically through the lower branches of shrubs and trees. Its habit of constantly flicking its wings is a key identification clue. This bird la a large clutch of eggs—up to 12 in a single nest. The entire clutch may weigh as much as the female herse

MALE

MALE

FEMALE

FEMALE

RANGE MAP

Nonbreeding
Year-round

SIZE & SHAPE Red-breasted Nuthatches are small, compact songbirds with slightly upturned, pointed bills, extremely short tails, and almost no neck. The body is plump or barrel-chested, and the short wings are very broad. It is slightly smaller than a sparrow.

COLOR PATTERN Both sexes are blue gray above. Males have cinnamon underparts, while the females' are a peach color. The male has a black cap, white stripe above the eye, and black stripe through the eye. The female's dark head markings are gray. Immature and adult birds look similar.

BEHAVIOR Red-breasted Nuthatches creep up, down, and sideways over trunks and branches, probing for food in crevices and under flakes of bark. They don't lean against their tail as woodpeckers do. Their flight is short and bouncy.

HABITAT Red-breasted Nuthatches live mainly in coniferous forests. Eastern populations use some broadleaf woods. During some winters, they may "irrupt" or move far south of their normal range.

e **Red-breasted Nuthatch** is a tiny, active songbird of northern woods and western mountains. It travels ough the canopy with chickadees, kinglets, and woodpeckers but sticks to tree trunks and branches, arching for hidden food. Its excitable *yank-yank* call sounds like a tiny horn honking in the treetops.

ADULT FEMALE (EASTERN)

ADULT MALE (EASTERN)

ADULT FEMALE (INTERIOR WEST)

ADULT MALE (INTERIOR WEST)

SIZE & SHAPE The White-breasted Nuthatch is small, with a large head and almost no apparent neck. The tail is very short, and the long, narrow, sharp bill is straight or slightly upturned. It is sparrow-sized.

COLOR PATTERN White-breasted Nuthatches are gray blue on the back, with a frosty white face and underparts. The lower belly and under the tail are often chestnut. The black or gray cap (male or female, respectively) and nape make it look like this bird is hooded. Size of the hood varies by region.

BEHAVIOR Like other nuthatches, they creep along trunks, probing into furrows with their bills and often turning sideways or upside down as they forage. Unlike woodpeckers, they don't use their tails to brace against a vertical trunk.

HABITAT Look for White-breasted Nuthatches in mature broadleaf woods, woodland edges, parks, wooded suburbs, and backyards. They're rarely found in coniferous woods, where Red-breasted Nuthatches are more likely.

RANGE MAP

Nonbreeding
Year-round

A common feeder bird, the **White-breasted Nuthatch** is an active, agile little bird with an appetite for insects and large, meaty seeds. It gets its common name from its habit of jamming large nuts and acorns into tree bark, then whacking them with its sharp bill to "hatch" out the seed from the inside.

RANGE MAP

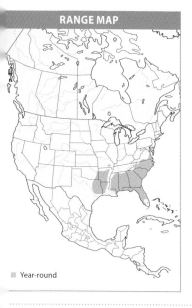

■ Year-round

SIZE & SHAPE The Brown-headed Nuthatch is a tiny, compact bird with a large head. It appears rather round thanks to its short tail, legs, and neck. It also has a chisel-like bill that looks a little too big for its body. It is smaller than a sparrow.

COLOR PATTERN Brown-headed Nuthatches are bluish gray with a clean brown cap neatly set off from the whitish face and throat. The underparts are pale grayish white. Males, females, and immature birds look similar.

BEHAVIOR Nuthatches zigzag up and down tree trunks and branches high in the canopy, squeaking as they go. Although they aren't very loud, there's usually more than one in a group calling, so they won't go unheard.

HABITAT Brown-headed Nuthatches live in or around pine forests of the southeastern U.S., especially in open, mature forests of loblolly, shortleaf, slash, and longleaf pine where natural fire patterns have been maintained.

ok for **Brown-headed Nuthatches** in southern pine forests, deftly climbing on pine trunks and branches. ey cling to bark with their strong feet rather than leaning on their tails like a woodpecker. These social ds travel in noisy family groups; offspring from previous years may help their parents raise young.

SIZE & SHAPE The Brown Creeper is a tiny and delicate songbird with a long, spine-tipped tail, slim body, and a slender, decurved bill.

COLOR PATTERN Streaked brown and buff above, with their white underparts usually hidden against a tree trunk, Brown Creepers blend easily into bark. Their brownish heads show a broad, buffy stripe over the eye. Adult and immature birds look similar.

BEHAVIOR Brown Creepers search for small insects and spiders by hitching upward in a spiral around tree trunks and limbs. They move with short, jerky motions using their stiff tails for support. To move to a new tree, they fly weakly to its base and resume climbing up. Brown Creepers sing a high, warbling song.

HABITAT Look for these birds in broadleaf or coniferous forests with large, live trees. In summer, they're often among hemlock, pine, fir, and cypress. In winter, they use a wider variety of wooded habitats, parks, and yards.

RANGE MAP

- Breeding
- Nonbreeding
- Year-round

Listen for the piercing call of the **Brown Creeper**, a tiny woodland bird with an affinity for the biggest tree it can find. They spiral up stout trunks and main branches, probing crevices and picking at loose bark with their slender, downcurved bills. They build hammock-shaped nests behind peeling bark.

BREEDING MALE (WESTERN)

BREEDING MALE (EASTERN)

JUVENILE (WESTERN)

ADULT FEMALE / NONBREEDING MALE

RANGE MAP

- Breeding
- Migration
- Nonbreeding
- Year-round

SIZE & SHAPE Blue-gray Gnatcatchers are tiny, slim songbirds with long legs, a long tail, and a thin, straight bill.

COLOR PATTERN These blue-gray birds have pale gray underparts and a mostly black tail with white edges. The face is highlighted by white eyerings. In summer, males sport a black 'V' on their foreheads. Young birds tend to be brownish gray.

BEHAVIOR The energetic Blue-gray Gnatcatcher rarely slows down, fluttering after small insects among shrubs and trees with its tail cocked at a jaunty angle. Blue-gray Gnatcatchers often take food from spiderwebs and also abscond with strands of webbing for their tiny nests, which are shaped like tree knots.

HABITAT In the East, gnatcatchers breed in broadleaf forests and near forest edges. In the West, look for them in shorter woodlands and shrublands including pinyon-juniper and oak woodlands.

The tiny **Blue-gray Gnatcatcher** makes itself known in broadleaf forests by its soft but insistent calls and constant motion. It forages in dense outer foliage for insects and spiders, flicking its tail from side to side to scare up prey. Pairs use spiderweb and lichens to build small, neat nests, which sit on top of branches.

ADULT

ADULT

JUVENILE

ADULT

SIZE & SHAPE The Rock Wren is a medium-sized wren with a long tail and a long, thin bill. It is sparrow-sized.

COLOR PATTERN The Rock Wren is pale brown above and whitish below with a slightly buffy or peachy wash on the lower belly. The long tail is barred, and the back and wings are finely speckled. Note the pale eyebrow stripe. Juveniles look like adults, but are a little more ragged and have a cleaner white belly.

BEHAVIOR Rock Wrens glean prey from rocks or remove prey from spiderwebs. They have a habit of bobbing quickly up and down while standing. They also repeatedly hop up vertically from the ground to capture flying insects. The Rock Wren usually builds a pavement or walkway of small, flat stones or pebbles that leads to the nest cavity. The nest is usually located in a rock crevice out of sight, but the pavement may give away the nest's location.

HABITAT Rock Wrens inhabit arid or semiarid areas with exposed rock, anywhere from desert to alpine habitats.

RANGE MAP

■ Breeding
  Migration
  Nonbreeding
■ Year-round

A pale gray bird of rocky areas, the **Rock Wren** is found throughout arid western North America. The male Rock Wren is a truly remarkable singer and can have a large song repertoire of 100 or more song types, many of which seem to be learned from neighbors.

RANGE MAP

■ Year-round

SIZE & SHAPE The Canyon Wren is a distinctive, pot-bellied, sparrow-sized wren with a long, slender, slightly curved bill, a fairly long tail, and strong, short legs. The wings are short and rounded.

COLOR PATTERN Canyon Wrens are rusty brown birds with a neat white throat. The crown is a grayer brown than the body and speckled with white, while the tail is a brighter rusty brown than the back. The wings and tail are barred with black. Juveniles are similar, but their upperparts are more textured and less spotted, and their flanks lack barring. Adult and immature birds look otherwise similar.

BEHAVIOR Canyon Wrens cling to rock walls like nuthatches, scaling even vertical surfaces with ease. They move deliberately and deftly, looking into crevices that might hold prey, which they extract with quick jabs of the fine bill. Males sing from favored rocky song perches in spring and summer and sometimes in winter. Females sing on occasion.

HABITAT Look for Canyon Wrens on cliffs, rocky outcrops, and boulder piles, and in canyons.

iny bird with a big voice, the **Canyon Wren** sings a gorgeous series of sweet, cascading whistles that echo the rocky walls of its canyon habitat. They are incredibly agile birds that hunt for insects mostly among ks, scaling cliff faces and using their long, slender bills to probe into crevices with surgical precision.

ADULT

ADULT

ADULT / IMMATURE

ADULT

SIZE & SHAPE The House Wren is small and compact, with a flat head and fairly long, thin, curved bill. It has short wings and a longish tail that it keeps either cocked above the line of the body or slightly drooped. Juveniles and late-summer molting adult birds may have little or no tail.

COLOR PATTERN The House Wren is subdued brown overall with darker barring on the wings and tail. The pale eyebrow that is characteristic of so many wren species is much fainter or completely lacking in House Wrens.

BEHAVIOR Bubbly and energetic, House Wrens hop or flit quickly through tangles and low branches. They call attention to themselves year-round with harsh scolding chatter and, in spring and summer, frequent singing.

HABITAT House Wrens live in habitats featuring trees, shrubs, and tangles interspersed with clearings. They thrive around humans, often exploring the nooks and crannies in houses, garages, and play spaces.

RANGE MAP

- Breeding
- Migration
- Nonbreeding
- Year-round

A plain brown bird with an effervescent voice, the **House Wren** is a common backyard bird. Listen for its rush-and-jumble song in summer to find it zipping through foliage, snatching at insects. House Wrens wil' use nestboxes, but you may also find their twig-filled nests in old cans, boots, or boxes in your garage.

RANGE MAP

■ Year-round
- - Year-round (scarce)

SIZE & SHAPE The Carolina Wren is a small but chunky bird with a round body and long tail, often cocked upward. The head is large with little apparent neck, and the distinctive long, slender, and downcurved bill marks it as a wren.

COLOR PATTERN Both sexes are a bright reddish brown above and warm buffy orange below, with a long, white eyebrow stripe, dark bill, and white throat. Adult and immature birds look similar.

BEHAVIOR The Carolina Wren scoots up and down tree trunks in search of insects and fruit. It explores yards, garages, and woodpiles, sometimes nesting there. It often cocks its tail upward while foraging and holds it down when singing. This wren defends its territory with constant singing and will aggressively chase off intruders.

HABITAT Look for Carolina Wrens singing or calling from dense vegetation in wooded areas, especially in forest ravines and neighborhoods. They move low through tangled understory, and frequent backyard brush piles and areas with vines and bushes.

hough the **Carolina Wren** is a shy bird that can be hard to see, it delivers an amazing number of decibels its size. Follow its *teakettle-teakettle* and other piercing exclamations through backyard or forest, and you y be rewarded with glimpses of this bird's rich cinnamon plumage and long, upward-cocked tail.

ADULT · ADULT · ADULT · ADULT

SIZE & SHAPE Bewick's Wrens are medium-sized wrens with a slender body and a strikingly long tail often held upright. They have long, slender bills that are slightly downcurved.

COLOR PATTERN Bewick's Wrens are subdued brown-and-gray wrens with a long, white stripe over the eye. The back and wings are plain brown, underparts are grayish white, and the long tail is barred with black and tipped with white spots. Males, females, and immature birds look similar.

BEHAVIOR Bewick's Wrens cock their long tails up over their backs, often flicking their tails from side to side or fanning them as they skulk through tangles of branches and leaves searching for insects. During breeding season, males sing vigorously from prominent perches.

HABITAT Bewick's Wrens favor dry brushy areas, chaparral, scrub, thickets in open country, and open woodlands near rivers and streams. They are at home in gardens, residential areas, and parks in cities and suburbs.

RANGE MAP

■ Breeding
■ Nonbreeding
■ Year-round

Look for the hyperactive **Bewick's Wren** flicking its long tail as it hops between branches in much of weste North America. These master vocalists belt out a string of whistles, warbles, burrs, and trills to attract mate and defend their territory. Unfortunately, these birds have virtually disappeared from the East.

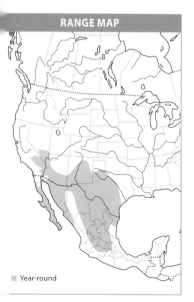

RANGE MAP

■ Year-round

SIZE & SHAPE The Cactus Wren is a large, chunky wren with a long, heavy bill, a long, rounded tail, and short, rounded wings. The Cactus Wren is the largest wren in the United States and is similar in size to a Spotted Towhee.

COLOR PATTERN Both sexes are speckled brown with red eyes and white eyebrows reaching from bill to nape. They have cinnamon sides and a white chest with dark speckles. The brown back has white streaks, and the tail is barred white and black. Adult and immature birds look similar.

BEHAVIOR The Cactus Wren seems to have no fear. It perches atop cactuses and other shrubs to announce its presence and forages out in the open. Unlike many other wrens, they fan their tail feathers, flashing white tail tips.

HABITAT Cactus Wrens live in deserts, arid foothills, coastal sage scrub, and urban areas throughout the deserts of the Southwest, especially in areas with thorny shrubs, cholla, and prickly pear.

ctus Wrens are true southwestern desert dwellers and can survive without needing to drink freestanding ter. They utter a scratchy noise and are always hopping on the ground, fanning their tails, scolding ighbors, or singing atop cacti. Their nests are the size and shape of footballs and used year-round.

BREEDING ADULT

NONBREEDING ADULT

ADULT

JUVENILE

SIZE & SHAPE Starlings are chunky and blackbird-sized, with short tails and long, slender bills. In flight, their wings are short and pointed. They are larger than sparrows but smaller than robins.

COLOR PATTERN At a distance, starlings look black. In summer, they are iridescent purplish green with yellow beaks, and in fresh winter plumage, they are brown and covered in brilliant white spots, that look like stars in a night sky (giving them their name). Juveniles are pale brown overall.

BEHAVIOR Boisterous starlings travel in large groups, often with blackbirds and grackles. They race across fields, beak down and probing the grass for food; or sit high on wires or trees. They make a bewildering variety of sounds, from thin whistles, to rattles, to imitations of birds, including Red-tailed Hawks, American Robins, and others.

HABITAT Starlings are common in towns, suburbs, farms, and countryside near human settlements. They feed on lawns, fields, sidewalks, and in parking lots. They perch and roost high on wires, trees, and buildings.

RANGE MAP

■ Year-round

All **European Starlings** in North America descended from 100 birds released in New York's Central Park in the early 1890s by a group who wanted America to have all the birds mentioned by Shakespeare. Today, more than 200 million starlings range from Alaska to Mexico and are largely considered pests.

ADULT / IMMATURE

ADULT / IMMATURE

JUVENILE

ADULT / IMMATURE

RANGE MAP

Breeding
Migration
Nonbreeding
Year-round

SIZE & SHAPE The Gray Catbird is a medium-sized, slender songbird with a long, round-tipped tail and a narrow, straight bill. Catbirds are fairly long-legged and have broad, rounded wings.

COLOR PATTERN Catbirds give the impression of being entirely slate gray. Looking closer, you may see the small black cap, blackish tail, and rich rufous-brown patch under the tail. Adult and immature birds look alike.

BEHAVIOR Catbirds are secretive but energetic, hopping and fluttering from branch to branch through tangles of vegetation. Singing males sit atop shrubs and small trees. Catbirds are reluctant to fly across open areas, preferring quick, low flights over vegetation.

HABITAT Look for Gray Catbirds in dense tangles of shrubs, small trees, and vines, along forest edges, streamside thickets, old fields, and fence rows. They are often found in backyards that have shrubs or thickets.

rt learning bird calls by listening in thickets and vine tangles for the **Gray Catbird**, whose catty *mew* is forgettable. They are relatives of mockingbirds and thrashers, and they share that group's vocal abilities, ying the sounds of other species and stringing them together to make their own song.

ADULT

ADULT

JUVENILE

ADULT

SIZE & SHAPE The Curve-billed Thrasher is a long-bodied, slim bird about the size of a robin with a long, curved bill, long tail, and thick legs.

COLOR PATTERN Curve-billed Thrashers are grayish brown above and paler off-white below mottled with indistinct gray-brown speckling, and pale peach undertail coverts. The eyes are orangey yellow. Juveniles have a shorter bill.

BEHAVIOR Males often perch prominently on a shrub or cactus, surveying their territory and, during the nesting season, singing during the early morning. These birds are agile and active hunters, incessantly overturning ground vegetation in search of insects, spiders, and other prey. When disturbed, they fly short distances or run through thorny habitat.

HABITAT Curve-billed Thrashers dwell in deserts (especially with cholla cactus), brushlands, thorn scrub, arid canyons, pinyon-oak scrub. They are also common in towns and cities.

RANGE MAP

■ Year-round

Curve-billed Thrashers hunt in deserts, canyons, and brushlands, using their long bill to keep long-legged insect prey at a safe distance. The bill also aids foraging and nesting among spiny plants. Its whistled *whit-wheet* call is often the first vocalization that bird watchers in deserts of the American Southwest learn.

ADULT

ADULT

JUVENILE

ADULT

RANGE MAP

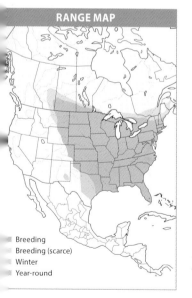

Breeding
Breeding (scarce)
Winter
Year-round

SIZE & SHAPE Brown Thrashers are fairly large, slender songbirds with long proportions. They have long sturdy legs, and a long and slightly downcurved bill. The long tail is often cocked upward.

COLOR PATTERN Brown Thrashers are foxy brown birds with heavy, dark streaking on their whitish underparts. The face is grayish brown, and the wings show two black-and-white wingbars. They have bright yellow eyes. Juveniles are paler brown with a scalloped-looking back and a paler head.

BEHAVIOR Brown Thrashers skulk in shrubby tangles or below dense cover, but are more noticeable when they sing loud, complex songs from shrubs and treetops. They also make a distinctive, harsh *tsuck* note.

HABITAT Scrubby fields, dense regenerating woods, and forest edges are the primary habitats of Brown Thrashers. They rarely venture far from thick undergrowth into which they can easily retreat.

an be tricky to glimpse a **Brown Thrasher** in tangled shrubbery, but once you do you may wonder how h a boldly patterned, gangly bird could stay so hidden. The only thrasher species east of Texas, Brown ashers are exuberant singers, with one of the largest repertoires of any North American songbird.

ADULT

ADULT

JUVENILE

ADULT

SIZE & SHAPE This medium-sized songbird is more slender than a robin and has a longer tail. Mockingbirds have small heads, a long, thin bill with a hint of a downward curve, and long legs. Their wings are short, rounded, and broad, making the tail seem particularly long in flight.

COLOR PATTERN Mockingbirds are gray overall, paler on the breast and belly, with two white wingbars on each wing. A white patch in each wing is often visible on perched birds, and in flight these become large white flashes. The white outer tail feathers are also flashy in flight. Juveniles have spotted breasts.

BEHAVIOR The Northern Mockingbird enjoys making its presence known. It sits conspicuously on fences or wires, or runs and hops along the ground. Found alone or in pairs, mockingbirds aggressively chase off intruders.

HABITAT Look for Northern Mockingbirds in towns, suburbs, backyards, parks, forest edges, and open land at low elevations.

RANGE MAP

- Breeding
- Nonbreeding (scarce)
- Year-round

If you've been hearing an endless string of 10 or 15 different birds singing outside your house, you migh have a **Northern Mockingbird** in your yard. These slender-bodied gray birds sing almost endlessly, ever sometimes at night, and flagrantly harass birds that intrude on their territories.

ADULT MALE

ADULT MALE

JUVENILE

ADULT FEMALE

RANGE MAP

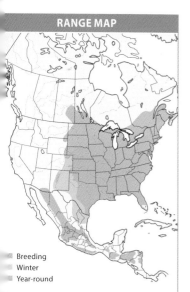

Breeding
Winter
Year-round

SIZE & SHAPE The Eastern Bluebird is a small thrush with a big, rounded head, large eye, plump body, and alert posture. The wings are long, but the tail and legs are fairly short. The bill is short and straight.

COLOR PATTERN Male Eastern Bluebirds are vivid blue above and rusty or brick red below. Blue in birds always depends on the light, and males often look plain gray brown from a distance. Females are grayish above with bluish wings and tail, and a subdued orange-brown breast. Juveniles have spotting on their back and chest with variable amounts of blue in the wings and tail.

BEHAVIOR Eastern Bluebirds perch erect on wires, posts, and low branches in open country, scanning the ground for prey. They drop to the ground onto insects to feed, or, in fall and winter, perch in trees to gulp down berries.

HABITAT Eastern Bluebirds live in open country with scattered trees and sparse ground cover, such as frequently burned pine savannas, forest openings, pastures, agricultural fields, parks, spacious backyards, and golf courses.

summer, look for **Eastern Bluebirds** on telephone wires or perched on a nest box, calling out in a short, vering voice or abruptly dropping to the ground after an insect. Marvelous birds to see in binoculars, e Eastern Bluebirds are brilliant blue on the back and head, and warm red brown on the breast.

ADULT MALE

ADULT FEMALE

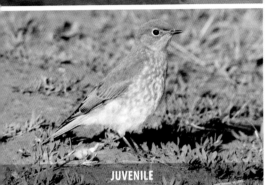

JUVENILE

ADULT FEMALE

SIZE & SHAPE Mountain Bluebirds are fairly small thrushes with round heads and straight, thin bills. Compared with other bluebirds, they are lanky and long-winged, with a long tail.

COLOR PATTERN Male Mountain Bluebirds are sky blue, a bit darker on wings and tail and paler below, with white under the tail. Females are mostly gray brown with tinges of pale blue in the wings and tail. They occasionally show a suffusion of orange brown on the chest. Mountain Bluebirds' bills are black. Juveniles have fewer spots than the young of other bluebirds and lack spotting on the back.

BEHAVIOR Unlike other bluebirds, they often hover while foraging and pounce on insect prey from elevated perches. In winter, they occur in large flocks, wandering the landscape and feasting on berries.

HABITAT Mountain Bluebirds are common in the West's wide open spaces, particularly at middle and higher elevations.

RANGE MAP

■ Breeding
■ Nonbreeding
■ Year-round

Male **Mountain Bluebirds** lend a bit of cerulean sparkle to open habitats across much of western North America. These cavity nesters flit between perches in mountain meadows, in burned or cut-over areas, o where prairie meets forest—especially in places where people have provided nest boxes.

ADULT

ADULT

IMMATURE

IMMATURE

RANGE MAP

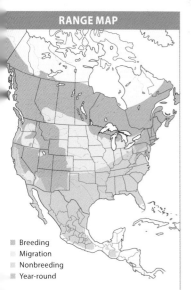

- Breeding
- Migration
- Nonbreeding
- Year-round

SIZE & SHAPE Hermit Thrushes have a chunky shape similar to an American Robin, but they are smaller. They stand upright, often with the slender, straight bill slightly raised. Like other thrushes, the head is round and the tail fairly long.

COLOR PATTERN The Hermit Thrush is soft brown on the head and back, with a distinctly warm, reddish tail. The underparts are pale with distinct spots on the throat and smudged spots on the breast. Look closely for a thin, pale eyering. Immature birds have pale wingbars that are lacking in adults.

BEHAVIOR Hermit Thrushes hop and scrape in leaf litter while foraging. They perch low to the ground and often wander into open areas such as forest clearings. They have a habit of raising the tail and then lowering it slowly.

HABITAT Hermit Thrushes breed in open areas inside boreal forests, broadleaf woods, and mountain forests. In winter, they often occupy lower elevation forests with dense understory and berry bushes.

unassuming bird with a lovely, melancholy song, the **Hermit Thrush** lurks in the understories of far rthern forests in summer and is a frequent winter companion across much of the U.S. and Mexico. It ages on the forest floor by rummaging through leaf litter or seizing insects with its bill.

SIZE & SHAPE The Wood Thrush's plump body, medium-length tail, straight bill, big head, and upright posture give it the profile of a scaled-down American Robin.

COLOR PATTERN Wood Thrushes are warm reddish brown above and white, with bold black spots on their underparts. Juveniles show a somewhat muted version of the same pattern, plus a faint wingbar. All have a bold, white eyering.

BEHAVIOR The reclusive Wood Thrush hops through leaf litter on the forest floor, probing for insects, bobbing upright between spurts of digging and leaf-turning. The male's clear, flutelike song echoes through forest in spring and early summer at dawn and dusk. Both sexes make distinctive, machine-gun-like alarm notes.

HABITAT The Wood Thrush breeds in broadleaf and mixed forests in the eastern U.S., where there are large trees, shade, and abundant leaf litter for foraging. It winters in lowland tropical forests in Mexico and Central America.

RANGE MAP

Breeding
Migration
Nonbreeding

The **Wood Thrush's** loud, flute-clear *ee-oh-lay* song rings through the broadleaf forests of the eastern U.S. and southeastern Canada in summer. This reclusive bird stays camouflaged as it scrabbles for leaf-litter invertebrates deep in the forest, though it pops upright frequently to peer about, revealing a boldly spotted white breast

ADULT MALE (SPRING / SUMMER)

ADULT FEMALE / IMMATURE MALE (FALL / WINTER)

JUVENILE

ADULT FEMALE (SPRING / SUMMER)

RANGE MAP

Breeding
Year-round
Winter

SIZE & SHAPE American Robins are among the largest songbirds with a round body, long legs, and fairly long tail. Robins are among the largest of the North American thrushes and are a good reference point for comparing the size and shape of other birds, too.

COLOR PATTERN American Robins are gray-brown birds with warm orange underparts and dark heads. Compared with males, females sometimes have paler heads that contrast less with the gray back. In fall and winter, birds are covered with pale feather edges. Juveniles are spotted.

BEHAVIOR American Robins are industrious birds that bound across lawns or stand erect, beak tilted upward, to survey their environs. When alighting, they habitually flick their tails downward several times. In fall and winter, they form large flocks and gather in trees to roost or eat berries.

HABITAT You'll find American Robins on lawns, fields, and in city parks, as well as more wild places like forests and mountains up to near treeline, recently burned forests, and tundra.

Quintessential early birds, **American Robins** are common across temperate North America, where they are often seen tugging earthworms from lawns. Robins are popular for their cheery song, and appearance at the end of winter. They are also at home in wild areas, like mountain forests and the Alaskan wilderness.

ADULT

ADULT

JUVENILE

IMMATURE (FIRST YEAR)

SIZE & SHAPE The Cedar Waxwing is a medium-sized, sleek bird with a large head, short neck, and short, wide bill. Its crest often lies flat, and its wings are broad and pointed, like a starling's. The tail is fairly short and square-tipped.

COLOR PATTERN Cedar Waxwings have a pale brown head and chest fading to gray wings with red, waxy tips that are not always easy to see. The belly is pale yellow, and the gray tail has a bright yellow tip, which may be orange due to diet. The face has a narrow black mask outlined in white. Immature birds lack the red tips on their wings. Juveniles are streaky below.

BEHAVIOR These social birds live in flocks when not nesting. They sit in fruiting trees, swallowing berries whole or plucking them with a brief, fluttering hover. They also course over water for insects, flying like tubby, slightly clumsy swallows.

HABITAT Cedar Waxwings live in broadleaf or coniferous forests, old fields, and sagebrush, especially near water. They're increasingly common in towns and suburbs, where ornamental fruit trees flourish.

RANGE MAP

■ Breeding
■ Nonbreeding
■ Year-round

In fall, **Cedar Waxwings** gather by the hundreds to eat berries, filling the air with their high, thin whistles. summer, you'll find them flitting about over rivers in pursuit of flying insects, where they show off dazzling aeronautics for a forest bird. To attract them to your yard, plant native trees and shrubs that bear small frui

ADULT MALE

ADULT MALE

ADULT FEMALE

JUVENILE

RANGE MAP

Nonbreeding
Year-round

SIZE & SHAPE The Phainopepla is a slender, long-tailed songbird with a distinct crest.

COLOR PATTERN Adult male Phainopeplas are glossy black with red eyes and large white patches in the wings (visible in flight). Adult females are mousy grayish brown with red eyes; immatures are similar but with brownish eyes.

BEHAVIOR Phainopeplas feed on mistletoe in winter, and on other berries and insects in spring through fall. Most of the year they are territorial, often perching for long periods to watch for intruders as they guard berries, nests, and territorial boundaries. Sometimes they nest in small colonies, and form large flocks after breeding. Most winter at lower elevations in deserts and move in warmer months to higher elevations.

HABITAT Phainopeplas are found mostly in desert washes with abundant mistletoe, orchards, chaparral, Joshua tree woodlands, and oak and sycamore woodlands.

singular silky-flycatcher of the Southwest, the **Phainopepla** is a brilliant sight in flight. These silky black rds occur in desert washes, where they eat mainly mistletoe berries, and in oak and sycamore woodlands California and Arizona. They often perch high in shrubs and catch insects on the wing.

BREEDING MALE

NONBREEDING MALE

JUVENILE

ADULT FEMALE

SIZE & SHAPE Introduced from Europe, House Sparrows aren't related to North American sparrows. They're chunkier and fuller in the chest, with a larger, rounded head, shorter tail, and stouter bill than most American sparrows.

COLOR PATTERN Males have a gray forehead, white cheeks, a black bib, and a rufous neck, although urban birds can be dull and grubby. Females are a buffy brown with dingy underparts. The backs of both are striped with buff, black, and brown.

BEHAVIOR House Sparrows flutter from eaves or hidden nests and hang around parking lots and outdoor cafés, waiting for crumbs. Their noisy, sociable *cheep cheep* calls are familiar wherever they are found.

HABITAT Look for House Sparrows on city streets, taking handouts in parks and zoos, or cheeping from a perch on trees in your yard. They are absent from undisturbed forests and grasslands, but common around farmsteads.

RANGE MAP

■ Year-round
  Year-round (scarce)

The **House Sparrow** was introduced into Brooklyn, New York, in 1851. By 1900, it had spread to the Rocky Mountains. Today they are some of our most common birds. They aggressively defend their nest holes and sometimes evict native birds from them. These include Eastern Bluebirds, Purple Martins, and Tree Swallows.

ADULT MALE

ADULT MALE

ADULT MALE (YELLOW VARIANT)

ADULT FEMALE

RANGE MAP

Year-round

SIZE & SHAPE House Finches are small with fairly large bills and somewhat long, flat heads. Wings are short, making the tail seem long. Tails have a relatively shallow notch when compared to other finches.

COLOR PATTERN Adult males are rosy red around the face and upper breast, with a streaky brown back, belly, and tail. In flight, the red rump is conspicuous. Adult females aren't red; they are plain grayish brown with thick, blurry streaks. Some adult males are decidedly more yellow than red. This is due to diet and can be temporary.

BEHAVIOR House Finches are gregarious birds that collect at feeders or perch high in nearby trees. They move fairly slowly and sit still as they crush seeds with rapid bites. Their flight is bouncy, like that of many finches.

HABITAT House Finches frequent city parks, backyards, urban centers, farms, and forest edges across the continent. In the West, you'll also find them in their native habitats of deserts, grassland, chaparral, and open woods.

e **House Finch** is a recent introduction from western into eastern North America (and Hawaii), but it has ceived a warmer reception than other arrivals like the European Starling and House Sparrow. That's partly e to the cheerful, long, twittering song, which can now be heard across much of the continent.

ADULT MALE (GREEN MORPH)

ADULT

ADULT / IMMATURE

ADULT / IMMATURE

SIZE & SHAPE Pine Siskins are very small songbirds with sharp, pointed bills and short, notched tails. Their uniquely shaped bill is more slender than that of most finches. In flight, look for their forked tails and pointed wingtips.

COLOR PATTERN Pine Siskins are brown and very streaky birds with subtle yellow edgings on wings and tails. Flashes of yellow can erupt as they take flight, flutter at branch tips, or display during mating. The occasional adult male is washed with green, but this is rare. Adults and immatures look mostly similar.

BEHAVIOR Pine Siskins often visit feeders in winter or cling to branch tips of pines and other conifers, sometimes hanging upside down to pick at seeds. They forage in tight flocks and twitter incessantly to each other, even in flight.

HABITAT Pine Siskins prefer coniferous or mixed coniferous-broadleaf forests with open canopies, but they'll forage in weedy fields, scrubby thickets, or yards and gardens. They flock at feeders in woodlands and suburbs.

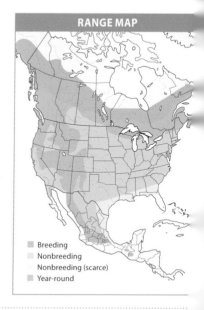

RANGE MAP

■ Breeding
  Nonbreeding
  Nonbreeding (scarce)
■ Year-round

Flocks of tiny **Pine Siskins** may monopolize your thistle feeder one winter and be absent the next. This nomadic finch ranges widely and erratically across the continent each winter in response to seed crops. These brown-streaked acrobats flash yellow wing markings as they flutter while feeding or explode into flight.

ADULT MALE (BLACK-BACKED)

ADULT MALE (GREEN-BACKED)

ADULT FEMALE / IMMATURE

ADULT FEMALE / IMMATURE

RANGE MAP

- Breeding
- Winter
- Year-round

SIZE & SHAPE Lesser Goldfinches are tiny, stub-billed songbirds with long, pointed wings, and short, notched tails.

COLOR PATTERN Males are bright yellow below with a glossy black cap and white patches in the wings. They have a black tail with large, white corners, and their backs range from dull green to black. Black-backed males are most prevalent in Texas. Green-backed adult males are green with varying amounts of black mixed in. Females and immatures have olive backs, dull yellow underparts, and black wings marked by two whitish wingbars.

BEHAVIOR Lesser Goldfinches feed in busy flocks of up to several hundred at a time. They cling to dried flower heads or hang upside down to reach seeds. On the wing, they have the same dipping, bouncy flight as the American Goldfinch.

HABITAT Lesser Goldfinches feed in weedy fields, budding treetops, and in brush of open areas and edges. Depending on food availability, they may concentrate in mountain canyons and desert oases, but are also fairly common in suburbs.

bbering clouds of yellow, green, and black, **Lesser Goldfinches** gather in scrubby oak, cottonwood, d willow habitats of the western U.S. They also visit backyards for seeds and water. Listen closely to their heezy songs, which often include snippets from the songs of other birds.

BREEDING MALE

NONBREEDING MALE

BREEDING FEMALE

NONBREEDING FEMALE / IMMATURE

SIZE & SHAPE The American Goldfinch is a small finch with a short, conical bill and small head, long wings, and short, notched tail.

COLOR PATTERN Adult males in spring and early summer are bright yellow with a black forehead, black wings with white markings, and white patches both above and beneath the tail. Adult females in spring and summer are duller yellow beneath, olive above. Nonbreeding winter birds are drab, unstreaked brown, with blackish wings and two pale wingbars. Immature birds have buffy wingbars on dark wings.

BEHAVIOR Active and acrobatic little finches that cling to weeds and seed socks, American Goldfinches sometimes mill about in large numbers at feeders or on the ground beneath them. They fly with a bouncy, undulating pattern and often call in flight, drawing attention to themselves.

HABITAT Their main natural habitats are weedy fields and floodplains, where plants such as thistles and asters are common. They're also found in cultivated areas, roadsides, orchards, and backyards. They show up at feeders any time of year, but most abundantly during winter.

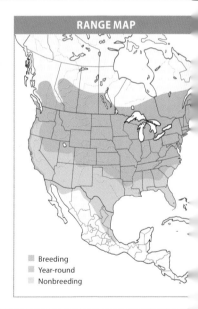
RANGE MAP

Breeding
Year-round
Nonbreeding

The **American Goldfinch** is our only finch that molts its body feathers twice a year, once in late winter and again, in late summer. The brightening yellow of male goldfinches is a welcome mark of approaching spring. Among the strictest vegans in the bird world, they select an entirely plant-based diet.

BREEDING MALE

BREEDING MALE

NONBREEDING MALE / IMMATURE MALE

ADULT FEMALE / IMMATURE

RANGE MAP

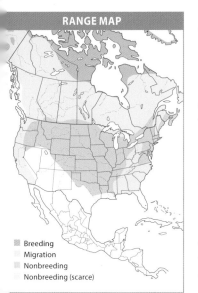

Breeding
Migration
Nonbreeding
Nonbreeding (scarce)

SIZE & SHAPE The Lapland Longspur is a sparrow-sized bird with a short, thick, pointed bill. It is quite compact, with a large head and a relatively short tail. The wings are relatively long.

COLOR PATTERN Breeding males have a bold black face bordered by a white line and a rufous patch on the back of the neck. Females are similar but lack the black face and look similar to a nonbreeding male. In winter, both sexes retain an echo of the face pattern but are overall pale brown and streaked. In all plumages, the tail is dark with white outer edges.

BEHAVIOR Lapland Longspurs walk or run across open landscapes, taking cover by crouching motionless on the ground, depending on camouflage to conceal them. Flushed birds often fly quite high and settle far from their original position.

HABITAT The Lapland Longspur breeds in Arctic tundra in wet meadows, grassy tussocks, and scrub. In migration and winter, look for them further south in plowed fields, stubble, and open grasslands.

The **Lapland Longspur** breeds in the High Arctic with continual daylight during the summer, and a breeding male may sing at any hour of the day. Despite the lack of a real dawn, the male tends to sing most in the early morning. Longspur refers to the elongated claw of the hind toe.

ADULT

ADULT

JUVENILE

ADULT

SIZE & SHAPE The Grasshopper Sparrow is small with a distinctive compact shape. The head is large and flat-crowned, with a conspicuous bill, and the tail is very short. It is among the smallest birds in its habitat.

COLOR PATTERN The Grasshopper Sparrow is a brown and tan bird with light streaking. The belly is white, but the entire breast is buffy. The back is mottled tan, black, and chestnut and isn't as streaky as other sparrows. The face is relatively plain with a conspicuous white eyering. They often show a yellow spot between the eye and bill (the lore) and on the bend of the wing. Juveniles have a band of streaks across the breast.

BEHAVIOR Grasshopper Sparrows stay close to the ground, preferring to run or walk rather than fly. During the breeding season, males sing from exposed perches near the tops of grass stalks or along barbed wire fences.

HABITAT This species breeds in open grasslands, prairies, hayfields, and pastures, typically with some bare ground. They usually avoid breeding in grasslands with shrub cover, but may inhabit them on migration and in winter.

RANGE MAP

- ▨ Breeding
- ▨ Breeding (scarce)
- ▨ Nonbreeding
- Nonbreeding (scarce)
- ▨ Year-round

When not singing a quiet, insectlike song from atop a stalk in a weedy pasture, the **Grasshopper Sparrow** disappears into grasses, running along the ground rather than flying. Appropriately, grasshoppers are the primary prey. Adults prepare them for chicks by vigorously shaking the legs off the insects.

ADULT

ADULT

JUVENILE

ADULT

RANGE MAP

Breeding
Year-round

SIZE & SHAPE The Black-throated Sparrow is a medium-sized sparrow with a large, round head, conical bill (perfect for eating seeds), and a medium-length tail.

COLOR PATTERN Black-throated Sparrows have a neat gray face bordered by two white stripes and a black triangular throat patch. The upperparts are grayish brown, and the underparts are a mix of cream and white. The tail is dark with white spots on the corners. Juveniles look like adults but lack the black throat patch and have faint streaks above and below.

BEHAVIOR Black-throated Sparrows hop along the ground, pecking for insects and seeds. They make short flights, low to the ground, across desert scrub areas. They often perch in trees and shrubs, giving quiet calls.

HABITAT These sparrows frequent semiopen areas with shrubs and small trees. They are common in canyons, desert washes, and desert scrub. In some parts of their range, they occur as high as 7,000 feet elevation in pinyon-juniper forests.

is resident of open, shrubby deserts is one of the sharpest looking of all sparrows. **Black-throated arrows** have neat gray faces with two bold white stripes and a black triangular patch on the throat. en intently for little tinkling calls as these quiet birds forage on the ground for seeds and insects.

ADULT

ADULT

IMMATURE

ADULT

SIZE & SHAPE The Lark Sparrow is large and long-tailed (for a sparrow). When perched, it often looks long-bodied with a thin neck and a round head.

COLOR PATTERN Adults have a very striking head pattern with a chestnut crown and cheek patch, a pale stripe over the eye, and a strong black malar or mustache stripe. Note the black spot in the center of the white breast. Immature Lark Sparrows have similar face patterns but lack the chestnut coloration in the crown and cheek.

BEHAVIOR Lark Sparrows usually feed on the ground for seeds and insects and will fly into trees and shrubs when disturbed. During the breeding season, males sing from elevated perches.

HABITAT Lark Sparrows breed in open grassy habitats like orchards, fallow fields, woodlands, mesquite grasslands, savanna, and sagebrush steppe. In migration and winter, look for them in pine-oak forest, thorn scrub, and agricultural areas.

RANGE MAP

- Breeding
- Breeding (scarce)
- Migration
- Nonbreeding
- Irruptive
- Year-round

This large, brown sparrow's harlequin facial pattern and white tail spots make it a standout among sparrow Male **Lark Sparrows** sing a melodious jumble of churrs, buzzes, and trills. Their unusual courtship involves hopping and crouching display, unlike other sparrows.

BREEDING MALE

ADULT MALE (EARLY SPRING)

ADULT FEMALE / IMMATURE

ADULT FEMALE / IMMATURE

RANGE MAP

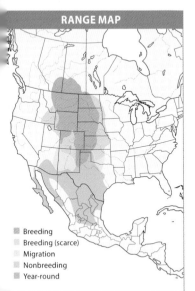

- Breeding
- Breeding (scarce)
- Migration
- Nonbreeding
- Year-round

SIZE & SHAPE The Lark Bunting is heavyset with a very large, conical bill, and a compact, robust body; larger than a House Sparrow's. The bill and overall shape are reminiscent of a grosbeak or bunting.

COLOR PATTERN Breeding males are an unmistakable black with white wing patches. Nonbreeding males, as well as females and immatures, are brownish above, pale with brown streaking below, with extensive white in the upperwing coverts and small white tips to the tail feathers. The bill is a distinctive pale blue gray.

BEHAVIOR Lark Buntings forage on or near open ground and may employ a gallop when pursuing fast insects, with one foot coming down just before the next. On migration and in winter, they form flocks of up to several hundred birds.

HABITAT Lark Buntings breed in open grasslands, usually with some element of sagebrush, but they may also forage and nest in hayfields and other agricultural fields. Wintering flocks are found in many similar habitats.

ark Buntings breed in beautiful, windswept habitats such as the grasslands and shrub-steppe of the eat Plains, where they prefer large expanses of native grasslands with sagebrush. Watch and listen for eeding males as they deliver their flight song, rising up and then gliding down to earth as they sing.

BREEDING ADULT

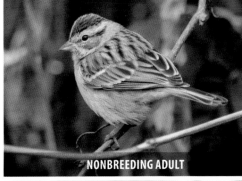
NONBREEDING ADULT

JUVENILE

NONBREEDING ADULT

SIZE & SHAPE The Chipping Sparrow is a tiny, slender, fairly long-tailed sparrow with a bill that is a bit small compared to those of some other sparrows.

COLOR PATTERN Summer Chipping Sparrows look clean and crisp, with frosty underparts, pale faces, a black line through the eyes, and a bright rusty crown to top them off. In winter, Chipping Sparrows are a subdued buff brown with darkly streaked upperparts. The black line through the eye is still visible, and the cap is a warm but more subdued reddish brown. Juveniles have streaked underparts and a streaked brown crown.

BEHAVIOR Chipping Sparrows feed on the ground, take cover in shrubs, and sing from the tops of small trees. You'll often see loose groups of them flitting up from open ground. When singing, they cling to high outer limbs.

HABITAT Look for Chipping Sparrows in open woodlands and forests with grassy clearings across North America, all the way up to the highest elevations. You'll also see them in parks, along roadsides, and in your backyard.

RANGE MAP

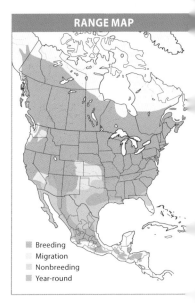

- Breeding
- Migration
- Nonbreeding
- Year-round

A crisp, pretty sparrow whose bright rufous cap provides a splash of color and makes adults fairly easy to identify. **Chipping Sparrows** are common across much of North America wherever trees are interspersed with grassy openings. Their loud, trilling songs are one of the most common sounds of spring.

ADULT

ADULT

JUVENILE

ADULT

RANGE MAP

Breeding
Nonbreeding
Year-round

SIZE & SHAPE Field Sparrows are small, slender sparrows with relatively short, conical bills, rounded heads, and somewhat long tails.

COLOR PATTERN Field Sparrows have a gray face with a distinct white eyering, pink conical bill, and rusty crown and eyeline. Underparts are pale gray with buff-orange highlights. The back is brown with black streaks, and the rump and tail are gray. Some birds, especially in the western portion of the range, lack rusty tones. Juveniles are streaky.

BEHAVIOR Field Sparrows would be easily overlooked but for the sweet accelerating song of territorial males. Individuals and small flocks quietly feed near the ground, flushing into shrubby cover when disturbed.

HABITAT Field Sparrows are so-called "old-field" specialists; look for them in areas of tall grass and brush that are growing up into small trees and shrubs, especially near thorny shrubs such as roses and briars.

e clear, bouncing-ball trill of the **Field Sparrow** is a familiar summer sound in brushy fields and roadsides the East and Midwest. Though still common, Field Sparrows have declined sharply in the last half-century, rtly because of the expansion of suburbs, where Field Sparrows will not nest.

BREEDING ADULT

BREEDING ADULT

JUVENILE

NONBREEDING ADULT

SIZE & SHAPE The Brewer's Sparrow is typical of the *Spizella* group of sparrows: dainty and slim, with a long, notched tail, short, rounded wings, and a small, sharply conical bill. Though its size varies, it is on average North America's smallest sparrow.

COLOR PATTERN Brewer's Sparrows are dusky gray brown, with grayish underparts and a thin white eyering. The back and nape are streaked. A faint gray stripe over the eye contrasts with a darker eyeline. The throat is grayish white. Juveniles are streaked below.

BEHAVIOR In spring and early summer, breeding males sing long, trilled songs from atop sagebrush. They forage in dense shrubs to glean insects and tend to stay out of open areas. In fall and winter, they often convene in large flocks with other *Spizella* sparrows.

HABITAT These birds live in the arid sagebrush steppe of the interior West—the region's most abundant bird. In some northwestern mountains, the "Timberline Sparrow" form lives in subalpine trees and dwarf shrubs.

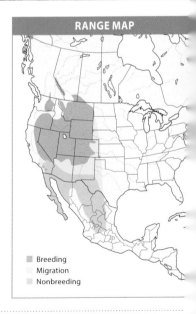

RANGE MAP

■ Breeding
■ Migration
■ Nonbreeding

Brewer's Sparrows are at first glance so subtly marked that they've been called the "bird without a field mark." These streaky, gray-brown sparrows are notable for their reliance on sagebrush breeding habitat, and their plumage is elegantly tuned to their muted, gray-green home.

ADULT (RED) ADULT (RED)

ADULT (RED) ADULT (RED)

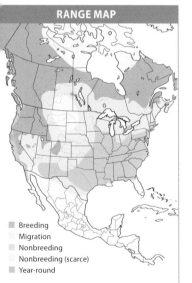

RANGE MAP

Breeding
Migration
Nonbreeding
Nonbreeding (scarce)
Year-round

SIZE & SHAPE Fox Sparrows are large, round-bodied sparrows with stout bills and medium-length tails.

COLOR PATTERN Fox Sparrows vary greatly across their range. "Red" Fox Sparrows, widely distributed across the boreal forest of northern North America, are rusty above with some pale gray on the head and rufous splotches on the underparts.

BEHAVIOR Fox Sparrows spend a lot of time on the ground, using their sturdy legs to kick away leaf litter in search of insects and seeds. They rarely venture far from cover, and often associate with other sparrows. In spring and summer, listen for their sweet, whistled song from scrub or forest; also, pay attention for a sharp *smack* call.

HABITAT Fox Sparrows breed in coniferous forest and dense mountain scrub. They spend winters in scrubby habitat and forest, when they are most likely to be seen kicking around under backyard bird feeders.

pically seen sending up a spray of leaf litter as they kick around in search of food, **Fox Sparrows** are dark, lotchy sparrows of dense thickets. Named for the rich red hues that many Fox Sparrows wear, this species nevertheless one of our most variable birds; they range from foxy red to gray to dark brown.

ADULT MALE (SLATE-COLORED)

ADULT MALE (PINK-SIDED)

ADULT MALE (GRAY-HEADED)

ADULT MALE (OREGON)

SIZE & SHAPE The Dark-eyed Junco has a rounded head, short, stout bill, and a fairly long tail.

COLOR PATTERN All juncos have pale bills and white outer tail feathers that they flash in flight. The male "Slate-colored" form is mostly gray with a white belly. "Pink-sided" birds have a pale gray head, a black mask, brown back, and pinkish brown sides. "Gray-headed" birds are gray with a dark face and a bright reddish brown back. The "Oregon" form has a black or brown hood (male and female, respectively), rusty or brown back, rusty to buffy sides, and a white belly. Female and immature birds are duller and browner in all forms. Juveniles are streaky.

BEHAVIOR Dark-eyed Juncos hop around the bases of trees and shrubs in forests or venture onto lawns looking for seeds. They give high *chip* notes while foraging or as they take short, low flights through cover.

HABITAT Dark-eyed Juncos breed in coniferous or broadleaf-coniferous forests across the United States. During winter, you'll find them in open woodlands, fields, parks, roadsides, and backyards.

RANGE MAP

- Breeding
- Nonbreeding
- Year-round

Dark-eyed Juncos are neat, even flashy little sparrows that flit about forest floors of the western mountain and Canada, then flood the rest of temperate North America for winter. They're easy to recognize by their crisp (though extremely variable) markings and the bright white tail feathers they habitually flash in flight.

ADULT (DARK-LORED)

IMMATURE (DARK-LORED)

ADULT (GAMBEL'S)

IMMATURE (GAMBEL'S)

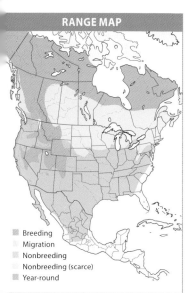

RANGE MAP

- Breeding
- Migration
- Nonbreeding
- Nonbreeding (scarce)
- Year-round

SIZE & SHAPE The White-crowned Sparrow is a large sparrow with a small bill and a long tail. The head can look either distinctly peaked or smooth and flat, depending on the bird's posture and activity.

COLOR PATTERN White-crowned Sparrows are gray-and-brown birds with large, bold, black-and-white stripes on the head. Dark-lored forms have pink bills and black between the bill and the eye. The Gambel's form has an orange bill and is pale between the bill and the eye. Young birds have rusty brown stripes on a gray head. Juveniles are streaky.

BEHAVIOR White-crowned Sparrows stay low near brushy habitat, hopping on the ground or on branches, usually below waist height. They're also found on open ground but will quickly retreat to nearby shrubs or trees to hide.

HABITAT White-crowned Sparrows live where safe tangles of brush mix with open or grassy ground for foraging. In much of the United States, they're most common in winter; they're found year-round in parts of the West.

White-crowned Sparrows appear in droves each winter over much of North America, gracing gardens and ails. Flocks scurry through brushy borders, overgrown fields, and backyards. As spring approaches, they art singing their sweet but buzzy song before and during migration.

BREEDING ADULT

NONBREEDING ADULT

IMMATURE (FIRST WINTER)

NONBREEDING ADULT

SIZE & SHAPE The Harris's Sparrow is a medium-sized songbird and very large for a sparrow. It has a rounded head and a moderately long tail.

COLOR PATTERN Harris's Sparrows are streaky brown and black overall with a black bib, face, and crown. A gray cheek and nape changes to brown in fall and winter, and obscures some of the hood. Immatures have very little black on the face or crown. The pinkish bill is unique among similar sparrows.

BEHAVIOR Harris's Sparrows feed on the ground, picking up seeds and occasionally insects. They often scratch in litter with both feet to reveal food. They also visit feeding stations, concentrating on the ground beneath feeders near cover.

HABITAT These sparrows breed at the edge of boreal forest and tundra. They winter along hedgerows, shelterbelts, agricultural fields, weed patches, and pastures, and visit feeders near brush piles or other low hiding places.

RANGE MAP

■ Breeding
■ Winter
■ Migration

It's not often that a sparrow takes center stage, but the **Harris's Sparrow** is a showstopper with a handsom black bib and pink bill. It is among North America's largest sparrows and the only songbird that breeds in Canada and nowhere else in the world. Unfortunately, its restricted range makes it vulnerable to habitat lo

ADULT (WHITE-STRIPED)

ADULT (WHITE-STRIPED)

ADULT (TAN-STRIPED)

ADULT (TAN-STRIPED)

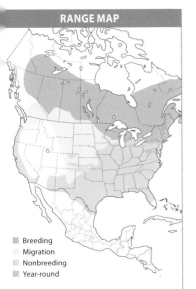

RANGE MAP

■ Breeding
■ Migration
■ Nonbreeding
■ Year-round

SIZE & SHAPE The White-throated Sparrow is a large, full-bodied sparrow with a fairly prominent bill, rounded head, long legs, and long, narrow tail.

COLOR PATTERN White-throated Sparrows are brown above and gray below. The "white-striped" form has a black-and-white-striped crown, bright white throat, and yellow between the eye and the gray bill. A second "tan-striped" form has a buff-on-brown face. The two forms persist because they almost always mate with a bird of the opposite morph.

BEHAVIOR White-throated Sparrows stay near the ground, scratching through leaves in search of food, often in flocks. In spring, look for them in bushes eating fresh buds. They sing their distinctive songs frequently, even in winter.

HABITAT Look for these sparrows in woods and forest edges, in regrowth following logging or fires, and at pond and bog edges. In winter, you can find them in thickets, overgrown fields, parks, and woodsy suburbs.

ısp facial markings make the **White-throated Sparrow** an attractive bird as well as a hopping, flying anatomy son. There's the black eyestripe, the white crown and eyebrow stripe, the yellow lores, and the white throat ⁏rdered by a black whisker, or malar stripe. Listen for their pretty, wavering whistle of *Oh-sweet-Canada*.

ADULT

ADULT

ADULT

ADULT

SIZE & SHAPE Savannah Sparrows are small sparrows with short, notched tails. The head appears small for the plump body, and the crown feathers often flare up to give the bird's head a small peak. The thick-based bill, perfectly shaped for eating seeds, is small for a sparrow.

COLOR PATTERN Savannah Sparrows are generally brown above with dark streaks. They are white below with thin brown or black streaks on the breast and flanks. They usually show a small yellow mark above and in front of the eye. The shade of brown varies regionally.

BEHAVIOR Savannah Sparrows forage on or near the ground. When flushed, they usually fly up, flare their short tails, and circle before landing a few yards away. Males sing from exposed, low perches such as fence posts.

HABITAT Savannah Sparrows breed on tundra, grasslands, marshes, and farmland. On their winter range, they stick to the ground or in low vegetation in open areas; look for them along the edges of roads adjacent to farms.

RANGE MAP

Breeding
Migration
Nonbreeding
Year-round

Savannah Sparrows are understated but distinctive, with a short tail, small head, and a telltale yellow sp before the eye. They're one of the most abundant songbirds in North American grasslands and fields, and in summer, their soft but distinctive insectlike song drifts lazily over farm fields and grasslands.

ADULT / IMMATURE

ADULT / IMMATURE

ADULT / IMMATURE

JUVENILE

RANGE MAP

Breeding
Nonbreeding
Year-round

SIZE & SHAPE Song Sparrows are medium-sized and fairly bulky sparrows. For a sparrow, the bill is short and stout and the head fairly rounded. The tail is long and rounded, and the wings are broad.

COLOR PATTERN Song Sparrows are brown with thick streaks on a white chest and flanks. The head is an attractive mix of warm red brown and slate gray, though these shades, and the amount of streaking, vary across its range. Adult and older, immature birds look similar. Juvenile birds have fine streaking on the breast.

BEHAVIOR Song Sparrows flit through dense vegetation, occasionally moving onto open ground after food. Flights are short, with a characteristic downward pumping tail. Males sing from exposed perches.

HABITAT Look for Song Sparrows in nearly any open habitat, including marsh edges, overgrown fields, backyards, desert washes, and forest edges. Song Sparrows commonly visit bird feeders and build nests in residential areas.

Song Sparrow is one of the most familiar North American sparrows. Don't let its bewildering variety of regional plumage differences deter you: if you see a streaky sparrow in an open, shrubby or wet area, perched on a low shrub and leaning back to sing a stuttering, clattering song, this is probably your bird.

ADULT

ADULT

ADULT

JUVENILE

SIZE & SHAPE The Lincoln's Sparrow is a medium-sized sparrow with a round belly and head, but the back of its head often looks pointed when it raises its crown feathers. Its tail is fairly short, and its conical bill is thinner than those of other sparrows.

COLOR PATTERN This bird is a streaky brown, buff, and gray with rusty wing and tail edges. Its chest and sides are buff with black streaking that fades to a white belly. A buffy mustache is outlined in brown, and it has a thin eyering. Its crown is striped brown and black.

BEHAVIOR Lincoln's Sparrows are secretive little birds that forage on or near the ground, rarely straying far from dense cover. During the breeding season, males sing either from exposed perches or tucked inside a shrub.

HABITAT Lincoln's Sparrows breed in wet meadows, patches of aspens, cottonwoods, and willows, and shrubby areas near streams. In winter, they use tropical and pine-oak forests, tropical scrub, weedy pastures, and shrubby fields.

RANGE MAP

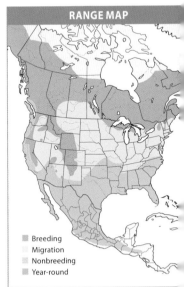

Breeding
Migration
Nonbreeding
Year-round

The dainty **Lincoln's Sparrow** has a talent for concealing itself. It sneaks around the ground amid willo thickets in wet meadows, rarely straying from cover. When it decides to pop up and sing from a willow twig, its sweet, jumbling song may seem more fitting of a House Wren than a sparrow.

ADULT

ADULT

ADULT

JUVENILE

RANGE MAP

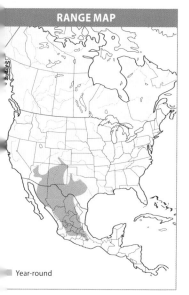

■ Year-round

SIZE & SHAPE Canyon Towhees are large sparrows with long tails, chunky bodies, and short rounded wings. The bill is short and thick at the base, and the legs are long.

COLOR PATTERN Overall, the Canyon Towhee is about as plain grayish brown as birds come. It has a warm rusty undertail, a buffy throat, a faint streaky necklace, and a hint of a reddish crown.

BEHAVIOR Watch for Canyon Towhees scurrying along the ground between bushes. They scratch and peck for seeds and insects, sometimes out in the open. Males perch atop short shrubs and cacti to sing in the breeding season.

HABITAT Within their fairly narrow range, look for Canyon Towhees in desert grasslands with scattered dense shrubs, rocky terrain, dry watercourses with mesquite, and other dry, scrubby areas. Unlike California Towhees, they more often shy away from suburban neighborhoods, favoring sparsely settled and remote areas.

yon Towhees keep a mostly low profile across their range in the desert Southwest. These big, warm-wn sparrows are common in a variety of scrubby habitats, but easily blend into the background. They k like the California Towhee (and were once considered the same species), but ranges don't overlap.

SIZE & SHAPE Rufous-crowned Sparrows are fairly large sparrows with flat to rounded heads and fairly long, rounded tails. The thick, pointed bill is fairly large.

COLOR PATTERN These are grayish sparrows with streaky backs and bright reddish brown crowns. They have a white eyering and a white whisker stripe that's bordered in black and contrasts with the gray face and underparts. Adult and immature birds look similar.

BEHAVIOR Rufous-crowned Sparrows spend much of their time under the cover of vegetation, often foraging or running across the ground instead of flying. Your best chance to see one in the open is to catch a male as he sings from a higher perch in a shrub or low tree.

HABITAT Look for Rufous-crowned Sparrows on steep, dry, rocky hillsides with plenty of grasses and a scattering of shrubs and small trees, such as sagebrush or scrub oaks. Recently burned areas can provide good, open habitat. The birds tend to avoid areas of dense shrubs.

RANGE MAP

■ Year-round

The hot, rocky hillsides of the Southwest can look inhospitable on a baking summer day, but they're exact the kind of place **Rufous-crowned Sparrows** call home. These bulky, long-tailed sparrows forage on the ground beneath sparse shrubs and grasses. Males sing a short, jumbled song with a bubbly quality.

ADULT

ADULT

JUVENILE

IMMATURE

RANGE MAP

- Breeding
- Migration
- Nonbreeding
- Year-round

SIZE & SHAPE Green-tailed Towhees are large, chunky sparrows with a big head, stocky body, and longish tail. The bill is thick and sparrowlike. They are larger than most sparrows and have shorter tails than most other towhees.

COLOR PATTERN Green-tailed Towhees are grayish birds with olive-yellow wings, back, and tail. The head is strongly marked with a bright rufous crown, white throat, and a dark "mustache" stripe. Juveniles are streaky and brownish but show a distinctive greenish yellow tinge to wings and tails.

BEHAVIOR Green-tailed Towhees forage on the ground or in dense shrubby foliage. They can be hard to see except when males sing from the top of a shrub. Their call, a quiet, catlike mew, can help you find them.

HABITAT Look for Green-tailed Towhees in shrubby habitats of the West, particularly disturbed areas of montane forest and open slopes in the Great Basin, sagebrush steppes, and high desert. In winter, they join mixed flocks in dense mesquite areas of desert washes.

ere's nothing quite like the color that gives the **Green-tailed Towhee** its name—from a deep olive to low-green on the edges of the wings and tail. Set off by a gray chest, white throat, and rufous crown, s large sparrow is a colorful resident of the West's shrubby mountainsides and sagebrush expanses.

ADULT MALE

ADULT MALE

JUVENILE

ADULT FEMALE

SIZE & SHAPE The Spotted Towhee is a large sparrow with a thick, pointed bill, short neck, chunky body, and long, rounded tail.

COLOR PATTERN Males have jet-black upperparts and throat; their wings and back are spotted bright white. The flanks are warm rufous, and the belly is white. Females have the same pattern but are grayish brown where males are black. In flight, look for white corners to the black tail. Juveniles are heavily streaked and brownish from the time they hatch into the fall.

BEHAVIOR Spotted Towhees hop over the ground beneath dense shrubs, scratching in leaf litter for food. They also climb into lower branches to search for insects and fruits, or to deliver their quick, buzzy song. Towhees can fly long distances, but more often make short, slow flights between patches of cover.

HABITAT Look for Spotted Towhees in open, shrubby habitat with thick undergrowth. Spotted Towhees are also at home in backyards, forest edges, and overgrown fields.

RANGE MAP

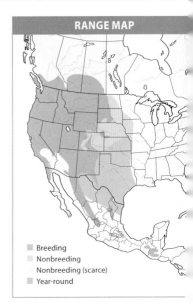

■ Breeding
■ Nonbreeding
Nonbreeding (scarce)
■ Year-round

The **Spotted Towhee** is a large, striking sparrow of sunbaked thickets of the West. When you catch sight of one, they're gleaming black above (females are grayish brown), and spotted and striped with brilliant white. Their warm rufous flanks match the dry leaves where they hop and scratch for food.

ADULT MALE

ADULT MALE

ADULT FEMALE

JUVENILE

RANGE MAP

Breeding
Migration
Nonbreeding
Nonbreeding (scarce)
Year-round

SIZE & SHAPE Towhees are a kind of large sparrow. Look for their thick, triangular, seed-cracking bill as a tip-off they're in the sparrow family. Also notice the chunky body and long, rounded tail.

COLOR PATTERN Males are a bold sooty black above and on the breast, with warm rufous sides and white on the belly. Females have the same pattern, but are rich brown where the males are black. Juveniles are brownish and heavily streaked from hatching into their first fall.

BEHAVIOR Eastern Towhees spend most of their time on the ground, scratching at leaves with both feet at the same time, in a kind of backwards hop. They spend lots of time concealed beneath thick underbrush. You may see this bird more often when it climbs into shrubs and low trees to sing.

HABITAT Look for Eastern Towhees at forest edges and in overgrown fields, woodlands, and scrubby backyards or thickets. The most important habitat qualities seem to be dense shrub cover with plenty of leaf litter.

stern Towhees are birds of the undergrowth, where their rummaging makes more noise than you would pect for their size. If you can get a clear look at it, it's a strikingly marked, oversized sparrow, feathered in ld black or chocolate brown and warm chestnut. Their *chewink* calls let you know how common they are.

ADULT

ADULT

ADULT

IMMATURE

SIZE & SHAPE The Yellow-breasted Chat is a small songbird about the size of a sparrow. It has a long tail, large head, and a relatively thick, heavy bill.

COLOR PATTERN Chats are olive green above with a bright yellow breast. The face is gray, with a white eyering that connects to the bill, forming "spectacles." They also have a white mustache stripe. The lower belly is white. Immature birds are duller overall.

BEHAVIOR Yellow-breasted Chats are loud birds that tend to skulk in low, thick brush. In spring, males may sing from an exposed perch, but otherwise these birds will typically stay well hidden. Calls include a low, chattering scold.

HABITAT Yellow-breasted Chats live in thickets and other dense, regrowing areas such as bramble bushes, clearcuts, powerline corridors, and shrubs along streams.

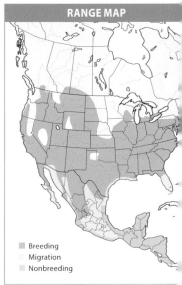

RANGE MAP

■ Breeding
  Migration
  Nonbreeding

The **Yellow-breasted Chat** offers a cascade of song in the spring, when males deliver streams of whistles, cackles, chuckles, and gurgles with the fluidity of improvisational jazz. It's seldom seen or heard during the rest of the year, when both males and females skulk silently in the shadows of dense thickets.

BREEDING ADULT

BREEDING ADULT

NONBREEDING ADULT / IMMATURE

NONBREEDING ADULT / IMMATURE

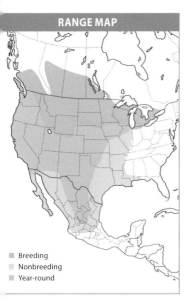

RANGE MAP

- Breeding
- Nonbreeding
- Year-round

SIZE & SHAPE The Western Meadowlark is the size of a robin but chunkier and shorter-tailed, with a flat head, long, slender bill, and a round-shouldered posture that conceals its neck. The wings are triangular (like a starling's), and the tail is short, stiff, and spiky.

COLOR PATTERN Western Meadowlarks have yellow underparts with intricately patterned brown, black, and buff upperparts. A black V crosses the bright yellow breast and yellow creeps up the cheek toward the eye. The tail has a small amount of white at the edges. Nonbreeding and immature birds are duller and covered in buffy markings that obscure the summer pattern.

BEHAVIOR Western Meadowlarks fly in brief bursts, alternating rapid, stiff wingbeats with short glides. In spring, males perform a "jump flight," springing straight up into the air with fluttering wings and legs hanging limp below.

HABITAT Western Meadowlarks seek wide open native grasslands, prairies, meadows, and agricultural fields ranging from sea level to 10,000 feet. Look for them among low- to medium-height grasses more so than in tall fields. They avoid wooded edges and areas with dense shrubs.

ore easily seen than heard, the colorful **Western Meadowlark** sings a flutelike melody across grasslands, eadows, pastures, and along marsh edges throughout the West and Midwest. Look and listen for flocks of ese stout ground feeders, strutting and feeding on seeds and insects.

BREEDING ADULT

BREEDING ADULT

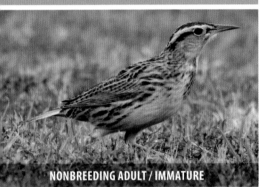

NONBREEDING ADULT / IMMATURE

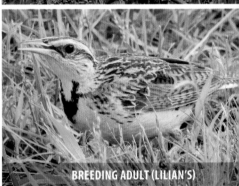

BREEDING ADULT (LILIAN'S)

SIZE & SHAPE Eastern Meadowlarks are chunky, medium-sized songbirds with short tails and long, spear-shaped bills. In flight, their rounded wings, short tails, and long bills help set them apart from other grassland songbirds.

COLOR PATTERN Eastern Meadowlarks are pale brown marked with black, with bright yellow underparts and a bold black V across the chest. The tail is barred brown in the center and extensively white on the edges. The "Lilian's" subspecies has more white in the tail and whiter cheeks. Nonbreeding and immature birds are duller overall.

BEHAVIOR Eastern Meadowlarks are hard to see as they walk on the ground concealed by grasses or crops. In summer, males sing beautiful, melancholic whistles from exposed perches, especially fence posts.

HABITAT Eastern Meadowlarks live in farm fields, native grasslands, and wet fields. They will breed in many kinds of grassy areas as long as they can find about six acres in which to create a territory.

RANGE MAP

- Breeding
- Nonbreeding
- Year-round

The sweet, lazy whistles of **Eastern Meadowlarks** waft over summer grasslands and farms in eastern Nor America. The birds themselves sing from fenceposts and telephone lines or stalk through the grasses, probing the ground for insects with their long, sharp bills.

ADULT MALE

IMMATURE MALE

ADULT FEMALE

ADULT FEMALE

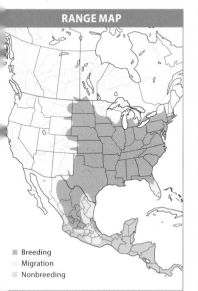

RANGE MAP

Breeding
Migration
Nonbreeding

SIZE & SHAPE Orchard Orioles are slim songbirds with medium-length tails, rounded heads, and a straight, sharply pointed bill. They are sparrow-sized and small for an oriole.

COLOR PATTERN Adult males are black above and rich reddish chestnut below. They have a black head and throat, with a reddish chestnut patch at the bend of the wing. Females are greenish yellow with two white wingbars and no black. Immature males look like females, but have black around the bill and throat; they may be blotched with orange and chestnut on the head and breast.

BEHAVIOR Orchard Orioles forage for insects in the tops of trees. They also drink nectar from flowers and, in fall, eat berries and other fruits. They sometimes visit hummingbird feeders or eat orange slices or jelly at feeding stations.

HABITAT Orchard Orioles spend summers in open woodlands and areas of scattered trees across the eastern United States. Look for them along river edges, in pastures, parks, and orchards.

he **Orchard Oriole** swaps the typical flame orange of other orioles for a deep, burnished russet. Hopping nong riverine shrubs or scattered trees, male Orchard Orioles sing a whistled, chattering song to attract ellow-green females. Orchard Orioles nest in groups, often with multiple nests in a single tree.

ADULT MALE (SPRING / SUMMER)

ADULT MALE (FALL / WINTER)

ADULT FEMALE

IMMATURE MALE

SIZE & SHAPE Hooded Orioles are sparrow-sized songbirds with longer and more delicate bodies than other orioles. They also have long rounded tails and longish necks. The bill is curved slightly downward, more so than in most other orioles.

COLOR PATTERN On adult males, the throat and wings are black, and they have yellow-to-orange rumps, hoods, and bellies. A black throat extends up the face, creating a mask around the eye and down the chest to make a bib. Adult males flash white wingbars. Females are olive yellow to orange yellow overall with gray backs and thin, white wingbars. Juvenile males look like females, but with black throats.

BEHAVIOR Hooded Orioles are acrobatic foragers and often hang upside down while they grab their prey, but tend to forage sluggishly among leaves and branches. They make flights between trees with strong wingbeats.

HABITAT Hooded Orioles live in open woodlands, towns, and deserts with scattered trees, including cottonwoods, willows, sycamores, and especially palm trees.

RANGE MAP

Breeding
Migration
Nonbreeding
Year-round

Flashing brilliant orange and black, **Hooded Orioles** light up open woodlands and parks as they pluck insects or sip nectar from flowers. Like other orioles, they weave hanging nests, often "sewing" them ont the undersides of palm leaves, leading to the nickname "palm-leaf oriole."

ADULT MALE

ADULT MALE

MALE

ADULT FEMALE

RANGE MAP

- Breeding
- Migration
- Nonbreeding
- Year-round

SIZE & SHAPE Bullock's Orioles are medium-sized songbirds, slightly smaller than robins, with slim but sturdy bodies and medium-long tails. Orioles are related to blackbirds and share their long, thick-based, sharply pointed bills.

COLOR PATTERN Adult males are bright orange with a black back and throat, large white wing patch, orange face with a black line through the eye, and a black throat. Females and immatures are yellowish orange on the head and tail, with a grayish back and white-edged wing coverts. Immature males are similar to adult females, but show a black throat patch.

BEHAVIOR Bullock's Orioles feed in slender branches of trees and shrubs, catching caterpillars and also feeding on nectar or fruit. They are agile and active, often hanging upside down or stretching to reach prey.

HABITAT Look for Bullock's Orioles in open woodlands along streams, particularly among cottonwoods. They also favor orchards, parks, and oak or mesquite woodlands.

mble canopy dwellers of open woodlands, **Bullock's Orioles** dangle upside down from branches to tch insects, or while weaving their hanging nests. Listen for their whistling, chuckling song in tall trees ng rivers and streams. Both male and female Bullock's Orioles sing.

ADULT MALE

ADULT MALE

ADULT FEMALE

ADULT FEMALE

SIZE & SHAPE Baltimore Orioles are medium-sized, sturdy songbirds with a thick neck and long legs. Look for their long, thick-based, pointed bills, a hallmark of the blackbird family.

COLOR PATTERN Adult males are flame orange and black, with a solid black head and one white bar on their black wings. Females and immature males are yellow orange on the breast, grayish on the head and back, with two bold white wingbars and a yellow tail. Adult female plumage is highly variable, ranging from a brownish to yellowish head and back.

BEHAVIOR Baltimore Orioles are more often heard than seen as they feed high in trees, searching for insects, flowers, and fruit. You may also spot them lower down, plucking fruit from vines and bushes or sipping from hummingbird feeders. Watch for the male's slow, fluttering flights between treetops and listen for their characteristic *wink* or chatter calls.

HABITAT Look for Baltimore Orioles high in leafy broadleaf trees, but not in deep forests. They're found in open woodlands, forest edges, orchards, parks, and backyards.

RANGE MAP

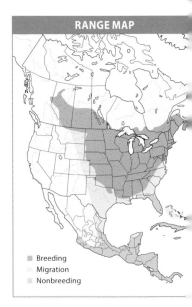

■ Breeding
▨ Migration
■ Nonbreeding

The rich, whistling song of the **Baltimore Oriole**, echoing from treetops near homes and parks, heralds spri in eastern portions of the U.S. and Canada. Look way up to find the male's orange plumage blazing from high branches. You might also spot the female weaving her remarkable hanging nest from slender fibers.

NONBREEDING MALE

ADULT MALE

ADULT FEMALES

IMMATURE MALE (FALL / WINTER)

RANGE MAP

- Breeding
- Nonbreeding
- Year-round

SIZE & SHAPE A stocky, broad-shouldered blackbird with a slender, conical bill and a medium-length tail. Red-winged Blackbirds often show a hump-backed silhouette while perched; males often sit with tail slightly flared.

COLOR PATTERN Male Red-winged Blackbirds are an even glossy black with red-and-yellow shoulder badges. The superficially sparrow-like females are crisply streaked and dark brownish overall, paler on the breast, and often show a whitish eyebrow. Immature and nonbreeding males have rufous feather edges.

BEHAVIOR Male birds sit on high perches and belt out a *conk-la-ree!* song all day long. Females skulk through vegetation for food and quietly weave their remarkable nests. In winter, they gather in huge mixed flocks to eat grains. Males display by holding their wings out to show off their red shoulder patches.

HABITAT Look for these birds in freshwater and saltwater marshes, along watercourses, and water hazards on golf courses, as well as drier meadows and old fields. In winter, you can find them at crop fields, feedlots, and pastures.

...e of the most abundant birds in North America, the **Red-winged Blackbird** is a familiar sight atop ttails, along roadsides, and on telephone wires. Males have scarlet-and-gold shoulder patches they can ff up or hide. Their *conk-la-ree!* songs are happy indications of the return of spring.

ADULT MALE

ADULT FEMALE (L) AND ADULT MALE (R)

ADULT FEMALE (WESTERN)

ADULT FEMALE (EASTERN)

SIZE & SHAPE The Bronzed Cowbird is a solidly built songbird with a thick-based, sharply pointed, slightly curved bill. Males have a thick neck, especially when they fluff out the feathers of the nape during displays.

COLOR PATTERN Adult males are black with a bronze sheen. The wings are bluish at close range. Females in the eastern part of the range are blackish; in the western part of the range, they are gray brown. Adults have vivid red eyes; these are dark in juveniles.

BEHAVIOR Bronzed Cowbirds forage in flocks, mostly on the ground, searching for seeds, grains, and insects. Males perform a "helicopter" display. Both sexes search for other birds in the process of building nests; the female lays eggs in other birds' nests.

HABITAT Bronzed Cowbirds can be found in open habitats such as chaparral, mesquite bosques, coastal prairie, farmland, pasture, golf courses, lightly wooded canyons, and riparian corridors. They also associate with Great-tailed Grackles in urban parking lots.

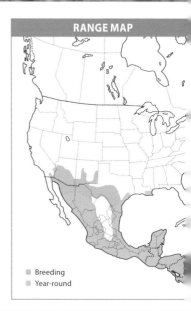

RANGE MAP

■ Breeding
■ Year-round

A bull-necked bird of open country, the **Bronzed Cowbird** forages for seeds and grains on the ground, usually in flocks. Like their relatives, the smaller Brown-headed Cowbirds, these unusual birds are "brood parasites"—they lay their eggs in other birds' nests, leaving the hosts to care for their young.

ADULT MALE

ADULT MALE

JUVENILE

ADULT FEMALE

RANGE MAP

- Breeding
- Nonbreeding
- Year-round

SIZE & SHAPE Brown-headed Cowbirds are smallish blackbirds, with a shorter tail and thicker head than most other blackbirds. The bill is much shorter and has a thicker base than other blackbirds. In flight, look for the shorter tail.

COLOR PATTERN Male Brown-headed Cowbirds have glossy black plumage and a rich brown head that looks black in low light or at distance. Females are gray-brown birds, lightest on the head and underparts, with fine streaking on the belly. Juveniles are brown overall with a scaly-looking back and streaked underparts.

BEHAVIOR Brown-headed Cowbirds feed on the ground in mixed flocks of blackbirds and starlings. Brown-headed Cowbirds are noisy, making a multitude of clicks, whistles, and chattering calls, in addition to a gurgling song.

HABITAT Brown-headed Cowbirds favor open habitats, such as fields, pastures, meadows, forest edges, and lawns. When not displaying or feeding on the ground, they often perch high on prominent tree branches.

male **Brown-headed Cowbirds** forgo building nests in favor of producing eggs, sometimes over three zen a summer. Eggs are laid in the nests of other birds and young are raised by foster parents, often at e expense of the hosts' chicks. Their numbers and range have grown as forests are fragmented.

ADULT MALE

IMMATURE MALE

ADULT FEMALE

ADULT FEMALE

SIZE & SHAPE The Brewer's Blackbird is a long-legged, robin-sized songbird with a fairly long tail balanced by a full body, round head, and long, thick-based beak. In perched birds, the tail appears widened and rounded toward the tip.

COLOR PATTERN Males are glossy black all over with a staring yellow eye and a purple sheen on the head grading to greenish on the body. Females are plainer brown, darkest on the wings and tail, and they have dark eyes. Occasionally, females will have a pale eye. Immature birds look like washed-out, lighter brown versions of the females.

BEHAVIOR Brewer's Blackbirds feed on open ground in parks and busy streets. Their long legs give them a head-jerking, chickenlike walk. In flocks, they rise and fall as they fly. When landing, birds may circle slowly before settling.

HABITAT Look for Brewer's Blackbirds in open habitats of the West, such as coastal scrub, grasslands, riversides, meadows, as well as lawns, golf courses, parks, and city streets.

RANGE MAP

Breeding
Migration
Nonbreeding
Year-round

A bird to be seen in the full sun, the male **Brewer's Blackbird** is a glossy combination of black, midnight blue, and metallic green. Females are a staid brown. Common in much of the West, you'll see these ground-foraging birds on sidewalks, in city parks, and chuckling in flocks atop shrubs, trees, and reeds.

ADULT MALE

ADULT MALE

JUVENILE

ADULT FEMALE

RANGE MAP

Breeding
Nonbreeding
Year-round

SIZE & SHAPE Common Grackles are large, lanky blackbirds with long legs. The head is flat, and the bill is longer than in most blackbirds, with the hint of a downward curve. In flight, wings appear short in comparison to the tail, which is very long and hangs down in the middle.

COLOR PATTERN Common Grackles appear black from afar, but up close, glossy blue-green heads contrast with bronzy iridescent bodies and a golden eye. Females are less glossy and have shorter tails than males. Juveniles are all dark brown with dark eyes and shorter tails.

BEHAVIOR Common Grackles form large flocks, flying or foraging on lawns and in agricultural fields. They strut on their long legs, pecking for food rather than scratching. At feeders, they dominate smaller birds. Their flight is direct, with stiff wingbeats.

HABITAT Common Grackles thrive around agricultural fields, feedlots, city parks, and suburban lawns. They're also common in open habitats including woodland, forest edges, meadows, and marshes.

mmon Grackles are blackbirds that look like they've been slightly stretched. They're taller and have a ger tail than a typical blackbird, with a longer, more tapered bill and glossy, iridescent bodies. Grackles k around lawns and fields on their long legs or gather in noisy groups high in trees, typically conifers.

ADULT MALE ADULT MALE

ADULT FEMALE ADULT FEMALE

SIZE & SHAPE Boat-tailed Grackles are huge, lanky songbirds with rounded crowns, long legs, and fairly long, pointed bills. Males have very long tails that make up almost half their body length. The center of the tail hangs below the rest, creating a V shape. Females are considerably smaller.

COLOR PATTERN Males are glossy black overall. Females are dark brown above and russet below, with a face pattern made up of a pale eyebrow, dark cheek, and pale "mustache" stripe. In Texas and Oklahoma, birds have dark eyes.

BEHAVIOR These scrappy blackbirds are supreme omnivores, feeding on everything from seeds and human food scraps to crustaceans scavenged from the shoreline.

HABITAT Boat-tailed Grackles are a strictly coastal species through most of their range; however, they live across much of the Florida peninsula, often well away from the immediate coast.

RANGE MAP

■ Breeding
■ Year-round

Blue-black **Boat-tailed Grackle** males are hard to miss with their ridiculously long tails on display from marsh grasses or telephone wires. The dark brown females are half the size of males and almost look like a different species. They often scavenge trash and hang out in busy urban areas, away from predators.

ADULT MALE

ADULT MALES

ADULT FEMALE

ADULT FEMALE

RANGE MAP

Breeding
Year-round

SIZE & SHAPE Males are huge, long-legged blackbirds with stout, straight bills. The center of the tapered tail hangs below the rest, creating a V or keel shape. Females are much smaller and have shorter tails.

COLOR PATTERN Adult males are iridescent black with black bills and legs, and striking yellow eyes. Adult females are dark brown above, paler below. Juveniles have the same coloring as females, but with streaked underparts and a dark eye.

BEHAVIOR You'll often see Great-tailed Grackles with other blackbirds pecking for food on lawns, fields, and at marsh edges, vying for trash in urban settings, or crowding in trees and on telephone lines in noisy roosts.

HABITAT Great-tailed Grackles forage in agricultural fields and feedlots, golf courses, cemeteries, parks, and neighborhood lawns. Large trees and vegetation edging marshes, lakes, parking lots, and lagoons provide roosting and breeding sites.

male **Great-tailed Grackle** shimmers in iridescent black and purple, trailing a striking tail. The rich wn female is about half the male's size. Flocks strut and hop on suburban lawns, golf courses, fields, and rshes. In the evening, flocks pack neighborhood trees, filling the sky with their ear-splitting voices.

ADULT MALE

ADULT MALE

ADULT MALE

ADULT FEMALE

SIZE & SHAPE Black-and-white Warblers are medium-sized warblers. They have a fairly long, slightly downcurved bill. The head often appears somewhat flat and streamlined, with a short neck. The wings are long, and the tail is short.

COLOR PATTERN These birds are boldly striped in black and white, with black wings highlighted by two wide, white wingbars. Adult males have more obvious black streaking, particularly on the underparts and cheek. Females (especially immatures) are paler, with less streaking and usually a wash of buff on the flanks. The undertail coverts have distinctive large black spots.

BEHAVIOR Black-and-white Warblers act more like nuthatches than warblers, foraging for hidden insects in the bark of trees by creeping up, down, and around branches and trunks.

HABITAT Broadleaf forest and mixed forest are the preferred summer habitats of Black-and-white Warblers, usually with trees of mixed ages. On migration, look for them in any forest or woodlot.

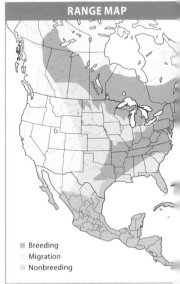

RANGE MAP

■ Breeding
Migration
■ Nonbreeding

The **Black-and-white Warbler's** thin, squeaky song is one of the first signs that spring birding has sprung. They creep along tree trunks and branches like a nimble nuthatch, probing the bark for insects with its slig curved bill. Though usually seen in trees, they build their little cup-shaped nests on the forest floor.

ADULT MALE

ADULT MALE

ADULT FEMALE / IMMATURE

ADULT

RANGE MAP

- Breeding
- Breeding (scarce)
- Migration
- Nonbreeding

SIZE & SHAPE The Prothonotary Warbler is a large, heavy-bodied warbler with a big head and bill. It has shorter legs, a shorter tail, and a heavier and longer bill than other warblers. It is sparrow-sized.

COLOR PATTERN This bird is bright golden yellow with blue-gray wings and tail and a yellow-olive back. Its beady black eye stands out on its solid yellow face. It has white in and under the tail. Females are duller than males.

BEHAVIOR This warbler often forages above standing or slow-moving water. It slowly hops along branches, twigs, and along fallen trees, keeping low or dropping to the ground in search of food. It flies between trees and shrubs with heavy wingbeats in an undulating pattern.

HABITAT Prothonotary Warblers breed in wooded swamps, flooded bottomland forests, and wooded areas near streams and lakes. They prefer forests that are flat and shady with standing dead trees that have old woodpecker holes for nests.

e brilliant **Prothonotary Warbler** bounces along branches like a golden flashlight in the dim understory swampy woodlands. This golden ray of light is unique among warblers with its beady black eye and ue-gray wings. It is also one of two warblers that build their nests in holes in standing dead trees.

SIZE & SHAPE Orange-crowned Warblers are small songbirds, smaller than a sparrow. Compared with other warblers, they have noticeably thin, sharply pointed bills. They have short wings and short, square tails.

COLOR PATTERN Orange-crowned Warblers are plain yellowish or olive, with a faint pale stripe over the eye, blackish line through the eye, and pale broken eyering. The undertail coverts are bright yellow. The orange crown may become visible if the bird is agitated, but is not often seen. Adult and immature birds look similar.

BEHAVIOR Orange-crowned Warblers forage in dense shrubbery and low trees. They tend to be unobtrusive, but their low foraging habits can help you spot them. They often give a high, faint contact call while foraging.

HABITAT Orange-crowned Warblers breed in dense broadleaf shrubs, usually within or adjacent to forest. During migration, you may find them in any habitat, though they still show a preference for dense, low vegetation.

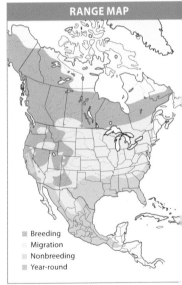

RANGE MAP

- Breeding
- Migration
- Nonbreeding
- Year-round

Orange-crowned Warblers aren't the most dazzling warblers, but they're useful to learn. These grayish olive-green birds have few bold markings. There's rarely any sign of an orange crown, which is usually on visible when the bird is excited. They are one of the few warblers that are more common in the West than the Ea

ADULT MALE

ADULT MALE

IMMATURE MALE

ADULT FEMALE

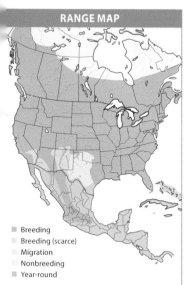

RANGE MAP

- Breeding
- Breeding (scarce)
- Migration
- Nonbreeding
- Year-round

SIZE & SHAPE Common Yellowthroats are small songbirds with chunky, rounded heads and medium-length, slightly rounded tails. They are smaller than sparrows.

COLOR PATTERN Adult males are bright yellow below, with a sharp black face mask and olive upperparts. A whitish line sets off the black mask from the head and neck. Immature males show traces of the full mask of adult males. Females are a plain olive brown, usually with yellow brightening the throat and under the tail. They lack the black mask.

BEHAVIOR Common Yellowthroats spend much of their time skulking low to the ground in dense thickets and fields, searching for small insects and spiders. Males sing a distinctive, rolling *wichety-wichety-wichety* song. During migration, this is often the most common warbler found in fields and edges.

HABITAT Yellowthroats live in open areas with thick, low vegetation, ranging from marsh to grassland to open pine forest. During migration, they use an even broader suite of habitats, including backyards and forests.

broad black mask lends a touch of highwayman's mystique to the male **Common Yellowthroat**. Look for ese furtive warblers skulking through tangled vegetation, often at the edges of marshes and wetlands. lowthroats are vocal, and their songs and distinctive call notes reveal their presence.

ADULT MALE

ADULT MALE

ADULT FEMALE / IMMATURE

ADULT FEMALE

SIZE & SHAPE Northern Parulas are small songbirds with a short tail and a thin, pointy bill. They are plump little warblers, slightly larger than a kinglet.

COLOR PATTERN Adult males are blue gray with a yellow-green back patch and two white wingbars. A chestnut band separates its yellow throat and chest. Adult females lack the breast band. Both sexes have white eye crescents. Immature birds lack the chestnut band.

BEHAVIOR These warblers flit mostly through the upper levels of the forest and subcanopy, but on migration, they also forage in the understory. They flutter at branch tips, quickly plucking insects. Males are very vocal during spring migration.

HABITAT In the southern part of their range, parulas are common in broadleaf forests, but in the northern part, they also use coniferous forests. They build their nests with Spanish "moss" or "old man's beard" lichen. In winter, look for them in scrub, forests, and plantations.

RANGE MAP

- Breeding
- Migration
- Nonbreeding
- Year-round

A small warbler of the upper canopy, the **Northern Parula** flutters at the edges of branches, plucking insects. It breeds in forests laden with Spanish "moss" or beard lichens, from Florida to the boreal forest. Males hop through branches singing a rising buzzy trill that pinches off at the end.

ADULT MALE

ADULT MALE

IMMATURE FEMALE (FIRST YEAR)

ADULT FEMALE

RANGE MAP

- Breeding
- Migration
- Nonbreeding
- Year-round

SIZE & SHAPE Yellow Warblers are small, evenly proportioned songbirds with medium-length tails and rounded heads. For a warbler, the straight, thin bill is relatively large.

COLOR PATTERN Yellow Warblers are uniformly yellow birds. Males are a bright, egg-yolk yellow with reddish streaks on the underparts. Females are yellow overall with a yellow-green back and mostly unstreaked yellow underparts. Both sexes flash yellow patches in the tail. The face is unmarked, accentuating the large black eye. Immatures are duller overall, and some can be almost entirely grayish.

BEHAVIOR Look for Yellow Warblers near the tops of tall shrubs and small trees. They forage with quick hops along small branches to glean caterpillars and other insects. Males sing a sweet, whistled song from high perches.

HABITAT Yellow Warblers breed in shrubby thickets and woods, particularly along watercourses and in wetlands. They are found in willows, alders, and cottonwoods across North America and up to 9,000 feet in the West. In winter, they mainly occur in mangrove forests of Mexico and Central and South America.

v warblers combine brilliant color and easy viewing quite like the **Yellow Warbler**. In summer, the ttery yellow males sing their sweet, whistled song from willows, wet thickets, and roadsides across much North America. Yellow Warblers eat mostly insects, so they don't come to backyard feeders.

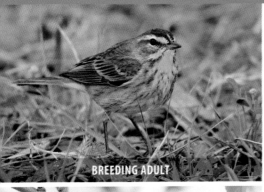

BREEDING ADULT

BREEDING ADULT

NONBREEDING ADULT

NONBREEDING ADULT

SIZE & SHAPE Palm Warblers are medium-sized warblers and may have a fuller looking belly. They stand more upright than most warblers. Their tails and legs are longer than most warblers, contributing to the pipitlike shape.

COLOR PATTERN Both sexes are grayish brown above and whitish streaked and dusky below with a yellow patch below the tail. Breeding birds have rusty caps and brighter yellow throats and breasts. Nonbreeding birds have a brownish crown and lack yellow on the throat and breast.

BEHAVIOR Look for this bird's near-constant tail-wagging. They forage on open ground or in low vegetation, rather than in forest canopy like other warblers, although they do sing from high perches in trees and shrubs.

HABITAT In migration and winter, these birds use weedy fields, forest edges, fence rows, and areas with scattered trees and shrubs. They breed in the boreal forest of the far north, in bogs with coniferous trees and thick ground cover.

RANGE MAP

▇ Breeding
  Migration
▨ Nonbreeding

A warbler that doesn't act like one, the **Palm Warbler** spends its time walking on the ground, wagging its tail up and down. They breed mainly in Canada's boreal forest but most people see them during migration or on wintering grounds foraging in open areas.

ADULT MALE

ADULT MALE

IMMATURE FEMALE

ADULT FEMALE

RANGE MAP

- Breeding
- Migration
- Nonbreeding
- Year-round

SIZE & SHAPE Pine Warblers are hefty, long-tailed warblers with stout bills. The tip of the tail usually appears to have a central notch. They are slightly smaller than sparrows.

COLOR PATTERN Pine Warblers are yellowish birds with olive backs, whitish bellies, and two prominent white wingbars on gray wings. Adult males are brightest; females and immatures are more subdued. Overall, Pine Warblers don't show the strong patterns of other warblers, but the face can look weakly "spectacled," with a pale, broken eyering connected to a pale stripe in front of the eye. Some immature females are gray overall, lacking any yellow coloration.

BEHAVIOR Pine Warblers are hard to see as they often stay high up in pines. They occasionally forage on the ground or come to feeders. Males sing even, rich trills from the tops of pines.

HABITAT Pine Warblers are well named—they spend most of their time in pine trees. This can be in pine forests or in broadleaf woods mixed with pine. In winter, they may visit backyard bird feeders for seeds and suet.

ue to its name, the **Pine Warbler** is common in many eastern pine forests and is rarely seen away from pines. ese yellowish warblers are hard to spot. Listen for their steady, musical trill, which sounds very like a Chipping arrow or Dark-eyed Junco, which are also common piney-woods sounds through much of the year.

ADULT MALE (AUDUBON'S)

ADULT FEMALE (AUDUBON'S)

ADULT MALE (MYRTLE)

IMMATURE (MYRTLE)

SIZE & SHAPE The Yellow-rumped Warbler is a small songbird, although fairly large and full-bodied for a warbler. It has a large head, sturdy but slender bill, and a fairly long, narrow tail.

COLOR PATTERN "Audubon's" adult males are charcoal gray and black with a yellow throat and rump, yellow patches on their sides, and a yellow crown. Adult male "Myrtle" birds are similarly marked but have bright white throats. Females are duller than males. Immature "Myrtle" birds are overall brown, with a pale throat patch that wraps up around the bottom of the ear, and brown streaks below. They may have some yellow patches like the adults, or none at all.

BEHAVIOR Yellow-rumped Warblers forage in outer branches at middle heights. They often fly out to catch insects in midair. In winter, they spend lots of time eating berries from shrubs, and often travel in large flocks.

HABITAT In summer, they live in open coniferous forests and edges, and to a lesser extent in broadleaf forests. In fall and winter, they move to open woods and shrubby habitats, including coastal areas, parks, and residential areas.

RANGE MAP

- ■ Breeding
-   Migration
-   Winter
- ■ Year-round

In fall, **Yellow-rumped Warblers** flood the continent, filling shrubs and trees with distinctive chirps. In sprin they molt to reveal a mix of bright yellow, charcoal gray, black, and bold white. In Texas and Oklahoma, both th western yellow-throated "Audubon's" form and the more widespread white-throated "Myrtle" form are commo

ADULT MALE

ADULT MALE

ADULT MALE

ADULT FEMALE

RANGE MAP

- Breeding
- Migration
- Nonbreeding
- Year-round

SIZE & SHAPE Yellow-throated Warblers are small, well-proportioned birds with sharp, pointed bills. Compared to other warblers, they are a bit more heavy-bodied with a longer and thicker bill. Note the blunt, slightly notched tail.

COLOR PATTERN Males have a gray back, yellow throat, and black side streaks, as well as a black triangle below the eye and a white eyebrow. They have a white belly, tail, and two white wingbars. Females and first-year males are duller overall.

BEHAVIOR These warblers forage by hopping along tree branches, probing into cracks, crevices, bundles of pine needles, and Spanish moss, much like a Brown Creeper or Black-and-White Warbler.

HABITAT Yellow-throated Warblers are found in pine forests, sycamore-bald cypress swamps, and woodlands near streams, especially areas with tall trees and an open understory.

spring and summer, the well-named **Yellow-throated Warbler** shows off its bright yellow throat in the nopy of forests in the southeastern United States. They tend to stick to the tops of the trees, so you might ly get a glimpse of their undersides; look for the bright white belly and slightly notched white tail.

ADULT MALE

ADULT MALE

ADULT FEMALE/IMMATURE

ADULT FEMALE/IMMATURE

SIZE & SHAPE Wilson's Warblers are one of the smallest warblers. They have long, thin tails and small, thin bills. They appear rather round bodied and large headed for their size.

COLOR PATTERN Wilson's Warblers are bright yellow below and yellowish olive above. Black eyes stand out on plain cheeks. Adult males have a distinctive black cap. Females and immatures have an olive crown, but some females show a small dark cap.

BEHAVIOR Wilson's Warblers flit restlessly between perches and make direct flights with rapid wingbeats through the understory. Unlike many warblers, they spend much of their time in the understory.

HABITAT Wilson's Warblers breed in mountain meadows and thickets near streams, especially those with willows and alders. They also breed along the edges of lakes, bogs, and aspen stands. During migration they use woodlands, suburban areas, desert scrub, and shrubby areas near streams.

RANGE MAP

■ Breeding
  Migration
■ Nonbreeding

Small even by warbler standards, the **Wilson's Warbler** dances through wet thickets to the beat of its chatterir song. They breed in the north and mountains of the West but are widespread across most of the U.S. and Mexi on migration. They rarely slow down, dashing between shrubs, grabbing insects or popping up onto low perch

ADULT MALE

IMMATURE MALE

ADULT FEMALE

ADULT FEMALE

RANGE MAP

■ Breeding
Migration
■ Nonbreeding

SIZE & SHAPE Summer Tanagers are medium-sized, chunky songbirds with a big body, large head, and fairly long tail. They have a large, thick, blunt-tipped bill. They are slightly smaller than robins.

COLOR PATTERN Adult male Summer Tanagers are entirely bright red. Females and immature males are bright yellowish green—more yellow on the head and underparts, and slightly greener on the back and wings. The bill is pale. Molting immature males can be patchy yellow and red. Some (presumably older) females develop a strong orange/pinkish wash.

BEHAVIOR Summer Tanagers stay high in the forest canopy, where they catch insects midair, or move slowly along branches to glean food. Males have a song similar to an American Robin; both sexes give a distinctive *pit-ti-tuck* call.

HABITAT Summer Tanagers breed near gaps and edges of open forests, especially broadleaf or mixed pine-oak woodlands. In the Southwest, look for them along streams among willows, cottonwoods, mesquite, or saltcedar.

e only completely red bird in North America, the male **Summer Tanager** is eye-catching in the forest nopy. The female is harder to spot, though both sexes have a very distinctive chuckling call note. All year ng, they specialize in catching bees and wasps on the wing.

ADULT MALE

ADULT FEMALE

ADULT FEMALE

JUVENILE

SIZE & SHAPE The Northern Cardinal is a medium-sized, long-tailed songbird with a short, very thick bill and a prominent pointed crest. Cardinals often sit with a hunched-over posture and with the tail pointed straight down.

COLOR PATTERN Males are red all over, with a reddish bill and black area around the bill. Adult females are brown overall with red tinges in the wings, tail, and crest, and black around the red-orange bill. Fledglings lack the black face and red bill.

BEHAVIOR Northern Cardinals tend to sit low in shrubs and trees and forage on or near the ground, often in pairs. They are common at bird feeders but inconspicuous away from them, at least until you learn their loud, metallic *chip* note.

HABITAT Northern Cardinals live in open or fragmented habitat such as backyards, parks, woodlots, and shrubby forest edges, nesting in dense tangles of shrubs and vines. They're almost never found in large forest interiors.

RANGE MAP

■ Year-round

The male **Northern Cardinal** is a conspicuous red; the female is brown with a sharp crest and red accent Cardinals don't migrate, and the male doesn't molt into a dull plumage, so it's still breathtaking in winter backyards. In summer, the sweet, whistled song is one of the first sounds of morning.

ADULT MALE

ADULT MALE

ADULT FEMALE

IMMATURE

RANGE MAP

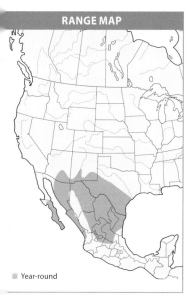

■ Year-round

SIZE & SHAPE Pyrrhuloxias are stocky, medium-sized songbirds with tall crests and long tails. They have heavy but short seed-cracking bills with a curved culmen, or upper edge.

COLOR PATTERN Males are crisp gray with a blood-red face and crest, a red stripe running down the breast, and a reddish tail. Females are buffy gray, with less red than males. Both sexes have yellowish bills and reddish highlights in the wings. Immatures look like females, but have a darker bill and fewer red highlights than adult males.

BEHAVIOR Pyrrhuloxias feed primarily on seeds on or near the ground, but will also eat insects. They make short, undulating flights when moving between patches of cover. Males frequently sing ringing, staccato melodies from exposed perches.

HABITAT Sedentary residents of desert regions, Pyrrhuloxias favor scrub, dry grasslands, open mesquite forest, and cactus gardens for nesting. In the winter, they may move short distances into more lush areas near water.

ne dapper **Pyrrhuloxia** is a tough-as-nails songbird of baking hot deserts in the American Southwest and orthern Mexico. During breeding season, Pyrrhuloxias are fiercely and vocally territorial, but in the winter ey forget their disputes and join together in large foraging flocks.

ADULT MALE

ADULT MALE

ADULT FEMALE

IMMATURE MALE

SIZE & SHAPE Rose-breasted Grosbeaks are stocky, medium-sized songbirds with oversized triangular bills. They are broad-chested, with a short neck and a medium-length, squared tail. They are slightly smaller than robins.

COLOR PATTERN Adult males are black and white with brilliant red from the throat to the center of the breast. Females and young are streaky brown, with a bold whitish stripe over the eye. Both sexes have white patches in the wings and tail. Immature males look like a cross between a male and female with a white eyebrow and a smaller red breast patch.

BEHAVIOR These chunky birds tend to sing from high in trees and may remain on the same perch for long periods. The sweet, rambling song of both sexes is familiar in eastern forests; the sharp *chink* calls are also very distinctive.

HABITAT Rose-breasted Grosbeaks breed in eastern coniferous and broadleaf forests and are most common in regenerating woodlands along forest edges and in parks. During migration, they gravitate to fruiting trees.

RANGE MAP

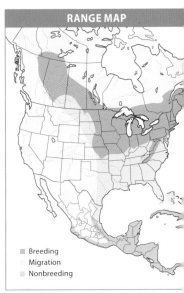

- Breeding
- Migration
- Nonbreeding

Rose-breasted Grosbeaks build such flimsy nests that eggs are often visible from below through the nest bottom. This bird's sweet, robinlike song has inspired many a bird watcher to pay tribute to it, calling it "entrancingly beautiful" and "far superior" to the songs of the American Robin and the Scarlet Tanager.

ADULT MALE

ADULT MALE

ADULT FEMALE / IMMATURE MALE

ADULT FEMALE / IMMATURE MALE

RANGE MAP

■ Breeding
Migration
■ Nonbreeding
■ Year-round

SIZE & SHAPE Black-headed Grosbeaks are hefty songbirds with large, conical bills that are thick at the base. They have large heads and short, thick necks. A short tail imparts a compact, chunky look. They are slightly smaller than robins.

COLOR PATTERN Breeding males are rich orange-cinnamon with a black head and black-and-white wings. Females and immature males are brown above with warm orange or buff on the breast, and some have streaks on the sides of the breast. Immature males tend to be a deeper orange underneath. All have grayish bills. In flight, they flash bright yellow under the wings.

BEHAVIOR Often hidden as they hop about in dense foliage gleaning insects and seeds, Black-headed Grosbeaks feed readily on sunflower seeds at feeders. Males sing in a rich, whistled lilt from treetops in spring and summer. The short, squeaky *chip* note is distinctive and can be a good way to find these birds.

HABITAT Look for Black-headed Grosbeaks in mixed woodlands and forest edges, from mountain forests to thickets along desert streams, to backyards and gardens. Ideal habitat includes some large trees and a diverse understory.

e male **Black-headed Grosbeak** does not get its adult breeding plumage until it is two years old. First-ar males can vary from looking like a female to looking nearly like an adult male. Only yearling males that st closely resemble adult males are able to defend a territory and attempt to breed.

BREEDING MALE

BREEDING MALE

NONBREEDING MALE

ADULT FEMALE

SIZE & SHAPE The Blue Grosbeak is a stocky songbird with a very large, triangular bill that seems to cover the entire front of its face, from throat to forehead. It is slightly larger than a House Sparrow.

COLOR PATTERN Adult males are a deep, rich blue with a tiny black mask in front of the eyes, chestnut wingbars, and a black-and-silver beak. Females are primarily rich cinnamon brown, paler underneath, with bluish tails. Nonbreeding males are patchy blue and cinnamon overall with chestnut wingbars.

BEHAVIOR Blue Grosbeaks are unobtrusive despite their bright colors, although in summer males frequently sing their pleasant, rich, warbling songs. Often they sing while perched at high points in the shrubs and small trees of their generally open or shrubby habitats. Listen for their loud, almost metallic *chink* call and watch for this species' odd habit of twitching its tail sideways.

HABITAT Blue Grosbeaks like old fields growing back into woodland. They breed in a mix of grass, forbs, and shrubs, with a few taller trees. In dry areas, they often use the shrubby growth along watercourses.

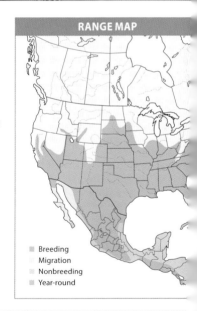

RANGE MAP

■ Breeding
  Migration
  Nonbreeding
■ Year-round

Blue Grosbeaks have expanded northward in the United States in the past century or two, possibly takir advantage of forest clearing. In the southern part of the Blue Grosbeak's breeding range, each mated pai may raise two broods of nestlings per year.

ADULT MALE (LATE WINTER / EARLY SPRING)

BREEDING MALE

ADULT FEMALE

JUVENILE

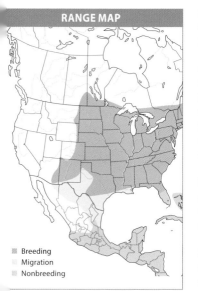

RANGE MAP

- Breeding
- Migration
- Nonbreeding

SIZE & SHAPE Indigo Buntings are small (roughly sparrow-sized), stocky birds with short tails and short, thick, conical bills. In flight, the birds appear plump with short, rounded tails.

COLOR PATTERN An Indigo Bunting breeding male is blue all over, with richer blue on his head and a shiny, silver-gray bill. Females are brown with faint streaking on the breast, a whitish throat, and sometimes a touch of blue on the wings, tail, or rump. Juveniles resemble adult females but have crisp wingbars. In fall and winter, adult males have buffy feather edges covering the blue.

BEHAVIOR Male Indigo Buntings sing from treetops, shrubs, and telephone lines all summer. This species can be attracted to backyards with thistle or nyjer seed. While perching, they often swish their tails from side to side.

HABITAT Look for Indigo Buntings in weedy and brushy areas, especially where fields meet forests. They love forest edges, hedgerows, overgrown patches, and brushy roadsides.

-blue male **Indigo Buntings** are common, widespread birds that whistle their songs through the late spring d summer across much of the eastern U.S. and southeastern Canada. Look for them in weedy fields and rubby areas near trees, singing atop the tallest perch or foraging for seeds and insects in low vegetation.

ADULT MALE

FEMALE / IMMATURE

FEMALE / IMMATURE

JUVENILE

SIZE & SHAPE Painted Buntings are small, sparrow-sized songbirds with stubby, thick bills that are perfectly shaped for eating seeds.

COLOR PATTERN Adult males are stunningly colored with blue heads, red underparts, and green backs. Females and immatures are bright greenish above and yellowish below, with a pale eyering. Though they are basically unpatterned, their overall color is greener and brighter than similar songbirds. Juveniles are drab and more gray but show some green on the rump.

BEHAVIOR Painted Buntings forage on the ground in dense cover, among grasses, or at seed feeders. Sometimes they venture out into grass to forage on seeds. On migration they form loose flocks with other seed-eating birds. Breeding males often perch out in the open to sing their jumbled, sweet songs.

HABITAT Painted Buntings breed in dense brush, often adjacent to thick, grassy areas or woodland edges. During migration and winter, they favor dense, weedy habitats as well as the understory of semiopen forest.

RANGE MAP

■ Breeding
■ Breeding (scarce)
■ Migration
■ Winter

With their vivid fusion of blue, green, yellow, and red, male **Painted Buntings** seem to have flown from a child's coloring book. Females and immatures are a distinctive bright green with a pale eyering. They are often sold illegally as cage birds, which puts pressure on their breeding populations.

ADULT MALE

ADULT MALE

ADULT FEMALE

IMMATURE

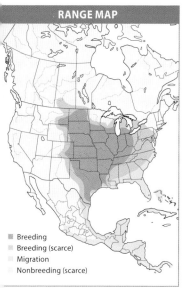

RANGE MAP

- Breeding
- Breeding (scarce)
- Migration
- Nonbreeding (scarce)

SIZE & SHAPE Dickcissels are compact and sparrowlike, with a full chest, a large, thick bill, and a relatively short tail. They are slightly larger than sparrows.

COLOR PATTERN Males are gray on the head with a yellow face and chest, crossed with a black V at the throat. The back is streaked brown and black, with reddish brown shoulders. Females are duller and lack the black V on the chest. Note the yellow eyebrow stripe. Immatures are browner, without the cool gray or bright yellow tones.

BEHAVIOR Dickcissels perch on stalks or shrubs, and sometimes fences, to pluck seeds. They also walk or hop on the ground, foraging for seeds. They will chase intruders with twisting flights that end with the birds fighting on the ground.

HABITAT In all seasons, Dickcissels are most commonly found in tall grasslands, including prairies, hayfields, lightly grazed pastures, and roadsides.

he curt song of the **Dickcissel** sounds like the bird's name, and it's part of the soundtrack of the North merican prairies. They are erratic wanderers—common across the middle of the continent, and a pleasant rprise whenever they turn up in pastures and fields elsewhere in the United States.

IMAGE CREDITS

Front matter photos: p. 11 Mallard ©Greg Gillson/Macaulay Library; p. 12 bird watcher ©Jill Leichter; p. 16 White-throated Sparrow ©Keenan Yakola/Macaulay Library; p. 18 Terns on a beach ©Jay McGowan/Macaulay Library; p. 19 Hairy Woodpecker ©Herb Elliott/Macaulay Library, Downy Woodpecker ©Evan Lipton/Macaulay Library; p. 20 Wilson's Warbler ©Ad Konings/Macaulay Library; p. 21 Lesser Scaup ©Brian L. Sullivan/Macaulay Library, Red-winged Blackbird ©Jonathan Eckerson/Macaulay Library; p. 22 Purple Finch ©Jay McGowan/Macaulay Library, House Finch ©Andrew Simon/Macaulay Library; p. 26 Herring Gulls ©Jay McGowan/Macaulay Library; p. 28 Ruby-throated Hummingbird ©Ian Davies/Macaulay Library; p. 31 binoculars ©Ivonne Wierink/Shutterstock; p. 32 birdfeeder ©Le Do/Shutterstock, scope ©Chokniti Khongchum/Shutterstock; p. 34 birders ©Jill Leichter; p. 35 Wood Thrush ©Ryan Schain/Macaulay Library; p. 36 camera ©EML/Shutterstock; p. 37 Sanderling ©Ryan Schain/Macaulay Library; p. 38 Rose-breasted Grosbeak ©Kevin J. McGowan/Macaulay Library; p. 39 American Goldfinch ©Kevin J. McGowan/Macaulay Library; p. 42 American Goldfinch ©Daniel Irons/Macaulay Library; p. 43 garden path ©Hannamariah/Shutterstock, bee ©Per-Boge/Shutterstock; p. 47 (top to bottom) ©NWStock/Shutterstock; ©spline_x/Shutterstock, ©Sarah Marchant/Shutterstock; p. 48 (top to bottom) ©motorolka/Shutterstock, ©ntstudio/Shutterstock; p. 49 (top to bottom) ©Tiger Images/Shutterstock, ©Jiang Zhongyan/Shutterstock, ©Roman Tsubin/Shutterstock, ©Mirek Kijewski/Shutterstock; p. 50 (top to bottom) ©Egor Rodynchenko/Shutterstock, ©matin/Shutterstock; p. 51 Blackburnian Warbler ©Terence Zahner/Macaulay Library; p. 52 birdhouse ©Feng Yu/Shutterstock; p. 64 Northern Cardinal ©Linda Petersen; p. 65 child and binoculars ©Pigprox/Shutterstock; p. 66 Song Sparrow nest ©Bob Vuxinic; p. 67 parade ©Karen Purcell; p. 68 cat ©Claudia Paulussen /Shutterstock; p. 69 Orange-crowned Warbler ©Brian L. Sullivan/Macaulay Library, cup of coffee ©Alina Rosanova/Shutterstock. All other photos are ©Shutterstock.

Front matter illustrations: p. 17 House Finch and silhouette ©Liz Clayton Fuller, Bartels Science Illustrator; How Big is It? ©Bird Academy; p. 24, 25, 29, 30 illustrations ©Cornell Lab of Ornithology; pp. 44, 45 feeder illustrations ©Virginia Greene/Bartels Science Illustrator; pp. 52–55 birdhouse illustrations ©NestWatch.

Photos in the *Guide to Species* section were primarily sourced from the Macaulay Library, a collection of photos and sound recordings contributed by citizen scientists from all over the world. The diagram on the right shows placement for photos in the book. We are especially grateful to the following Macaulay Library photographers who each contributed over 25 photographs to this series: Sue Barth, Shawn Billerman, Darren Clark, Ian Davies, Matt Davis, Herb Elliott, Paul Fenwick, Greg Gillson, Daniel Irons, Ad Konings, Alex Lamoreaux, Evan Lipton, Scott Martin, Jay McGowan, Ollie Oliver, Arlene Ripley, Ryan Schain, Brian L. Sullivan, Christopher Wood, and Terence Zahner. All photos are ©the photographer/Macaulay Library, except those marked with an asterisk.

Black-bellied Whistling-Duck
1. Ryan Shaw
2. Ian Davies
3. Sean Fitzgerald
4. Ian Davies

Snow Goose
1. Jay McGowan
2. Matt Brady
3. Marky Mutchler
4. Ryan Schain

Canada Goose
1. Liam Wolff
2. Jay McGowan
3. Paul Fenwick
4. Louis Hoeniger

Muscovy Duck
1. Melissa James
2. Kathryn Young
3. Adam Jackson
4. Eric Hoffstein

Wood Duck
1. Ryan Schain
2. Jay McGowan
3. Ollie Oliver
4. Paul Fenwick

Blue-winged Teal
1. Brad Imhoff
2. Jay McGowan
3. Jay McGowan
4. George Armistead

Northern Shoveler
1. Arlene Ripley
2. Christopher Wood
3. Paul Fenwick
4. Ryan Schain

Gadwall
1. Brian L. Sullivan
2. Ryan Schain
3. Melissa James
4. Terence Zahner

American Wigeon
1. Greg Gillson
2. Greg Gillson
3. Greg Gillson
4. Matt Davis

Mallard
1. Brian L. Sullivan
2. Greg Gillson
3. Evan Lipton
4. Evan Lipton

Mexican Duck
1. Michael Hilchey
2. Patrick Maurice
3. Ken Oeser
4. Ad Konings

Mottled Duck
1. Ian Davies
2. Ian Davies
3. Alex Lamoreaux
4. Dan Vickers

Northern Pintail
1. Louis Hoeniger
2. Scott Martin
3. Ryan Schain
4. Amanda Guercio

Canvasback
1. Brian L. Sullivan
2. Alex Lamoreaux
3. Matt Davis
4. Ian Davies

Redhead
1. Matt Davis
2. Greg Gillson
3. Jay McGowan
4. Jay McGowan

Lesser Scaup
1. Brian L. Sullivan
2. Dorian Anderson
3. Ryan Schain
4. Dorian Anderson

Ruddy Duck
1. Arlene Ripley
2. Ryan Schain
3. Liam Wolff
4. Louis Hoeniger

Northern Bobwhite
1. Jeff Maw
2. Don Danko
3. Alex Lamoreaux
4. Shawn Billerman

Scaled Quail
1. Christopher Wood
2. Jeff Maw
3. Arlene Ripley
4. Arlene Ripley

Wild Turkey
1. Andrew Simon
2. Ian Davies
3. Jay McGowan
4. Doug Hitchcox

Pied-billed Grebe
1. Ryan Schain
2. Matt Davis
3. Matt Davis
4. Paul Fenwick

Eared Grebe
1. Matt Davis
2. Matt Davis
3. Luke Seitz
4. Matt Davis

Rock Pigeon
1. Ryan Schain
2. Matt Davis
3. Sue Barth
4. Dan Vickers

Eurasian Collared-Dove
1. Jay McGowan
2. Steven G. Mlodinow
3. Ryan Schain
4. Louis Hoeniger

Inca Dove
1. Louis Hoeniger
2. Jeffrey Moore
3. Matt Brady
4. Shawn Billerman

Common Ground Dove
1. Jeff Maw
2. Dan Vickers
3. Jeffrey Moore
4. Ad Konings

White-winged Dove
1. Evan Lipton
2. Arlene Ripley
3. Don Sterba
4. William Byers

Mourning Dove
1. Ryan Schain
2. Terence Zahner
3. Arlene Ripley
4. Nick Pulcinella

Greater Roadrunner
1. Jerry Ting
2. Matt Davis
3. Nancy Christensen
4. Ad Konings

Yellow-billed Cuckoo
1. Sue Barth
2. Jay McGowan
3. Ryan Schain
4. Dan Vickers

Lesser Nighthawk
1. Brian L. Sullivan
2. Caleb Strand
3. Dan Vickers
4. Usha Tatini

Common Nighthawk
1. Jane Mann
2. Jay McGowan
3. Herb Elliott
4. Mark Ludwick

Chimney Swift
1. Janet Rathjen
2. Katherine Edison
3. Brian L. Sullivan
4. Steve Calver

White-throated Swift
1. Matt Davis
2. Jay McGowan
3. Brian L. Sullivan
4. Paul Fenwick

Ruby-throated Hummingbird
1. Ian Davies
2. Jay McGowan
3. Ad Konings
4. Alex Lamoreaux

Black-chinned Hummingbird
1. Herb Elliott
2. Ad Konings
3. Kyle Blaney
4. Ad Konings

Rufous Hummingbird
1. Kent Leland
2. Matthew Pendleton
3. Matt Davis
4. Paul Fenwick

Calliope Hummingbird
1. Matthew Pendleton
2. Marya Moosman
3. Louis Hoeniger
4. Ad Konings

Buff-bellied Hummingbird
1. Jay McGowan
2. Alex Lamoreaux
3. Ian Davies
4. Alisha Flanary

Sora
1. Marky Mutchler
2. Ad Konings
3. Brad Imhoff
4. Matt Davis

Common Gallinule
1. Sean Fitzgerald
2. Matt Davis
3. Matt Davis
4. Matt Davis

American Coot
1. Brad Imhoff
2. Melissa James
3. Ad Konings
4. August Davidson-Onsgard

Purple Gallinule
1. Christopher Wood
2. Luke Seitz
3. Alex Lamoreaux
4. Alex Lamoreaux

Sandhill Crane
1. Paul Fenwick
2. Paul Fenwick
3. Matt Davis
4. Ad Konings

Black-necked Stilt
1. Sean Fitzgerald
2. Dorian Anderson
3. Shawn Billerman
4. Alex Lamoreaux

American Oystercatcher
1. Terence Zahner
2. Ryan Schain
3. Evan Lipton
4. Evan Lipton

Black-bellied Plover
1. Matt Davis
2. Dorian Anderson
3. Sue Barth
4. Paul Fenwick

American Golden-Plover
1. Ian Davies
2. Christopher Wood
3. Chris S. Wood
4. Christopher Wood

Killdeer
1. Jay McGowan
2. Brian L. Sullivan
3. Jay McGowan
4. Ollie Oliver

Upland Sandpiper
1. Brian L. Sullivan
2. Liam Wolff
3. Jay McGowan
4. Alex Lamoreaux

Long-billed Curlew
1. Brian L. Sullivan
2. Brian L. Sullivan
3. Brian L. Sullivan
4. Brian L. Sullivan

Marbled Godwit
1. Matt Davis
2. Brian L. Sullivan
3. Kent Leland
4. Dorian Anderson

Ruddy Turnstone
1. Jay McGowan
2. Jay McGowan
3. Ryan Schain
4. Shawn Billerman

Sanderling
1. Ryan Schain
2. Matt Davis
3. Paul Fenwick
4. David Wilson

Western Sandpiper
1. Ian Davies
2. Ian Davies
3. Matthew Pendleton
4. Brian L. Sullivan

Spotted Sandpiper
1. Matt Brady
2. Ian Davies
3. Jay McGowan
4. Ad Konings

Willet
1. Evan Lipton
2. Evan Lipton
3. Steve Calver
4. Patrick Maurice

Laughing Gull
1. Jay McGowan
2. Ollie Oliver
3. Shawn Billerman
4. Adam Jackson

Franklin's Gull
1. Brian L. Sullivan
2. Alan Versaw
3. Sue Barth
4. Brian L. Sullivan

Ring-billed Gull
1. Paul Fenwick
2. Liam Wolff
3. Herb Elliott
4. Jay McGowan

Herring Gull
1. Darren Clark
2. Brian L. Sullivan
3. Evan Lipton
4. Christopher Wood

Least Tern
1. Jonathan Eckerson
2. Dorian Anderson
3. Dorian Anderson
4. Paul Fenwick

Caspian Tern
1. Brian L. Sullivan
2. Jay McGowan
3. Paul Fenwick
4. Herb Elliott

Black Tern
1. Paul Fenwick
2. Melissa James
3. Daniel Irons
4. Ryan Schain

Common Tern
1. Doug Hitchcox
2. Doug Hitchcox
3. Jay McGowan
4. Melissa James

Forster's Tern
1. August Davidson-Onsgard
2. Steve Tucker
3. Ryan Schain
4. David Wilson

Royal Tern
1. Paul Fenwick
2. Ian Davies
3. Ryan Schain
4. Shawn Billerman

Black Skimmer
1. Bryan Calk
2. Ian Davies
3. Chris S. Wood
4. Dorian Anderson

Common Loon
1. Brad Imhoff
2. Matt Davis
3. Brian L. Sullivan
4. Patrick Maurice

Wood Stork
1. Patrick Maurice
2. Ian Davies
3. Andrew Simon
4. Dan Vickers

Anhinga
1. Alex Lamoreaux
2. Dan Vickers
3. Alex Lamoreaux
4. Liam Wolf

Neotropic Cormorant
1. Louis Hoeniger
2. Darren Clark
3. Louis Hoeniger
4. Chris S. Wood

Double-crested Cormorant
1. Evan Lipton
2. Terence Zahner
3. Steve Kolbe
4. Jane Mann

American White Pelican
1. Jerry Ting
2. Paul Fenwick
3. Herb Elliott
4. Gordon W. Dimmig

Brown Pelican
1. Daniel Irons
2. Alex Lamoreaux
3. Alex Lamoreaux
4. Brad Imhoff

Great Blue Heron
1. Herb Elliott
2. Daniel Irons
3. Shawn Billerman
4. Terence Zahner

Great Egret
1. Jonathan Eckerson
2. Melissa James
3. Alex Lamoreaux
4. Matt Davis

Snowy Egret
1. Evan Lipton
2. Jay McGowan
3. Jay McGowan
4. Melissa James

Little Blue Heron
1. Ad Konings
2. Ryan Schain
3. Greg Gillson
4. Alex Lamoreaux

Tricolored Heron
1. Paul Fenwick
2. Ian Davies
3. Daniel Irons
4. Scott Martin

Cattle Egret
1. Steve Kolbe
2. Brian L. Sullivan
3. Samuel Paul Galick
4. Steve Calver

Green Heron
1. Evan Lipton
2. Brad Imhoff
3. Evan Lipton
4. Paul Fenwick

Black-crowned Night-Heron
1. Ad Konings
2. Matt Davis
3. Alex Lamoreaux
4. Evan Lipton

Yellow-crowned Night-Heron
1. Evan Lipton
2. Paul Fenwick
3. Evan Lipton
4. Ad Konings

White Ibis
1. Melissa James
2. Ryan Schain
3. Ian Davies
4. Jay McGowan

White-faced Ibis
1. Ad Konings
2. Paul Fenwick
3. Matt Davis
4. Matt Davis

Roseate Spoonbill
1. Darren Clark
2. Paul Fenwick
3. Jay McGowan
4. Steve Calver

Black Vulture
1. Brian L. Sullivan
2. Ian Davies
3. David Wilson
4. Kathryn Young

Turkey Vulture
1. Louis Hoeniger
2. Paul Fenwick
3. Ryan Shaw
4. Brian L. Sullivan

Osprey
1. Matt Davis
2. Matt Davis
3. Jay McGowan
4. Melissa James

White-tailed Kite
1. Matt Davis
2. Brian L. Sullivan
3. Matt Davis
4. Brian L. Sullivan

Mississippi Kite
1. Brian L. Sullivan
2. Arlene Ripley
3. Brian Smith
4. Jim Merritt

Northern Harrier
1. Brian L. Sullivan
2. Matt Davis
3. Brian L. Sullivan
4. Brian L. Sullivan

Cooper's Hawk
1. Evan Lipton
2. Ryan Schain
3. Sue Barth
4. Alan Versaw

Bald Eagle
1. Sue Barth
2. Chris S. Wood
3. Scott Martin
4. Jay McGowan

Harris's Hawk
1. Jack L. Sheldon, Jr.
2. Brian L. Sullivan
3. Usha Tatini
4. Chris S. Wood

Red-shouldered Hawk
1. Liam Wolff
2. Steve Calver
3. Gordon W. Dimmig
4. Ian Davies

Swainson's Hawk
1. Steven G. Mlodinow
2. Matt Davis
3. Brian L. Sullivan
4. Brian L. Sullivan

Red-tailed Hawk
1. Arlene Ripley
2. Alan Versaw
3. Paul Fenwick
4. Herb Elliott

Rough-legged Hawk
1. Matthew Pendleton
2. Jay McGowan
3. Christopher Wood
4. Brian L. Sullivan

Eastern Screech-Owl
1. Andrew Simon
2. Ryan Schain
3. Jay McGowan
4. Ryan Schain

Great Horned Owl
1. Ad Konings
2. Terence Zahner
3. Ryan Schain
4. Lawrence Haller

Burrowing Owl
1. Shawn Billerman
2. Darren Clark
3. Janine McCabe
4. Terence Zahner

Barred Owl
1. Luke Seitz
2. Alex Lamoreaux
3. Alex Lamoreaux
4. Jay McGowan

Belted Kingfisher
1. John D. Reynolds
2. Louis Hoeniger
3. William Higgins
4. Matthew Pendleton

Yellow-bellied Sapsucker
1. Jay McGowan
2. Alex Lamoreaux
3. Ryan Schain
4. Dan Vickers

Red-headed Woodpecker
1. Steve Calver
2. Jay McGowan
3. Jay McGowan
4. Jay McGowan

Acorn Woodpecker
1. Brian L. Sullivan
2. Charlie Jackson
3. George Gibbs
4. Matt Davis

Golden-fronted Woodpecker
1. Darren Clark
2. Aaron Boone
3. Bryan Calk
4. Dina Perry

Red-bellied Woodpecker
1. Scott Martin
2. Scott Martin
3. Scott Martin
4. Sue Barth

Downy Woodpecker
1. Evan Lipton
2. Steve Calver
3. Alex Lamoreaux
4. Jay McGowan

Ladder-backed Woodpecker
1. Don Danko
2. Alex Lamoreaux
3. Herb Elliott
4. Arlene Ripley

Hairy Woodpecker
1. Terence Zahner
2. Herb Elliott
3. Christopher Wood
4. Joe Wing

Pileated Woodpecker
1. David Wilson
2. Shawn Billerman
3. Jay McGowan
4. Shawn Billerman

Northern Flicker
1. Ian Davies
2. Matt Davis
3. Warren Lynn
4. Greg Gillson

Crested Caracara
1. Dan Vickers
2. Brian L. Sullivan
3. Melissa James
4. Ad Konings

American Kestrel
1. Matthew Pendleton
2. Sue Barth
3. Dorian Anderson
4. Ad Konings

Peregrine Falcon
1. Ryan Schain
2. Brian L. Sullivan
3. Jay McGowan
4. Ryan Schain

Monk Parakeet
1. Jay McGowan
2. Jay McGowan
3. Marya Moosman
4. Shawn Billerman

Western Wood-Pewee
1. Darren Clark
2. Steve Calver
3. Ryan Schain
4. Evan Lipton

Eastern Wood-Pewee
1. Daniel Irons
2. Linda Petersen*
3. Ian Davies
4. Terence Zahner

Least Flycatcher
1. Jay McGowan
2. Ian Davies
3. Terence Zahner
4. Russ Morgan

Black Phoebe
1. Ian Davies
2. Paul Fenwick
3. Don Danko
4. Ad Konings

Eastern Phoebe
1. Ryan Schain
2. Jay McGowan
3. Ian Davies
4. Jay McGowan

Say's Phoebe
1. Arlene Ripley
2. Sean Fitzgerald
3. Arlene Ripley
4. Brian L. Sullivan

Vermilion Flycatcher
1. Matt Davis
2. Brian L. Sullivan
3. Louis Hoeniger
4. Evan Lipton

Ash-throated Flycatcher
1. Robert Hamilton
2. Alan Versaw
3. Brian L. Sullivan
4. Luke Seitz

Great Crested Flycatcher
1. Ryan Schain
2. Keenan Yakola
3. Steve Kolbe
4. Shawn Billerman

Great Kiskadee
1. Ian Davies
2. Ad Konings
3. Scott Martin
4. Patrick Maurice

Western Kingbird
1. Jerry Ting
2. Ryan Schain
3. Ad Konings
4. Steve Calver

Eastern Kingbird
1. Scott Martin
2. Josh Ketry
3. Jay McGowan
4. Russ Morgan

Scissor-tailed Flycatcher
1. Ryan Shaw
2. Evan Lipton
3. Jay McGowan
4. Lawrence Haller

Yellow-throated Vireo
1. Andrew Simon
2. Adam Jackson
3. Jay McGowan
4. Sue Barth

Warbling Vireo
1. Ad Konings
2. Shawn Billerman
3. Jay McGowan
4. Jay McGowan

Red-eyed Vireo
1. Gordon W. Dimmig
2. Scott Martin
3. Evan Lipton
4. Ryan Schain

Loggerhead Shrike
1. Matthew Pendleton
2. Matt Davis
3. Dorian Anderson
4. Evan Lipton

Green Jay
1. Scott Martin
2. Ian Davies
3. Marky Mutchler
4. Dina Perry

Blue Jay
1. Scott Martin
2. Patrick Maurice
3. Jay McGowan
4. Dan Vickers

Woodhouse's Scrub-Jay
1. Christopher Wood
2. Arlene Ripley
3. Carol Morgan
4. Ad Konings

American Crow
1. Alan Versaw
2. Steven Kolbe
3. Steven G. Mlodinow
4. Sue Barth

Fish Crow
1. Alex Lamoreaux
2. Shawn Billerman
3. Alex Lamoreaux
4. Tom Lally

Common Raven
1. Brian L. Sullivan
2. Matt Davis
3. Greg Gillson
4. Brian L. Sullivan

Carolina Chickadee
1. Daniel Irons
2. Ryan Shaw
3. Kathryn Young
4. Steve Calver

Tufted Titmouse
1. Evan Lipton
2. Evan Lipton
3. Scott Martin
4. Ryan Schain

Black-crested Titmouse
1. Scott Martin
2. Andrew Simon
3. Ad Konings
4. Michael L. P. Retter*

Verdin
1. Dan Vickers
2. Ad Konings
3. Ad Konings
4. Arlene Ripley

Horned Lark
1. Alan Versaw
2. Linda Petersen*
3. Sue Barth
4. Ad Konings

Purple Martin
1. Bryan Calk
2. Mark Ludwick
3. Terence Zahner
4. Alex Lamoreaux

Tree Swallow
1. Greg Gillson
2. Phil McNeil
3. Matt Davis
4. Noah Strycker

Barn Swallow
1. Alex Lamoreaux
2. Paul Fenwick
3. Brian L. Sullivan
4. Arlene Ripley

Cliff Swallow
1. Dorian Anderson
2. Dorian Anderson
3. Dan Vickers
4. Laurens Halsey

Cave Swallow
1. Jack Chiles
2. Jay McGowan
3. Ryan Schain
4. Ad Konings

Bushtit
1. Darren Clark
2. Tim DeJonghe
3. Michael Andersen
4. Aaron Boone

Golden-crowned Kinglet
1. Ryan Schain
2. Luke Seitz
3. Gates Dupont
4. Ian Davies

Ruby-crowned Kinglet
1. Jay McGowan
2. Brian L. Sullivan
3. Matt Davis
4. Luke Seitz

Red-breasted Nuthatch
1. Scott Martin
2. Ryan Schain
3. Christopher Wood
4. Shawn Billerman

White-breasted Nuthatch
1. Ian Davies
2. Evan Lipton
3. Louis Hoeniger
4. Herb Elliott

Brown-headed Nuthatch
1. Ian Davies
2. Daniel Irons
3. Steve Calver
4. Andrew Simon

Brown Creeper
1. Scott Martin
2. Scott Martin
3. Scott Martin
4. Adam Jackson

Blue-gray Gnatcatcher
1. Liam Wolff
2. Brad Imhoff
3. Keith Leland
4. Alex Lamoreaux

Rock Wren
1. Ryan Schain
2. Bryan Calk
3. Darren Clark
4. Matt Davis

Canyon Wren
1. Arlene Ripley
2. Herb Elliott
3. Kent Leland
4. Nancy Christensen

House Wren
1. Matt Brady
2. Ryan Schain
3. Evan Lipton
4. Ad Konings

Carolina Wren
1. Evan Lipton
2. Melissa James
3. Ryan Schain
4. Daniel Irons

Bewick's Wren
1. Darren Clark
2. Bryan Calk
3. Jerry Ting
4. Russ Morgan

Cactus Wren
1. Robert A. Hamilton
2. Daniel Irons
3. Ad Konings
4. Nick Dorian

European Starling
1. Matt Davis
2. Ryan Schain
3. Jay McGowan
4. Linda Petersen*

Gray Catbird
1. Ryan Schain
2. Bryan Calk
3. Jay McGowan
4. Evan Lipton

Curve-billed Thrasher
1. Don Danko
2. Jeffrey Moore
3. Jeffrey Moore
4. Jeffrey Moore

Brown Thrasher
1. Brad Imhoff
2. David Wilson
3. Melissa James
4. Linda Petersen*

Northern Mockingbird
1. Evan Lipton
2. Sue Barth
3. Arlene Ripley
4. Ian Davies

Eastern Bluebird
1. Brad Imhoff
2. Brad Imhoff
3. Terence Zahner
4. Jay McGowan

Mountain Bluebird
1. Christopher Wood
2. Brian L. Sullivan
3. Shawn Billerman
4. Arlene Ripley

Hermit Thrush
1. Alan Versaw
2. Sue Barth
3. Sue Barth
4. Terence Zahner

Wood Thrush
1. Evan Lipton
2. Sue Barth
3. Ian Davies
4. Ryan Schain

American Robin
1. Christopher Wood
2. Evan Lipton
3. Jay McGowan
4. David Wilson

Cedar Waxwing
1. Terence Zahner
2. Jay McGowan
3. Jane Bain
4. Evan Lipton

Phainopepla
1. Eric Gofreed
2. Louis Hoeniger
3. Arlene Ripley
4. Arlene Ripley

House Sparrow
1. Evan Lipton
2. Louis Hoeniger
3. Paul Fenwick
4. Ad Konings

House Finch
1. Scott Martin
2. Jay McGowan
3. Paul Fenwick
4. Ryan Schain

Pine Siskin
1. Matthew Pendleton
2. Matt Davis
3. Luke Seitz
4. Jim Merritt

Lesser Goldfinch
1. Jim Merritt
2. Matthew Pendleton
3. Paul Fenwick
4. Arlene Ripley

American Goldfinch
1. Don Danko
2. Ian Davies
3. Linda Petersen*
4. Daniel Irons

Lapland Longspur
1. Ian Davies
2. Ian Davies
3. Andrew Simon
4. Andrew Simon

Grasshopper Sparrow
1. Ian Davies
2. Melissa James
3. Matt Davis
4. Scott Martin

Black-throated Sparrow
1. Luke Seitz
2. Arlene Ripley
3. Arlene Ripley
4. Chris S. Wood

Lark Sparrow
1. Matt Davis
2. Paul Fenwick
3. Scott Martin
4. Brian L. Sullivan

Lark Bunting
1. Jay McGowan
2. Marky Mutchler
3. Ad Konings
4. Ad Konings

Chipping Sparrow
1. Evan Lipton
2. Daniel Irons
3. Jay McGowan
4. Jay McGowan

Field Sparrow
1. Daniel Irons
2. Evan Lipton
3. Ian Davies
4. Dan Vickers

Brewer's Sparrow
1. Matt Davis
2. Doug Hitchcox
3. Steven G. Mlodinow
4. Ad Konings

Fox Sparrow
1. Ian Davies
2. Jay McGowan
3. Ryan Schain
4. Terence Zahner

Dark-eyed Junco
1. Scott Martin
2. Christopher Wood
3. Christopher Wood
4. Greg Gillson

White-crowned Sparrow
1. Linda Petersen*
2. Sue Barth
3. Daniel Irons
4. Jay McGowan

Harris's Sparrow
1. Ian Davies
2. Scott Martins
3. Steve Calver
4. Alex Lamoureaux

White-throated Sparrow
1. Jay McGowan
2. Keenan Yakola
3. Adam Jackson
4. Shawn Billerman

Savannah Sparrow
1. Matt Davis
2. Bryan Calk
3. Arlene Ripley
4. Don Blecha

Song Sparrow
1. Ryan Schain
2. Shawn Billerman
3. Linda Petersen*
4. Linda Petersen*

Lincoln's Sparrow
1. Scott Martin
2. Darren Clark
3. Linda Petersen*
4. Sue Barth

Canyon Towhee
1. Matt Davis
2. Jim Merritt
3. Ad Konings
4. Arlene Ripley

Rufous-crowned Sparrow
1. Arlene Ripley
2. Matt Davis
3. Paul Fenwick
4. Kent Leland

Green-tailed Towhee
1. Noah Strycker
2. Don Danko
3. Tom Lally
4. Arlene Ripley

Spotted Towhee
1. Terence Zahner
2. Ad Konings
3. Brian L. Sullivan
4. Kent Leland

Eastern Towhee
1. Davey Walters
2. Steve Calver
3. Shawn Billerman
4. Melissa James

Yellow-breasted Chat
1. Bryan Calk
2. Ad Konings
3. Ad Konings
4. Ryan Schain

Western Meadowlark
1. Alan Versaw
2. Matt Davis
3. Matt Davis
4. Alex Lamoureaux

Eastern Meadowlark
1. Marky Mutchler
2. Dan Vickers
3. Steve Calver
4. Ad Konings

Orchard Oriole
1. Bryan Calk
2. Sue Barth
3. Jay McGowan
4. Ryan Schain

Hooded Oriole
1. Louis Hoeniger
2. Arlene Ripley
3. Greg Gillson
4. Arlene Ripley

Bullock's Oriole
1. Arlene Ripley
2. Matt Davis
3. Arlene Ripley
4. Don Sterba

Baltimore Oriole
1. Ryan Schain
2. Steve Kolbe
3. Ryan Schain
4. Linda Petersen

Red-winged Blackbird
1. Ryan Schain
2. Jonathan Eckerson
3. Dan Vickers
4. Sue Barth

Bronzed Cowbird
1. Brian L. Sullivan
2. Brian L. Sullivan
3. Arlene Ripley
4. Nic Allen

Brown-headed Cowbird
1. Brian L. Sullivan
2. Arlene Ripley
3. Shawn Billerman
4. Linda Petersen*

Brewer's Blackbird
1. Brian L. Sullivan
2. Matt Davis
3. Shawn Billerman
4. Jack Bushong

Common Grackle
1. Christopher Wood
2. Herb Elliott
3. Jay McGowan
4. Evan Lipton

Boat-tailed Grackle
1. Caleb Strand
2. Brian L. Sullivan
3. Tom Lally
4. Paul Fenwick

Great-tailed Grackle
1. Darren Clark
2. Ian Davies
3. Bob Walker
4. Ian Davies

Black-and-white Warbler
1. Ryan Schain
2. Daniel Irons
3. Ryan Schain
4. Ryan Schain

Prothonotary Warbler
1. Ryan Schain
2. Sue Barth
3. Steve Calver
4. Jay McGowan

Orange-crowned Warbler
1. Ryan Schain
2. Paul Fenwick
3. Ryan Schain
4. Ryan Schain

Common Yellowthroat
1. Paul Fenwick
2. Brad Imhoff
3. Darren Clark
4. Shawn Billerman

Northern Parula
1. Sue Barth
2. Evan Lipton
3. Ian Davies
4. Jay McGowan

Yellow Warbler
1. Ryan Schain
2. Shawn Billerman
3. Sue Barth
4. Ryan Schain

Palm Warbler
1. Alex Lamoureaux
2. Sue Barth
3. Sue Barth
4. Paul Fenwick

Pine Warbler
1. Ryan Schain
2. Evan Lipton
3. Ryan Schain
4. Ryan Schain

Yellow-rumped Warbler
1. Matthew Pendleton
2. Arlene Ripley
3. Tom Lally
4. Ryan Schain

Yellow-throated Warbler
1. Brad Imhoff
2. Brad Imhoff
3. Brad Imhoff
4. Luke Seitz

Wilson's Warbler
1. Ryan Schain
2. Ian Davies
3. Ryan Schain
4. Jay McGowan

Summer Tanager
1. Matt Brady
2. Sue Barth
3. Paul Fenwick
4. Brad Imhoff

Northern Cardinal
1. Ryan Schain
2. Shawn Billerman
3. Terence Zahner
4. Terence Zahner

Pyrrhuloxia
1. Christopher Wood
2. Scott Martin
3. Arlene Ripley
4. Dean LaTray

Rose-breasted Grosbeak
1. Ryan Shain
2. Warren Lynn
3. Terence Zahner
4. Jay McGowan

Black-headed Grosbeak
1. Herb Elliott
2. Robert A. Hamilton
3. Jim Merritt
4. Herb Elliott

Blue Grosbeak
1. Daniel Irons
2. Arlene Ripley
3. David Disher
4. Arlene Ripley

Indigo Bunting
1. Sue Barth
2. Ryan Schain
3. Shawn Billerman
4. Alex Lamoreaux

Painted Bunting
1. Dan Vickers
2. Scott Martin
3. Sue Barth
4. Mary McSparen

Dickcissel
1. Alex Lamoreaux
2. Jim Merritt
3. Luke Seitz
4. Evan Lipton

INDEX

ACKNOWLEDGMENTS

These guides were put together with the help of many people. The bird species profiles are derived from the more comprehensive accounts in the *All About Birds Online Bird Guide*, authored by numerous expert contributors throughout the year, with editing and many recent additions made possible by Hugh Powell, Kathi Borgmann, and Ned Brinkley. Maps are based on original *All About Birds* base maps featuring data from NatureServe and updated to reflect known ranges. Early on, Jessie Barry and Ian Davies shared what they would like to see in a new field-guide series. Hugh Powell wrote much of the helpful information on ID at the front of the guides. Tilden Chao provided a selection of photos to begin our search for ID photos. Robyn Bailey, Jenna Curtis, Marilu Lopez Fretts, Holly Grant, Emma Greig, Jay McGowan, Becca Rodomsky-Bish, and Bobby Stickel provided updates on projects and technology. Rachel Lodder's eagle eyes proofread many versions of these books. Caroline Watkins filled spreadsheets and edited copy, assisted with photo permission requests, and hunted down images. Diane Tessaglia-Hymes' design skills brought this project to the finish line with finesse and grace. Miyoko Chu smoothed over the many road bumps along the way, and Brian L. Sockin gave guidance and support. Michael L. P. Retter provided crucial feedback on photographs, range-map adjustments, and copy. Michael's boundless knowledge, enthusiasm, and energy kept the project moving forward.

Last, but certainly not least, I would like to thank every photographer/citizen scientist who contributes photos to the Macaulay Library, the contents of which I scoured for birds of all ages and plumages. For a complete list of image credits, please see pages 310–315. A special thanks to the following photographers who granted use of any of their photographs in this book. I admire their skill and appreciate their generosity: Sue Barth, Shawn Billerman, Jeff Bleam, Matt Brady, Steve Calver, August Davidson-Onsgard, Ian Davies, Matt Davis, Herb Elliott, Paul Fenwick, Fred Forssell, Greg Gillson, Louis Hoeniger, Adam Jackson, Melissa James, Ad Konings, Tom Lally, Alex Lamoreaux, Kent Leland, Evan Lipton, Mark Ludwick, Scott Martin, Patrick Maurice, Jeff Maw, Jay McGowan, Jim Merritt, Marya Moosman, Russ Morgan, Ollie Oliver, Matthew Pendleton, Arlene Ripley, Ryan Schain, Luke Seitz, Andrew Simon, Caleb Strand, Brian L. Sullivan, Usha Tatini, Alan Versaw, Dan Vickers, David Wilson, Liam Wolff, Chris S. Wood, Christopher Wood, Kathryn Young, and Terence Zahner.

Jill Leichter, Editor